International Social Work Policy and Practice

International Social Work Policy and Practice:

Practical Insights and Perspectives

Edited by

Carolyn J. Tice
Dennis D. Long

WILEY

John Wiley & Sons, Inc.

Published by John Wiley & Sons, Inc., Hoboken, New Jersey.
Published simultaneously in Canada.

For general information on our other products and services please contact our Customer Care Department within the U.S. at (800) 762-2974, outside the United States at (317) 572-3993 or fax (317) 572-4002.

Wiley also publishes its books in a variety of electronic formats. Some content that appears in print may not be available in electronic books. For more information about Wiley products, visit our website at www.wiley.com.

Library of Congress Cataloging-in-Publication Data:

International social work policy and practice : practical insights and perspectives / edited by Carolyn J. Tice, Dennis D. Long.
p.   cm.
ISBN 978-0-470-25286-4 (pbk.)
1. Social service.   2. Social policy.   I. Tice, Carolyn J.   II. Long, Dennis D.
HV40.I556   2009
361.3--dc22

2009000843

Printed in the United States of America

10 9 8 7 6 5 4 3 2 1

This book is dedicated to the memory of Andrew
Dennis Long, beloved youngest son of Joan and Dennis Long.
Allow Andrew's thirst for knowledge, passion for embracing the
ways of people, and kindness toward others act as a source of
inspiration in your reading of this work.

—DENNIS

My work on this book is dedicated to Mark T. Wieland, the
Wieland reunions and a shared sense of family.

—CAROLYN

Contents

About the Editors

Carolyn J. Tice, DSW, ACSW, is Professor and Associate Dean of Social Work at the University of Maryland, Baltimore County. However, the majority of her professional career was spent in the Appalachian region. Dr. Tice received her MSW from Temple University and DSW from the University of Pennsylvania, where she worked extensively in the Hmong community. Dr. Tice's international experience includes living for approximately three years in Europe with extended stays in France, Israel, Sweden, and Turkey. In the last five years she traveled to Portugal and China to support the design of educational programs. In 2008, Dr. Tice was named a Senior Fulbright Specialist and traveled to Mongolia, where she worked with social work programs in curriculum and field education development. Dr. Tice has published numerous articles on the strengths perspective in social work practice and is the coauthor of three textbooks. Her teaching interest is social welfare policy. Dr. Tice serves as a member of the Council on Leadership Development of the Council on Social Work Education and is on the editorial board of the *Journal of Teaching in Social Work*.

Dennis D. Long, Ph.D., ACSW, is Professor and Chair of the Department of Social Work at the University of North Carolina at Charlotte, where he currently serves as an interim Associate Dean in the College of Health and Human Services. Dr. Long received his MSW from The Ohio State University (1979) and Ph.D. in sociology with a concentration in social psychology from the University of Cincinnati (1985). His scholarly interests and research center on macro–social work practice. International experience includes participation in a service learning program in Nepal and, most recently (2007) with Dr. Blanca Ramos, exploration of cultural exchange and collaborative opportunities in Lima and Chiclayo, Peru. Dr. Long has published numerous articles examining the impact of larger social systems and is the coauthor of two other macro-oriented textbooks. His teaching interests are in the areas of human behavior and the social environment and social change. Dr. Long serves as a member of the Board of Trustees at Charlotte Emergency Housing and of the National Board of Examiners in Optometry.

About the Contributors

Mery L. Botton is an experienced social work educator who has held faculty positions at the Universidad Católica del Perú and the Universidad National Villarreal. She is former Dean of the Colegio de Asistentes Sociales del Perú. As a member of LIBECO, a non-governmental organization, she planned and delivered a number of workshops and training institutes for social work faculty and practitioners, and has served as consultant to government social service agencies. She is collaborating with U.S. faculty developing curricula on community practice with immigrants, a project funded by IASSW. She has participated in international forums in Mexico, Belgium, the US, Dominican Republic, and throughout Latin America.

Lisa E. Cox, Ph.D., LCSW, MSW, is Associate Professor of Social Work and Gerontology: The Richard Stockton College of New Jersey. Spain was the first country Dr. Lisa Cox traveled to while a college sophomore double majoring in History/Political Science and Spanish. Later her travel took her to other parts of Europe, the Caribbean, Central America, Australia, Mexico, Ireland, Scotland, England, Nepal, and India. Since joining The Richard Stockton College of New Jersey's Social Work Program in 1999, she has taught courses on Costa Rican Life and Culture and guided students as they enrolled in a Spanish Immersion Seminar/Study Tour and traversed the biodiverse countryside of Costa Rica. Dr. Cox's additional teaching and research interests include gerontology, health and neurobiology.

Ann Dinan, Ph.D., M.S.S.A., C.P.C.C., has traveled extensively around the world and lived and worked in Asia for five years. Upon returning to the United States, she continued working in the international arena by focusing her research, coaching, and training efforts in South Africa as well as around the globe. Dr. Dinan is currently the CEO of Dinan & Associates, a global firm with worldwide affiliates focused in the area of personal leadership. Currently Dr. Dinan teaches Personal Leadership in the MBA program at Xavier University in Ohio.

Blanca M. Ramos, Ph.D., is Associate Professor of Social Work and Latin American Studies at the University of North Carolina at Charlotte. Her international experience includes teaching at universities in Peru, leading study abroad programs to Mexico and Peru, and conducting transnational research on domestic violence, community leadership, and health and healthcare. She has published in the US, Spain, and Russia, and has delivered professional presentations in Europe, Canada, and Latin America. She is on the editorial board of the international journal *Tzhoecoen* and consultant to NGOs in Peru. She was recently inducted into the Phi Beta Delta Honor Society for International Scholars.

Diana Rowan, Ph.D., MSW, LCSW, has experience working with HIV/AIDS affected communities in several eastern countries of Sub-Saharan Africa. She has conducted international research funded by the International Association of Schools of Social Work and recently collaborated on research studying the response to the HIV orphan crisis in Malawi. She is currently the MSW Program Coordinator at the University of North Carolina at Charlotte and her research centers around domestic and international dimensions of HIV/AIDS and social work. She is a member of Phi Beta Delta Honor Society for International Scholars.

Susan Kiss Sarnoff, DSW, MSW, is Associate Professor and Chair of the Department of Social Work at Ohio University. She is the author of two books, *Paying for Crime*, a study of victim compensation programs, and *Sanctified Snake Oil*, a study of how public policy is corrupted by "junk" social science. Further, Dr. Sarnoff is the author of numerous peer-reviewed journal articles, book chapters and other publications and has received funding for several research and program development projects. Dr. Sarnoff received the Jeanette Graselli Brown Outstanding Teaching Award from the College of Arts and Sciences for the 2004 academic year.

Her areas of expertise include ethnicity, ethics, technology, and rural social work practice.

Gary A. Wright, Ph.D., is Professor Emeritus at the University at Albany. He has conducted research in Turkey, Israel, France, and Peru. Dr. Wright has published articles and books on Middle Eastern and North American prehistory and ethnohistory, and most recently on social work in Peru. His major teaching interests are in archeological theory and the historical dimensions of cultural and ethnic diversity.

Preface

Social workers have become increasingly aware of the importance of an international perspective in the development of their policy and practice skills. In part, this recognition reflects the undeniable global interconnection of critical issues (e.g., poverty, health disparities, migration, and exploitation of the environment) confronting humankind. In addition, social work's embrace of international practice is also indicative of our profession's commitment to social and distributive justice. Social workers seek and engage in social change to promote opportunities and access to resources and services. In doing so, they must exhibit sensitivity to and understanding about social conditions and cultural, racial, and ethnic diversity in a changing and increasingly complex world.

Typically, the contemporary social worker is engaged in professional help with consumers of services from a myriad of backgrounds and places. With this in mind, *International Social Work Policy and Practice: Practical Insights and Perspectives* was written to provide social work students, educators, and practitioners with examples and reflective exercises for contemplating the application of theory and research in social work practice in venues from around the globe. We encourage you to become excited about the prospect of working with clients from and in various venues with a newfound realization that wherever social workers practice geographically, they must embrace ethically sound practice and strive to keep the historical, political, social, and cultural components of location and people at the forefront of intervention, policy development, and change processes.

International Social Work Policy and Practice: Practical Insights and Perspectives is intended for use as supplementary reading in upper-level practice and policy course work in undergraduate curriculums and foundation-level graduate social work education. This text is especially suited for specialized undergraduate and graduate courses emphasizing international policy and practice. You will find that country-based chapters follow a pattern of organization, beginning with pertinent information on each featured country. Using the country's profile as a backdrop, examples of practice and policy are introduced, providing readers with an opportunity to grapple with ethical issues, complex life situations, interpersonal relationships, and dynamic social-environmental conditions.

Reflective exercises are integrated throughout all the chapters. These exercises are designed to encourage readers to think beyond the written word by examining online references, Web sites, databases, and readings or through identified activities related to chapter content. Ideally, exercises provide readers the ability to pause and contemplate assumptions, assess values and beliefs, and consider the appropriateness and applicability of social work theory, research, and practice to diverse populations and a variety of contexts and situations. The authors contend that intentional examination, reflection, synthesis, and discovery in relationship to various examples of practice and policy can be helpful for advancing professional abilities in international social work practice and encourage a paradigm shift from a monocultural, Eurocentric framework to approaches that build on the history, culture, and experiences of global communities.

Finally, *International Social Work Policy and Practice: Practical Insights and Perspectives* depicts social workers as professional adventurers or pioneers, often traveling to the far corners of the world to learn about and adopt culturally appropriate practice, resulting in lasting relationships and indelible memories. Without doubt, each of the contributors would agree that gains from their international experiences far outweigh any inconveniences, trials, or tribulations. Our hope is that this text will serve as a source of inspiration for readers to seek and embrace possibilities for practice with new and different people, organizations, and communities, both in their native land and beyond, in efforts to enrich the professional self, human well-being, and the profession of social work.

Acknowledgments

Throughout the writing of this book, Lisa Gebo served as a guiding and passionate force and powerful influence. For well over a decade, Lisa has been a cherished colleague and friend. The consummate multitask editor, Lisa always took time to inquire and ask about our lives, families, and pets. It was Lisa who brought this book to life. We are especially thankful for her relentless encouragement of our work, camaraderie, and compassion toward all living beings.

The authors would also like to express appreciation to Sweta Gupta, Stevie Belchak, Susan Moran, and Rachel Livsey, for their dedicated work and contributions to the production of this book. A special recognition goes to Karen Kraft, Andrea Judson, and Kelly McDonald, for their assistance in this once-in-a-lifetime adventure.

CHAPTER

1

International Social Work Education and Practice

DENNIS D. LONG

Social workers should recognize and respect the ethnic and cultural diversity of the societies in which they practice, taking account of individual, family, group and community differences.
—International Federation of Social Workers/
International Association of Schools
of Social Work (2008)

Acurrent buzz and source of excitement in social work education and the profession of social work involves the international nature and globalization of practice. The enthusiasm surrounding social work's many efforts to reach across the world and embrace various population groups is profound. Dr. Elvira Craig de Silva, president of the National Association of Social Workers (NASW), acknowledges, "In the social work profession, there is much interest in furthering our nation's involvement in issues that affect the global scene. Fortunately, social workers have the training and worldview to be an important part of this effort" (2008, p. 3).

1

Many social workers find it difficult to attend a conference, workshop, meeting, or continuing education event without entering a conversation or discussion regarding the international context and nature of contemporary social work education and practice.

> Enthusiasm for international social work education is bubbling over among students, faculty, and practitioners. The International Association of Schools of Social Work and the International Federation of Social Workers are even working on new definitions of social work, noting that the profession in the twenty-first century is dynamic and evolving. New avenues for partnerships are being sought. (Leggett, 2008, p. 48)

Regardless of specialty or area of practice, many social workers would agree that the realities of modern-day practice necessitate an enriched and informed understanding of people, social-economic issues, cultural context, politics, and social systems from both near and far.

It is social work's long-standing commitment to assessment and change involving the social environment, especially with larger social systems (e.g., communities and societies), that positions the field for a leadership role in grappling with the human elements and challenges associated with globalization. Unlike other helping professionals, social workers have historically embraced the rich and comprehensive nature of the social environment in everyday life. Social work has a unique tradition in America of working with a variety of population groups to promote human well-being by promoting living wages, safe housing, affordable transportation, nurturing daycare, comprehensive health coverage, and quality education. When considering the social-economic and technological interconnected and interdependent nature of our contemporary world, it seems only logical for social work to be at the forefront of efforts to provide a broader, more comprehensive approach for examining and addressing both the positive and negative consequences of globalization.

In order to grasp the changing nature of living conditions, social circumstances, and practice opportunities and challenges across the globe, social work practice is challenged to identify new and creative ways for keeping informed about various cultures and the profession's responses to the needs of people in and from other countries. Educational opportunities include scholarly readings, course work, workshops, conferences, training sessions, internet sites, and educational trips. As with any form of social work practice, social workers also learn from their experiences with consumers of services. There is no formal substitute for the educational benefit obtained from critical thought and analysis of the cultural relevance of values, customs, beliefs, and behaviors as expressed by clients. Social workers and clients prosper when education is bidirectional, concerted, and ongoing.

In keeping with the NASW *Code of Ethics*, social workers will also want to document "competence in provision of services that are sensitive to clients' cultures and to differences among people and cultural groups" (NASW, 1996, p. 9). In our litigious age that emphasizes credentialing and limiting practice to defined scopes of practice, social workers will continue to be called on by regulatory entities (e.g., state licensing boards) and funding sources to provide evidence of their abilities and competency in practice. Arguably, it is no longer sufficient in many locales and jurisdictions simply to seek to understand the nature of social and cultural diversity. Instead, social workers need to document and be able to demonstrate in concrete ways (e.g., certificates of completion) sensitivity and competence in working with clients from various cultures. Indeed, as a means to assist social workers to keep abreast of current literature and best practices in areas of expertise, the NASW has initiated teleconferences for specialty practice sections for continuing education units. Using technological advancement for continuing education holds promise for learning about and documenting knowledge and competency in working with a variety of populations groups as well as innovation in international practice.

Some social workers believe that our profession is being challenged to "rethink whether a traditional professional approach is well-suited to the needs of a complex, diverse and divided world" (Mohan, 2005, p. 246). If globalization and the international nature of life are prompting and calling for adaptation in professional practice, then social workers, social work educators, and students of social work must be willing to step out of their comfort zones in order to consider and embrace occurrences, concepts, terms, beliefs, behaviors, practices, modes of change, policies, interests, values, and realities that are unfamiliar and must be willing to appropriately challenge conventional wisdom and modes of intervention.

This book presents examples of social work practice and policy in various countries for analysis and contemplation. With each example of international practice, allow yourself to imagine being in another country and become immersed into the national context, social situation, presenting circumstances, and social work responses. Frame thinking with the assumption that differences in intervention, policies, and programs are to be expected and reflect time, place, culture, and people. It is hoped that the various examples will serve as an impetus for learning more about situations, struggles, and the strengths of people in the countries discussed and promote additional professional involvement in addressing and improving social-economic conditions of people across the globe.

BASIC CONCEPTS AND TERMS

Few would disagree that the current interest in international social work "stems mainly from increased global interdependence. As such, many social work practitioners and scholars have argued that the field of social work must 'internationalize' itself to address these new, complex social problems stemming from the international context" (Xu, 2006, p. 679). Some social workers argue the ramifications of a global economy for social justices are multiple and complex and constitute one of the most important challenges for social work in the 21st century (Polack, 2004). However, this is not to suggest that international social work should be viewed solely on the basis of technological strides and trends toward social-economic interconnectedness that have been experienced over recent years. It is important to recognize that U.S. social workers have a history of involvement in humanitarian efforts across the globe, as evidenced by the contributions of social workers in the International Red Cross Movement and organizations such as the Peace Corps, the United Nations Relief and Rehabilitation Administration, and the United Nations Children's Fund.

Over three decades ago, Friedlander (1975) acknowledged social work's broader, global perspective in helping and in the conceptualization of the social environment. "For years, a number of social workers have taken it upon themselves to work for international development agencies and non-governmental organizations in direct services, administration, program planning, and development" (Fred, 2005, p. 4). Hence, social work's commitment to problems around the world and initiatives across national boundaries is not simply or solely attributable to recent trends involving globalization. Instead, social work has been pursuing and building momentum for international work based on the profession's long-standing devotion to principles of human rights and social justice. It is important to remember that "globalization is not new. It has been under way for centuries. What is new is the pace and the transforming effects" (Ramos & Briar-Lawson, 2004, p. 365).

So, what is international social work? There is not a simple answer to this question. Healy (2001) states: "The definition of the term *international social work* has been the subject of much debate. . . . international can mean any of the following: between or among two or more nations, of or pertaining to two or more nations or their citizens, pertaining to the relations between nations, having members or activities in several nations, or transcending national boundaries or viewpoints" (p. 5). Regardless of definition, Healy has identified four dimensions to international action—"internationally related domestic practice and advocacy, professional exchange, international practice, and international policy development and advocacy" (p. 7).

In an abstract fashion, the phrase "international social work" can be thought of and defined as focusing "on the profession and practice in different countries, the different roles that social workers perform, the practice methods they use, the problems they deal with, and the many challenges they face" (Hokenstad, Khinduka, & Midgley, 1992, p. 4). Using this definition, and consistent with the impetus of this book, the primary focus of international social work involves social work practice as defined and implemented in various countries. In social work practice and education, professionals and students learn and can benefit from thoughtful analysis of examples of practice and policy in other countries. International social work promotes an awareness and exchange of information about perspectives, approaches, and techniques utilized in social work that are grounded in a specific country's traditions, laws, culture, geographical setting, and social environment.

In their education in the United States, many social workers have been introduced or exposed to social policies and human services from other countries. Projects and papers typically are designed with the intention to expand thinking, examine the merits of practices from different countries, and analyze the influence of culture and values on policy formation and the provision of services. An example is the critical analysis of the strengths and limitations of universal healthcare policies in Canada as compared to the privatization of healthcare in the United States. When confronted with such an assignment, students often grapple with the appropriateness and applicability of policies and service delivery as defined and implemented in another country. This type of analysis is called *international social welfare* or *comparative social policy*.

A growing body of literature in social work is dedicated to the study of people living across country boundaries. Furman and Negi (2007) identify and describe "the emergence of a population of migrants who live their lives across transnational borders" (p. 107). The term "transnational migration" refers to people "engaged in lives across countries and cultures for economic reasons, while immigrants and traditional migrants discontinue such consistent movement across boundaries with the passing of time" (Furman & Negi, 2007, p. 108). When working with transnational migrants, social workers need an understanding of two or more cultures as well as family structure, political influences, social-economic conditions, and technical capabilities (e.g., communication and transportation technology) that necessitate, support, and challenge transnational lifestyles.

Xu (2006) proposes an expansive yet sensible definition of international social work that emphasizes the influence of organizations and agencies in determining professional practice and exchange across national boundaries. For example, are community-based agencies willing to engage in international partnerships, and at what cost or benefit? This perspective recognizes that the definition of international social work practice in many settings is influenced directly by the perceptions of agency and community leaders and stakeholders concerning the impact of globalization and migration for a particular geographical area (Xu, 2006, p. 684). An agency-oriented approach is needs based, highlighting the reality that many organizations and communities become involved in programming, services, and educational efforts in a reactive rather than proactive fashion—based on organizational or community need(s).

Finally, as mentioned at the beginning of this chapter, the International Federation of Social Workers (IFSW) has worked with various international organizations, including the International Association of Schools of Social Work, to create a commonly accepted definition of social work that transcends national boundaries. The IFSW (2005) defines social work in this manner:

> The social work profession promotes social change, problem solving in human relationships and the empowerment and liberation of people to enhance well-being. Utilising theories of human behaviour and social systems, social work intervenes at the points where people interact with their environments. Principles of human rights and social justice are fundamental to social work. (p. 1)

While one could debate the specifics of any number of definitional aspects, this definition is an important milestone for providing social workers with

Reflection Exercises

1. Visit the homepage of the International Federation of Social Workers/ International Association of Schools of Social Work (http://www.ifsw .org/home) and read about the organization's mission, value and principle statement, and planned activities. What are the themes of the information? What information do you find especially helpful when considering an international experience?
2. Group Debate: Randomly divide class members into two groups. The first group supports the agency's decision (presented next) and describes the merits of the decision. The second group points out the negative consequences of such a decision.

   My child welfare agency is experiencing appreciable budget problems. These financial woes have forced leadership to prioritize the needs of consumers in the community over the plight of people from and in other parts of the world. For example, the agency plans to eliminate international adoptions, the refugee relocation program, and emergency services for people unable to document their legal status in the United States.

a strong foundation for structuring thought and action for practice in international arenas.

CONSIDERATIONS FOR TRANSITIONING TO AND EMPLOYMENT IN A FOREIGN COUNTRY

Social workers fortunate enough to have spent time in foreign lands often have a romantic approach to travel and learning about different places, ways, and people. Reading about, encountering, and contemplating everyday life in another country can be personally and professionally enriching and inspirational. Both opportunities and challenges are presented to social workers when studying and practicing abroad. Salient considerations include: language acquisition, meeting people, developing new relationships, securing reliable sources of information, safety concerns, the country's political stability, culture shock (e.g., unfamiliarity with local customs), and the presence of infrastructure (e.g., agencies and organizations) for professional oversight to process important issues or dilemmas.

In reality, most visitors and professionals in a foreign country must learn to rely on acquaintances and friends on the ground to support everyday functioning and activities. It is common to rely on a trustworthy go-to person or host family to help address the complexities of everyday existence (e.g., transportation, shelter, food, laws, and customs). Especially when language is a barrier, seemingly simple and basic tasks can become overwhelming. As an example, in many developing countries, commodes are not regularly available. "Squatters" and makeshift holes in the ground may be the norm. Sanitary toilet paper can be scarce. Imagine trying to go to the bathroom without anyone explaining the local scene and the dos and don'ts.

When considering employment in social work in a different country, White (2006) suggests sensitivity to and understanding of "differences in social welfare systems and legislation; in the organization of human services and role expectations; and in communication styles, professional terminology and perhaps also in language spoke, as well as in professional qualifications" (p. 631). The tradition and current implementation of the practice of social work and human services in any particular country is especially relevant. A primary consideration involves the professional authority and stature of social workers: expectations, rights, and ethical responsibilities. In a practical sense, what types of activities and functions can social workers perform with consumers of services?

Across borders, do not assume a common definition, understanding, or credentialing of social workers. In some countries, the term *social worker* refers to a formally recognized status that requires an educational degree in social work. Indeed, social work practice could be differentiated by basic versus advanced practice, contingent on degree level and/or number of years of practice. In other countries, becoming a social worker is more an artifact of experience in social welfare organizations, a special certification, or governmental designation (classification). In the United States, status as a social worker is regulated by state law and differs appreciably from state to state.

Additionally, expect theoretical orientations or the epistemological basis of social work practice to vary from nation to nation. In some countries, social work practice is more clearly grounded in problem solving and less oriented to an examination of the strengths of people, as can be seen in the IFSW's definition of social work. Other countries emphasize cognitive-behavioral and evidence-based approaches, as currently can be found in many parts of the United States. Conversely, other parts of the world view social work practice as more of an art than science with little consideration of measurable outcomes. The challenge in these realms for international social workers is to avoid the undue imposition or exclusion of modes of practice, especially biases derived from one's country of origin. Lum (2007) states:

> If the mission of social work is truly to promote social and economic justice, we must translate that commitment into culturally relevant and nonoppressive social work practice. Social workers need to do their own work in relation to understanding their own boundaries of moral exclusion and developing a stance of inclusion, in which all people are entitled to the same values, rules, and considerations of fairness. (p. 89)

The pragmatic aspects of obtaining employment across country borders "can be easier if transnational arrangements already exist for worker mobility between specified countries" (White, 2006, p. 632). For the European Union, there is the European Job Mobility Portal (www.europa.eu.int/eures). This is a good example of how countries can use technology to collaborate to provide information and guidance concerning employment opportunities in allied countries. When regularly updated, this kind of portal system can facilitate the fluid movement of professionals across national boundaries and effectively assist organizations in addressing labor market needs.

The recognition and validation of professional social work degrees and credentials relies heavily on designated national regulatory organizations. For example, in the United States, the Council on Social Work Education (CSWE) examines and makes a determination concerning the comparability (equivalency) of a social work degree from another country with a bachelor's of social work (BSW) or master's of social work (MSW) earned from an American university. "According to Todd Lennon of CSWE . . . CSWE considers admission criteria, level and duration of course work length and supervision of field instruction and the content of the program from which the degree was received" (White, 2006, p. 635).

Other practical considerations for social workers hoping to practice in other countries involve the cost and time involved in the processing of visas and work permits. Understanding the myriad of regulations and forms to move paperwork through embassies, consulates, and immigration offices can be challenging and a barrier for employment. It is not unusual for people to hire attorneys or other professionals who specialize in obtaining visas and work permits. Employing a reputable person to prepare and efficiently process applications is often a huge advantage that assists people in receiving services.

CONTEMPLATE MOTIVATIONS FOR INVOLVEMENT IN INTERNATIONAL SOCIAL WORK PRACTICE

Before engaging in international social work practice, ask yourself two important questions: Why here, and why now? As with any form of social work practice, the primary motivation for engagement in practice must center on the needs and concerns of consumers of services and one's professional preparation and strengths. Even the most cursory of assessments of the effects of globalization on the human condition would suggest that social-economic inequality, poverty, oppression, and strife over human rights can be found in many nations and across the globe. Indeed, many social scientists would argue that "in general, a significant economic change is likely to benefit some while hurting others. Globalization is not just about dollars and cents: globalization takes place with a social context where it [regularly] impacts upon people and their environments" (Ramos & Briar-Lawson, 2004, p. 372).

Involvement in international social work practice should be intentional, meaningful, and centered on using one's talents for the benefit of consumer groups. A conscious and concerted effort should be made to ensure that international practice is advantageous to the identified client populations, not a vacationlike adventure in a foreign land. Social workers participating in efforts abroad have a value-added effect as opposed to being a drain on scarce resources. For example, in writing this book, the authors were careful to not burden or pull social workers away from their practices and work with client populations. In one instance, the authors of this book decided not to request a contribution from a social worker whose personal and professional commitments abroad were so great that writing would have presented an undue hardship.

Like other forms of social work practice, international practice should not be a self-centered, self-serving endeavor primarily for personal or professional gain. Although social workers certainly benefit intellectually and otherwise and can enjoy and learn from experiences abroad, international social work practice is predicated on improving the well-being of consumers of social services. When considering participation in international social work and international exchanges, it is important to acquire an understanding and overview of the other country; identify the benefits and costs for you and others associated with your practice; and clarify the specific expectations, roles, and responsibilities associated with the new social work position (Mathiesen & Lager, 2007).

Networking, knowing and developing an ability to interact with people and professionals with an organization(s) in another country, along with

Reflection Exercises

1. Go to http://go.hrw.com/atlas/norm_htm/world.htm and click on particular countries with which you are familiar as a result of reading or experiences. What do you recall about the countries, and why? Now click on countries that are totally unfamiliar to you. Discover at least three points of interest about one of these countries. Why are some countries more familiar to you than others? What are the points of contact we have with the world around us?

2. Go to http://www.gksoft.com/govt/en and explore the governmental structures of the countries that interest you. What can you surmise about the country from its form of government? Consider how the role or possible role of social work is influenced by a country's form of government.

---

an interest in and a passion for learning more about a particular culture are common sources of motivation for work, travel, and developing affiliations abroad. In this book, the examples of international social work practice reflect these functional realities. People tend to migrate toward and network with people on the basis of familiarity, interest, and interpersonal contacts. Many of the contributors to this book have long-standing professional relationships with each other. As suggested by Healy (2001), countries selected for inclusion in this book could have been chosen on the basis of a host of dimensions (e.g., state of development, status of the profession of social work, rankings of well-being, geographical region). The examples of international social work practice you are about to read, much like the migration of many social workers across national boundaries, came about primarily as a result of relationship building, contacts in social work, and the professional experiences of the authors. For the most part, country selection was predicated on professional relationships from social work practice and education.

READING EXAMPLES OF INTERNATIONAL SOCIAL WORK PRACTICE AND POLICY

In the chapters to come, you will be presented with thought-provoking examples of international social work practice and policy. For analytical and critical thinking, consider these criteria when reading each example of practice and policy analysis:

- Foundation areas and core competencies
- Culture
- Organizational context
- Issues of safety and self-care in international social work practice
- Ethical considerations

These elements can be points of discussion for use in class or in conversations with classmates and professional colleagues.

Foundation Areas and Core Competencies

Traditionally, social work education has identified foundation areas (e.g., research, practice, social policy and services, values and ethics, etc.) that when considered collectively identify social work as having a body of knowledge, value orientation, and skill base for professional development. For many social workers, Greenwood's (1957) article "Attributes of a Profession" stimulated thinking about and analysis of the unique nature, authority, and subculture of our profession. As social workers, we constitute "people who 'profess' or claim to know something special about particular phenomena. This claim to special knowledge is not an insignificant thing, for it is on the basis of such claims that doctors, lawyers, social workers, and other professional groups maintain privileged positions in society" (Gilbert, Miller, & Specht, 1980, p. 14).

Aligned with each example of international social work practice in this book is a different knowledge area typically associated with the profession of social work. In 2008, the CSWE endorsed new standards (Educational Policy and Accreditation, 2008 Standards) reconceptualizing foundation (knowledge) areas into "core competencies" for the preparation of social workers. In writing this book, a conscious and concerted attempt has been made to pay homage to traditionally recognized foundation areas in social work as well as to embrace the spirit of newly transformed CSWE standards delineating core competencies in social work education, emphasizing critical thinking, ethical practice, human diversity, research-informed practice, human behavior and the social environment, social and economic well-being, policy practice, field education, and practice with clients at multiple levels.

When examining examples of practice in another country, ask yourself a variety of questions about the appropriateness, applicability, and unique nature of each foundation/competency area for social work practice. For example, is research for informed practice in South Africa (Chapter 6) the same or different from research in your native land? How might field education, now defined as signature pedagogy in social work education, differ in Portugal (Chapter 4) from that of other countries? How is human behavior and the social environment uniquely defined in Costa Rica (Chapter 7)? Ultimately, in a comparative fashion, one of your tasks should be to focus on the merits of how knowledge, skills, and the value orientation of social work are implemented in a unique fashion in each specific country and how they differ from your own national experience.

Try to approach each chapter with a creative yet skeptical spirit. Lindsey (2005) suggests six general themes for use when engaged in study abroad and contemplating foreign countries; these include: "opening the mind to new ways of thinking; awareness and insight into one's own values and beliefs; social awareness and challenges to societal values and beliefs; appreciation of difference, cultural sensitivity, and anti-discriminatory practice; social justice; and professional identity development" (p. 229). Attentiveness to these themes will be helpful for understanding and deciphering the relevance of each identified knowledge area within a national context. As an example, how does cultural awareness and knowledge of values and beliefs in Mongolia (Chapter 5) inform and assist the reader to think about engagement, assessment, intervention, and evaluation of practice with individuals and families?

Culture

Upon return from a foreign land, it is not uncommon for interested coworkers, friends, and family members to ask: "So, what was it like living and working in [insert name of the country]?" Frequently, returnees hesitate to share a mere glimpse of their experience abroad. They can be apprehensive about entering brief conversations to describe complicated matters in complex cultural environments. One fear or source of caution involves the ability to accurately and fully describe and share the culture of another country. A person may think: How can I ever do justice in communicating to friends and colleagues my immersion in another country?

Historically, a country's culture has been conceptualized as a binding force or the social glue of a nation that involves shared knowledge, beliefs, morals, and customs, passed from generation to generation. Culture can be thought of as a blueprint for living or a prescription for life in a country—advancing ever-changing expectations and standards for members of a society concerning acceptable values, beliefs, behaviors, and activities.

For social workers engaged in international practice, the ability to understand culture and acquire a worldview between cultures for helpers and help seekers is crucial for participation in culturally appropriate practice and policy-oriented endeavors in foreign lands (Kee, 2003). For international practice, either through structured opportunities (e.g., classes, readings, and workshops) or less formal, experiential means, social workers need to understand and reconcile differences and develop a cognitive synthesis between their new and old society and culture (Kee, 2003). Making a deliberate effort to front-load information, taking preparatory steps for immersion into another country, and reflecting on one's own culturally bound values and beliefs are important ingredients for combating culture shock and forming an appreciation of difference and cultural sensitivity to engage in antidiscriminatory practice (Lindsey, 2005).

In most societies, language, verbal and nonverbal, is a primary mode of communicating and sharing cultural aspects. Culture is socially transmitted through communication from members to members, individually and via groups and technology (e.g., media). Because language structures communication, one of the most relevant considerations for international practice involves "the importance of language in communicating with others . . . how language structures not only thinking, but the ways in which individuals perceive and make sense of their world and subsequently use these understandings in their interactions with others" (Dominelli, 2004, p. 515).

Before traveling abroad, you will have to make a decision concerning language and its role in learning about culture and subcultures of any land. Can you rely on your native language to understand another country's culture and effectively communicate with people? If necessary, how quickly can you adopt another language? Will you need to rely on a translator(s) to function successfully in another country? What are the limitations of depending on others for translation?

Organizational Context

Each of the examples of international social work practice or policy in this book takes place in and/or refers to organizational contexts. Organizations constitute a specific form of social unit where people unite and are structured to accomplish a common goal(s). In modern societies, organizations are known for placing "a high moral value on rationality, effectiveness, and efficiency . . . by coordinating a large number of human actions, the organizations create a powerful social tool" (Etzioni, 1964, p. 1). In developing countries, organizations may be less formal, rationale, and purposeful, emphasizing social-emotional and relational aspects.

Given Etzioni's definition, it can be seen that the unique features of any organization, be it a social service agency, business, or club, are influenced by its societal and cultural context on the basis of common goals of people. More specifically, human service organizations tend to be built with the size, complexity, division of labor, and diversity of services needed to address identified goals and needs.

If organizations are open social systems and seek input from the broader environment for forming and adapting to "serve the various needs of society and its citizens" (Etzioni, 1964, p. 1), special attention needs to be given to how agency goals are established as well as which values influence the creation and development of organizational goals. For example, try to assess how the broader national context (e.g., political, religious, and economic conditions) and culture (e.g., beliefs and values) have impacted the organizational context of social work practice in each particular country. Management style, philosophical orientation to helping, ritualized practices, artwork, agency symbols, use of technology, jargon, shared assumptions about consumers of services as well as a variety of other elements can be dictated by organizational climate and culture (Ott, 1989).

Given the interconnected nature of countries and the movement of people across and between national boundaries (transnational migration) in the current era, Furman and Negi (2007) suggest that in many countries, an "important service need is to establish multi-service social welfare agencies that are capable of responding to transnational populations" (p. 42). Multiservice agencies are human service organizations that offer a variety of goods and services to address the needs of identified population groups. As you read examples in this book, seek to identify the presence of multiservice social welfare agencies in each country. To and from which nations-states are people moving, and why? Would multiservice agencies be a realistic consideration in each identified country—why or why not? What type of expertise (e.g., language, knowledge of cultural and economic circumstances) is needed to practice social work in multiservice agencies with transnational population groups?

Issues of Safety and Self-Care in International Social Work Practice

As you contemplate social work practice in a variety of national settings, an essential consideration involves the safety, health, and overall well-being of each social worker. In order to help others, a professional needs to take care of her- or himself. A cardinal rule is to avoid placing oneself in danger. Familiarity with surroundings and the establishment of policies, procedures, and personnel to create a safe workplace are essential.

While social work practice in another country can be perilous, the quest and excitement for learning about people and cultures in other lands can cloud judgment and place a social worker at risk. In international social work practice, especially practice in developing countries, social workers can be tempted to circumvent typical safeguards in practice (e.g., supervisory oversight and safety procedures) in favor of very fluid, merging, undefined, and unstructured work environments. Caution is required to ensure that the passion for helping people abroad does not taint or supersede practice wisdom for maintaining safety. As examples, traveling alone, venturing into unknown surroundings, eating strange foods (dietary considerations), exposure to disease, and defying local norms, values, and laws can have disastrous consequences. As you read each chapter, identify obvious or seemingly inherent risks for each social worker.

Concerning self-care, Gibelman and Furman (2008) state, "An emotionally volatile worker is of little use to clients" (p. 222). Social workers need to identify their vulnerabilities in working with people and take appropriate actions to ensure responsible, professional action with consumers of services. Taking time off, seeking professional help, maintaining sound and supportive supervision, surrounding oneself with positive and constructive colleagues, and establishing clear boundaries between professional and personal self are examples of ways to promote and enhance self-care. Stresses and tensions for social workers engaged in international social work practice can be uniquely challenging and idiosyncratic. In each chapter, take a few moments and make a special effort to ascertain what you think would constitute sources of stress or strain for a social worker. Given these demands, how might a social worker effectively embrace self-care?

Ethical Considerations

No matter the venue, many social workers would readily agree that ethical awareness and conduct is a foundation of professional social work practice. However, one of the most important considerations for a social worker participating in international practice and research involves "considering ethical matters . . . within the social, economic, and political reality of the host country" (Young, Johnson, & Bryant, 2002, p. 89). These social, economic, and political realities provide the context for and often shape beliefs concerning what constitutes ethical behavior and action by social workers, producing the potential for considerable variability in definition of ethical principles and acceptable professional conduct from country to country.

In an effort to promote ethical standards for social workers worldwide, the International Federation of Social Workers and the International Association of Schools of Social Work (IASSW) have developed a document to cut across borders to delineate general principles and guidelines on professional conduct "to encourage social workers across the world to reflect on the challenges and dilemmas that face them and make ethically informed decisions about how to act" (IFSW, 2005, p. 3). Consistent with many national codes of ethics, these ethical principles and guidelines, titled "Ethics in Social Work, Statement of Principles," were approved by the IFSW and IASSW in 2004 and emphasize respect of human rights and dignity, social justice, competence, integrity, compassion, professionalism, confidentiality, accountability, collaboration, ethically informed decision making, and evaluation of national codes. The complete and most recent version of this statement can be found on the IFSW's Web site at www .IFSW.org.

Most chapters in this book highlight an ethical dilemma grounded in a country context for your reflection and thought. Consider each chapter's ethical consideration with the IFSW's "Ethics in Social Work, Statement of Principles" as well as your native country's code of ethics for social workers. How do each country's social-economic and political conditions influence relevance and applicability of the ethnical issue? If you were assigned to an ethics panel to review each situation, how would you respond as a professional to each ethical concern or allegation?

FORMING AN IMAGINATION FOR INQUIRY

In a seminal book, C. Wright Mills (1959) called on social scientists to look beyond their everyday lives (work, family, and circumstances) to critically examine the experiences and social patterns of people in connection with corresponding social structures (e.g., countries) given a specific time in history. He sought a conscious and deliberate, not necessarily scientific, examination of the social-cultural environment and ways of life of others. Mills referred to this ability as the sociological imagination.

When applied to the examination of social work practice and policy in foreign lands, the quest becomes to identify and critically analyze the essential features and qualities of each country, group of people, organization, social structure, and form of social work practice and policy. In order to embrace Mills's sociological imagination, strive to leave behind your own unique worries, trials, and realities of everyday life. Concentrate on content in each chapter, and attempt to immerse yourself in the examples of international practice and policy, as if you actually were the social worker in each country. Cognitively place yourself in each national context and imagine the pleasures, trials, and enjoyment of each experience. Who knows; someday you may experience a social work practice as professional in a distant land.

SUMMARY

An increasing number of social workers are engaging in international practice. Certainly the profession of social work recognizes globalization as a feature that needs to be addressed through curriculum, workshops, seminars, conferences, research agendas, professional travel, and the thoughtful consideration of the experiences of social workers around the world. Globalization challenges social workers to expand their fields of practice and knowledge and to consider social justice from a broader, worldwide perspective.

This chapter introduces you to the idea of international social work by discussing key concepts and suggesting that you consider unfamiliar countries and customs. Placing social work in a larger context promises exciting adventures for social workers interested in a variety of cultural and political factors across consumer systems. As you read each country-based chapter, live vicariously. Allow yourself to take the role of the other and cognitively assume the status of a social worker in another country. This approach promises to be liberating, filled with contextually relevant ideas, thoughts, experiences, challenges, and modes of professional engagement from the everyday lives and experiences of colleagues committed to the ideals of professional social work.

REFERENCES

Craig de Silva, E. (2008). Reaching out across the world. NASW News, 52, no. 3, 3.

Dominelli, L. (2004). Crossing international divides: Language and communication within international settings. Social Work Education: The International Journal, 23, 515–525.

Etzioni, A. (1964). Modern organizations. Englewood Cliffs, NJ: Prentice-Hall.

Fred, Sheryl (2005). Building an international field of practice. NASW News, 50, no. 4, 4.

Friedlander, W. (1975). International social welfare. Englewood Cliffs, NJ: Prentice-Hall.

Furman, R., & Negi, N. J. (2007). Social work practice with transnational Latino populations. International Social Work, 50, 107–112.

Gibelman, M., & Furman, R. (2008). *Navigating human service organizations.* Chicago: Lyceum Books.

Gilbert, N., Miller, H., & Specht, H. (1980). *An introduction to social work practice.* Englewood Cliffs, NJ: Prentice-Hall.

Greenwood, E. (1957). Attributes of a profession. *Social Work, 2,* 45–55.

Healy, L. M. (2001). *International social work: Professional action in an interdependent world.* New York: Oxford University Press.

Hokenstad, M., Khinduka, S., & Midgley, J. (1992). *Profiles in international social work.* Washington, DC: National Association of Social Workers.

International Federation of Social Workers. (2005). Definition of social work. Retrieved June 10, 2008, from http://ifsw.org/en/p38000208.html?print=true.

International Federation of Social Workers/International Association of Schools of Social Work. (2008). Ethics in social work: Statement of principles. Retrieved September 18, 2008, from http://www.ifsw.org/home.

Kee, L. (2003). Drawing lessons from local designated helpers to develop culturally appropriate social work practice. *Asia Pacific Journal of Social Work, 2,* 26–45.

Leggett, K. (2008). Making a world of difference. *International Educator, 17,* 42–49.

Lindsey, E. W. (2005). Study abroad and values development in social work students. *Journal of Social Work Education, 41,* 229–249.

Lum, D. (2007). *Culturally competent practice: A framework for understanding diverse groups and justice issues.* Belmont, CA: Thomson Brooks/Cole.

Mathiesen, S., & Lager, P. (2007). A model for developing international student exchanges. *Social Work Education: The International Journal, 26,* 280–291.

Mills, C. W. (1959). *The sociological imagination.* New York: Oxford University Press.

Mohan, B. (2005). New internationalism: Social work's dilemmas, dreams, and delusions. *International Social Work, 48,* 241–250.

National Association of Social Workers. (1996). *Code of ethics.* Washington, DC: Author.

Ott, J. S. (1989). *The organizational culture perspective.* Pacific Grove, CA: Brooks/Cole.

Polack, R. J. (2004). Social justice and the global economy: New challenges for social work in the 21st century. *Social Work, 49,* 281–290.

Ramos, B. M., & Briar-Lawson, K. (2004). Globalization and international social work. In A. L. Sallee (Ed.), *Social work & social welfare: An introduction* (pp. 356–378). Peosta, IA: Eddie Bowers.

White, R. (2006). Opportunities and challenges for social workers crossing borders. *International Social Work, 49*, 629–640.

Xu, G. (2006). Defining international social work: A social service agency perspective. *International Social Work, 49*, 679–692.

Young, L., Johnson, K. W., & Bryant, D. (2002). Conducting a therapeutic community training experiment in Peru: research design and implementation issues. *Journal of Social Work Research and Evaluation, 3*, 89–102.

2

Perspectives on the Relevance of Examples of International Practice and Policy

Dennis D. Long

Begin where the learner is. . . . Use whatever past experiences the individual brings to the situation as a foundation for more learning.

—C. Towle (1945, p. 146)

A *perspective* is a way of looking at or viewing an event or occurrence. In this chapter, the relevance and merit of examples of international social work practice and policy are examined from a variety of perspectives. Entertaining various perspectives for the analysis of examples assists the reader to identify and think about the salience and importance of content from an assortment of standpoints (e.g., scientific, diversity, ways of knowing, and theoretical). Enabling and training yourself to think about expectations, beliefs, behaviors, and actions in a host of ways lies at the heart of a liberal arts education and is an essential ingredient for informing judgments and decision making in social work practice.

When conceptualizing the structure and format of this book, the authors were deliberate in deciding to solicit and examine nonscientific examples of practice and policy. The primary intent of chapters highlighting examples of international social work practice and policy is to plunge authors and readers in an unbridled and unrestricted fashion into real-life experiences of social workers and human service professionals in an effort to expand and broaden analytical thought. Chapters represent unique opportunities to delve into the lives of social workers in various countries. Presentations of experiences in practice and policy in various countries are intended to prompt and facilitate the analysis of each country's cultural values, social structures, and social welfare system as well as the contributions of social welfare and services to empower, strengthen, challenge, oppress, marginalize, and/or privilege its citizens.

As you read from chapter to chapter, commonalities and distinctions across national states and borders concerning human rights, freedoms, safety, shared (public) needs, human dignity, environmental assets, standards of living, technological capabilities, and the availability and delivery of goods and services will become apparent and are worth noting and thinking about. Of particular interest are the various outlooks and strategies utilized and implemented by social workers in each country to promote human and civil rights, social justice, and sustainable social change. Given today's global interconnectedness, social workers often need to be resourceful and proactive in thinking about and responding to human needs in a variety of ways, given the societal context of practice. A particular technique, intervention, program, and/or policy may be of great use in one country but inappropriate or unsuitable for use in another setting. Chapter content is designed to enable the reader to consider and debate the relevancy of problems, policies, services, programs, interventions, and helping strategies in relation to societal realities and trends for practice with individuals, families, and groups (microsystems) as well as change with organizations, communities, and societies (macrosystems).

HOW NONSCIENTIFIC EXAMPLES DIFFER FROM CASE STUDIES

The various country-based examples offered in this book do not constitute case studies. As you may have already learned in introductory research coursework, case studies are designed and implemented with scientific rigor and scrutiny to address specific research questions. Case studies are purposeful and intended to collect data in an objective and structured fashion for analysis by researchers. In a case study, data and findings are linked and ultimately evaluated in relationship to the premises and propositions set forth by the study's research question(s). Frequently they are used as a means for concept formation and/or to address how and/or why questions in a real-life context (Baker, 1999, pp. 322–323).

In the social sciences, case studies are characterized by an in-depth study of a specific unit of analysis (e.g., a single event, family, group, organization, town, community, country). As such, results cannot be viewed as representative of similar cases or the basis for generalizations to similar units of analysis. The examples of international practice and policy found in this book lack the overall descriptive detail for addressing in any great length or depth "how" and "why" questions. Examples are intended to be instances or illustrations that provide the reader with a glimpse of practice and policy from abroad to produce insight and stimulate thoughtful consideration, reflection, and social comparison (e.g., across countries).

The same caution concerning generalizability applies to the examples of practice and policy presented in this book. Examples are not intended to be generalized for use in social work practice. The circumstances and situations confronted by people in various countries constitute complex phenomena typically involving a host of factors. As such, it would be simplistic, misleading, and naive to suggest that a specific experience or example of intervention with a family or group of people in one country would be directly applicable to another family or group in that same or a similar (kindred) country.

Examples constitute individual, unique occurrences; no two incidences are exactly the same. As with case studies, it is more appropriate to view examples of international practice and policy as being helpful in facilitating thought about the similarities and differences concerning specific happenings (e.g., social and cultural situations, events, definitions of need, interventions, service delivery, and efforts for planned change) across countries and as information for prompting and/or informing future scientific inquiry rather than as research evidence for shaping and dictating practice.

DIVERSITY

Appreciation of and concern for human diversity is at times an explicit and always an implicit goal in country-based examples of international practice and policy. Thoughtful examination and analysis of examples can be a useful tool for deciphering the meaning, role, and bearing of human diversity in social work practice. View yourself as an active learner embracing examples of practice and policy as a means to enter and contemplate unique societal bound realities. The diversity challenge is to conceptualize and understand the role and relevance of multiple dimensions of diversity (e.g., culture, race, ethnicity, gender, social-economic class, gender identity and expression, political ideology, religion, age, and sexual orientation) through the description of the lives of the human beings (social workers, clients, and citizens) involved in international social work practice. Strive to enter the cultural context of another country, respecting each nation's potential and avoiding the temptation to view a country and its conditions and the actions of its people on the basis of your own preconceived beliefs, values, and standards (Freire, 1970).

Lindsey (2005) suggests that when studying social practice from abroad, social workers should work diligently to identify underlying values and philosophies and the relationship of value-laden tenets to social work intervention. As you read each example of practice and policy, pay special attention to "cultural diversity and examine differences in patterns of ethnicity and culture within each country" (Lindsey, 2005, p. 233). For example, make a special effort to identify and note any instances of what might be perceived as or constitute discriminatory behavior, institutional racism, cultural oppression, as well as cultural strengths in the delivery or implementation of both formal and informal social services and assistance.

Using a strengths orientation, Hurdle (2002) describes and advocates for what can be called *culture-centered practice*, placing a distinct emphasis on "recognition of the strengths of communities of color . . . [and] cultural practices into program delivery" (pp. 189–190). Human diversity and differences often constitute sources of identity, support, encouragement, and empowerment. Frequently people take pride in their cultural background and uniqueness and take pleasure in telling others about group accomplishments and advancement.

Reflection Exercise

Status of Women in Examples of International Practice and Policy

> While the majority of women worldwide live in patriarchal societies, there is great cross-cultural variation in the gendered challenges women face and how they face them. (Burn, 2005, p. 4)

Using this statement as a guiding premise, complete row A of Table 2.1 by briefly jotting down your thoughts and ideas for items 1 to 5. After you read each chapter of international practice and policy, return to this page and write some notes in the appropriate row. Use Internet search tools (e.g., Google) and/or supplementary readings to complement chapter readings in addressing items 1 to 5 for each country. Strive to become an informed citizen and professional concerning the strengths and challenges of women in each country.

Table 2.1   Cross-Cultural Examination of Strengths and Challenges for Women

Country/ Chapter	1. Apparent Struggles for Women	2. Identifiable Strengths of Women	3. How Do or Might Women Act as Agents for Change?	4. Is There Evidence via Social Policy or Social Work Practice of Specific Rights of Women?	5. How Does Culture Contribute to the Needs and Abilities of Women?
A Your Native Country					
B Mongolia (Chapter 4)					
C Portugal (Chapter 5)					
D South Africa (Chapter 6)					
E Costa Rica (Chapter 7)					
F United States: Appalachian Region (Chapter 8)					
G Malawi (Chapter 9)					
H Peru (Chapter 10)					

As you complete each row in this table, take a few minutes to examine perceived cultural differences and similarities for women across countries. The goal of this exercise is to illustrate that women's issues vary by society and are bound in components of culture—mainly societal values, traditions, beliefs, and norms. Society and cultural influences are important considerations for any meaningful analysis of gender rights, opportunities, and equality. Once again, take the role of the other by imagining that you are a woman living in each of the identified countries. Use role enactment to determine how it feels to face everyday demands that dictate interpersonal behavior and relationships in the home and workplace (e.g., as a wife, mother, and worker). Strive for specificity, and identify unique expectations governing the actions of and opportunities for women.

KNOWLEDGE VIA EXAMPLES OF INTERNATIONAL PRACTICE AND POLICY

The quest for knowledge and understanding has traditionally taken many forms and embraced a variety of paradigms—scientific, philosophical, theological, and historical, to name a few. Bacon (1970) states that "human understanding is most excited by that which strikes and enters the mind at once and suddenly, and by which the imagination is immediately filled and inflated" (p. 91). While an appreciable amount of academic study across the world is grounded in and dedicated to scientific pursuit and inquiry, clearly people learn and expand their thinking via a multitude of contemporary ways of knowing, such as life experiences, examples, television, Internet sites, blogs, newspapers, theoretical insight, and artistic expression and illustrations. Bias and accuracy are distinct concerns with any pursuit of knowledge, especially when the motive to sell (e.g., sell airtime and advertisements) or persuade (e.g., religious or political propaganda) can lead to exaggeration and distortion in the description of accounts of everyday life.

When seeking knowledge from examples of international social work policy and practice, it is important to temper the enthusiasm and excitement associated with learning about new and different ways of approaching social work practice with rational thinking—analytical thought, a sense of skepticism, and an inquisitive mind. Rather than accepting ideas and actions from another country at face value, attempt to contextualize information and seek to confirm the authenticity and relevancy of findings. As an illustration, in the United States, companies have been known to create zero-tolerance policies concerning discrimination. At face value, it would seem helpful that organizations in a formal and public way pronounce strong opposition to discriminatory actions and behavior in the workplace. However, what is the efficacy of zero-tolerance policies? Are such policies really intended to prohibit discrimination, or are they simply glib public relations ploys? It is crucial to look beyond the stated goal(s) of any policy and ascertain its practical meaning and implementation. A statement of zero tolerance tells us little about how an organization intends to react to instances of discriminatory behavior. Have people been terminated for exhibiting racist or sexist actions? Is the policy applied throughout the organization with the same force? Are there formal mechanisms for educating employees about discrimination and detecting and reporting discriminatory behavior? What does zero tolerance mean in the context it is being applied?

Neopositivists would have people believe that scientific, empirical study represents the true and substantiated way of knowing. Yet Mannheim and others have suggested historical shifts in the exploration of human life and phenomenon, including a contemporary diversion from spiritual, religious realities to the study of social and economic conditions (Speier, 1970, p. 271). While the analysis of examples does not constitute empirical investigation, careful and intentional contemplation of examples can be revealing and informative concerning spiritual, religious, political, social, economic, and familial factors as well as their interconnections for informing and influencing social work practice and policy.

In his writings on methodological considerations for examining cultural patterns, Wolff (1970) warns: "'Meaningful presentation of the culture' is its reinterpretation in such a way to make its uniqueness incorporable into the universe of discourse of the student's and of his [her] readers'" (p. 326). It is relatively safe to assume that the descriptions or depictions of country-based cultural patterns in this book constitute authors' interpretations of realities. Even when stringent research methods are used, cultural patterns and phenomena are susceptible to observation and perceptions of the viewer(s). Hence, examples of international social work in this book should be thought of as interpretative descriptions of practice and policy intended for meaningful professional discourse.

Many social workers conceptualize and depict practice as a unique mixture or blend of science and art. Professionals rely on science to qualify and quantify the strengths and problems of various population groups as well as empirically supported modes of intervention that reflect best practices. The "art" of social work refers to the less tangible, often culturally bound aspects of practice. Typically these aspects are derived from years of experience and the ability to identify and consider a variety of contextual circumstances and conditions that warrant reflection when working with population groups in a specific city, state, or region. In this book, the examples of practice and policy are meant to be thought provoking and revealing. They are to be used in conjunction with best practices in building relationships, assessment, and intervention, at multiple levels (micro and macro) in contemporary practice and policy formation and development across the globe.

To illustrate this observational (less scientific) element, in many rural areas in the United States, cultural norms continue to prohibit recognition of and respect for homosexuality. In many rural locales, practice and policy initiatives to promote protective physical and social environments (e.g., safe spaces and zones) to thwart harassment on the basis of sexual orientation face unique barriers, especially when compared to the situation in many cities in America (e.g., San Francisco and Seattle). Examples illustrating the way cultural values, norms, and patterns of action (e.g., specific discriminatory behaviors and "gay bashing") inhibit or promote social change can inform and promote effective social work practice and policy development to advance the rights of people on the basis of sexual orientation.

Finally, from a historical perspective, the use of examples has distinct and noteworthy limitations and restrictions. Mandelbaum (1938) suggests that occurrences reported at and about a specific historical point in time are: (1) difficult to be fully grasped given the vantage point of the reporter, (2) a selection of certain aspects of an event or occurrence,

⌐◥ Reflection Exercises

1. Enter a conversation with a classmate or colleague. Ask about her or his perspective with regard to a topical subject, such as war, taxation, global warming, or reproductive rights. What new knowledge did you gain from this conversation? What did you learn about your classmate or colleague's life philosophy that you did not know before the conversation?
2. Go to http://www.bbc.co.uk/religion. Use the tools provided there to develop a sense of the influence of religion on a country's societal and cultural norms, ethical principles, and historical perspective. Compare and contrast the major features of the various religions. How might this information be useful in international social work practice?

---

and (3) inherently "inadequate to the object which he [or her] seeks to describe" (pp. 22–23). In short, the reporting and description of an example represents an explanation of an occurrence(s) at a given point in time that is open to debate and interpretation. As such, examples should be considered a limited explanation of events and happenings from a specific vantage point.

EXAMPLES OF PRACTICE AND POLICY IN RELATIONSHIP TO SEPARATE, CONNECTED, AND EXPERIENTIAL KNOWING

People learn and come to know about human existence and experiences in a variety of ways. Traditionally, professors and teachers, often in an autocratic fashion, present theories, ideas, findings, examples, and concepts for comprehension, analysis, and reflection by students. This type of learning is prevalent in many classrooms, where teachers bestow information (e.g., lecture content, PowerPoint presentations, etc.) and students engage in memorization and critical thought concerning the materials. This form of education emphasizes recall, active thinking, and abstract analysis within academic disciplines and is called *separate knowing* (Enns, 1993). Reading, comprehending, analyzing, and reflecting on the examples of international social work practice and policy in this book for discussion in class constitutes an application of separate knowing.

Belenky, Clinchy, Goldberger, and Tarule (1986) advocate what has been termed "women's ways of knowing," or *connected knowing*. Intellectual maturation takes place via participatory forms of knowing that emphasize knowing by doing and collaborative learning and reflection. Connected knowing empowers people to embrace their educational environment and realize their potential in learning situations through interaction with others. Asserting control over learning and using the examples presented in this book to think about and enter into conversations with colleagues concerning your and their ideas and professional goals constitutes connected knowing. We encourage you to use the various examples in this book to build on your existing knowledge of countries and new situations, be sensitive to individual differences in interpreting the merits of international social work practice, and strive to actively listen to the opinions and reactions of colearners.

Enns (1993) also describes an *experiential learning model*. Experiential learning involves a degree of specific involvement in a concrete subject matter (e.g., experiencing an example of social work practice) as well as an action-reflection dimension that involves "seeking out the meaning of encounters" (p. 9). Approaching experiences from an experiential learning perspective has several distinct advantages: "[C]oncrete experience is associated with the activity of experiencing, reflective observation with examining, abstract conceptualization with explaining, and active experimentation with applying" (p. 9).

Many schools of social work offer immersion experiences, where students can spend a summer session or miniterm (e.g., 1–2 weeks) in another country with a faculty member to experience and study social welfare policy and practice. Our hope is that by reading examples of international social work practice and policy, you will imagine yourself being actively involved and engaged in social work practice in each country. Contemplate the meaning of each country-based example and ponder the application of methods and techniques in various society and cultural contexts. Indeed, after reading a chapter in this book, you may be inspired to enroll in an immersion course or seek some form of social work practice experience in a foreign land.

Table 2.2 Ways of Knowing and Considerations of Examples of International Social Work Practice and Policy

Way of Knowing	Emphasis	Considerations When Reading Chapters
Separate	Information is bestowed for critical analysis and reflection.	Question content and reflect on the relevance of information in examples for social work practice.
Connected	Learn through doing and interaction with others.	Identify specific ways that you can partner with classmates, social workers, and/or members of social service agencies to discuss and have debates, write papers, and collaborate on projects to learn from their ideas.
Experiential	Involvement in a specific phenomenon and reflection.	Imagine that you are actually present in each country and experiencing what is occurring. What are your thoughts and emotions? Identify educational and/or practice opportunities for an immersion experience in social work in a specific country.

Adapted from the work of Enns, 1993.

APPLYING FORMAL THEORIES TO EXAMPLES

Formal theories are organized statements of ideas for making sense of the each client's world. For example, psychological, cultural, and sociological theories can be used to provide insight for informed social work practice (Payne, 2005, pp. 4–6). Theories constitute abstract, general propositions that, when applied in a deductive, abstract to concrete fashion to specific situations and examples, provide social workers and other helping professionals with insight and plausible explanations about the actions and behaviors of service consumers.

In social work education, a variety of social work, psychological, sociological, economic, and political-oriented theories have been used to assist students make sense of client situations and circumstances in a host of settings. Ecological, system, psychodynamic, cognitive, behavioral, social construction, labeling, symbolic interactionism, feminism, conflict, class, strengths, and empowerment are examples of theoretical approaches often found in the social work literature. Social workers utilize these approaches to structure and organize their thinking about presenting situations for assessment, intervention, and evaluation in practice.

Take *systems theory* as an example. Contemporary systems theory focuses on and takes into account the importance and relevance of a variety of system levels (e.g., individuals, families, groups, organizations, communities, and societies) for analyzing and describing the impact of the social environment on human behavior. Social systems are viewed as being interrelated and interdependent with each other and having a powerful influence in people's lives. As any one system changes, other social systems change, compensate, and adapt. Few would disagree with the premise that one's family, friends, peer group, school, place of employment, community, and nation influence personal and group well-being. Systems are viewed as being dynamic and changing. Fluctuations in any one or more systems can result in major problems and challenges for the functioning of individuals and families in a variety of social contexts. Chetkow-Yannov (1992) notes, "Since human beings interact and grow within a variety of surrounding environments, a systems-derived person-environments model seems appropriate for social work intervention" (p. 6).

As you read each country-based example of social work practice and policy in this book, ask yourself which, if any, theories appear most applicable to the situation under study. The essence of *deductive reasoning* involves taking abstract ideas and concepts and, when possible, applying them to concrete situations and examples. As an illustration, systems theory often is helpful in enabling social workers to identify maladaptive and dysfunctional systems driving and causing disruption in the lives of clients. Families and individuals living in developing countries in the midst of modernization, technological change, and adoption of contemporary medicine can be caught in the transition from using long-standing cultural traditions (e.g., prayer and other spiritual-based practices) for promoting health and Western ways emphasizing vaccination and the use of sophisticated medicines. This type of societal change, exemplified by modernization in healthcare, seems particularly pertinent and critical for families in many countries in Africa struggling with effective prevention and treatment of AIDS.

Social construction theory is particularly valuable and relevant when reading examples of social work practice and policy from around the world. Social construction theory focuses on understanding how people construct, shape, and frame their identities, social world, and realities through the use of language (Payne, 2005, p. 161). This theory emphasizes communication and social and cultural determinants for "understanding how human beings use language and individually in social situations to give meaning to particular views of the world" (Payne, 2005, p. 162).

It is crucial to acknowledge that words, concepts, and terms found in many languages across the globe not only dictate how people conceptualize social realities and relationships but also do not necessarily have equivalences in other languages. Even within a country, it is not unusual for dialect and slang language to dominate conversation and thinking. Ride a public bus in a downtown urban area of the United States and listen to the conversation of school-age adolescents. The unique teen variation of the English language will likely seem strange and, at times, beyond comprehension. Similarly, regional differences in the United States involving enunciation and the meaning of terms connote alternative interpretations of behavior. For instance, in some areas in the South, the use of the phrase "Bless your heart" is not an expression of endearment involving a supreme being. Instead, this idiom can suggest that a person has done something wrong, unacceptable, or undesirable or that behavior is viewed as inappropriate. For example, a man wears a coat and pants with uncoordinated, clashing colors and patterns and someone says, "Bless his heart." In this context and use, the adage "Bless his heart" is meant to be negative and expresses displeasure with his selection of and taste in clothing.

As a final point, the examples of social work practice and policy in this book have been offered in English. In several chapters (e.g., Chapters 9 and 10), translating specific situations into English represented a challenge for the book's contributors. It is hoped that the essence of examples has not been lost in translation. However, the importance of terms and language should not be minimized. As you read each chapter, look for words, phrases, or situations that defy conceptualization or meaning in your native language. Consider how a particular social work practice or policy might be viewed differently or in an alternative fashion, if cast or implemented in a different language and context. As a case in point, the idea of a short-term solution, popular in the United States, would likely seem absurd in cultures and settings characterized by long-term relationships and prolonged forms of communication.

COMPARE CONTENT IN EXAMPLES WITH RESEARCH FINDINGS

As a general rule, educators recommend that social workers review the existing literature to identify articles describing their client population (problems and strengths) and the efficacy of helping interventions with population groups prior to engaging in practice. Research findings typically provide social workers with insight concerning their clients (e.g., descriptive information on their social-economic characteristics), the situations confronting them, and evidence suggesting the best way(s) to approach interpersonal and structural change to improve human functioning and well-being. Many social workers would argue that effective and responsible practice begins with a thorough knowledge and understanding of research findings pertinent to population, problems, and strategies for producing change.

In this book, the converse is suggested. After or as you read each chapter of social work practice and policy, use search tools and engines to access research articles examining various aspects of country-based problems and issues. Ask yourself these questions:

- Are you surprised by the number or lack of research articles on the topic?
- Are the articles published in blind, peer-reviewed research journals?
- Is information available or plentiful in research journals about the country? Why or why not?
- From your analysis, does it appear that research in the social and helping sciences is encouraged in this country?
- Why are research findings from one country not applicable or inappropriate to generalize to another country?
- Does the available research literature appear to support or conflict with premises and notions advanced in the chapter?

If you can identify research studies pertaining to country-based strategies for change (e.g., technique, intervention, policy, or program), view them skeptically and consider methodological limitations and strengths. As a general rule:

> clear linkage must be established between the intervention component and changes in client functioning in one or more areas. If the study is an investigation of theoretical change processes that are hypothesized to be activated by a specific intervention, a clear theoretical rationale must be defined before causal inferences can be made regarding the effect of a specific intervention component on client outcomes. Demonstrating *how* the treatment works is much more difficult than demonstrating that the intervention *does* work. (O'Hare, 2005, p. 44)

Ultimately, in our day and age of scientific inquiry, social workers aspire to engage in and be directed by "evidence-based" or informed practice. Ideally, this means that professionals should not rely on intuitive knowledge, common sense, practical wisdom, and/or theoretical assumptions. Instead, when available and applicable, research findings and validated knowledge concerning phenomena, population groups, and interventions need to be at the forefront of contemporary social work practice and decision making.

Of course, the more advanced the country and its scientific development and promotion of scientific inquiry, the more probable it is that research and findings for professional use are available. The building of research infrastructure, organizationally and nationally, is a costly venture. Dedication of resources (e.g., personnel, space, time, and technology) to support research constitutes a commitment on behalf of leaders, politicians, and public officials.

It is also important to remember that

> practice always entails an element of judgment, by which the practitioner must determine whether a particular situation represents a reasonable example of the larger population to which

the generalizations apply. . . . Therefore, the practitioner must continuously monitor the application of knowledge to determine whether the desired effects are being achieved in this practice situation [e.g., country and setting]. (Powers, Meenaghan, & Toomey, 1985, p. 15)

Hence, when examining country-based research, very important pragmatic considerations in social work practice include applicability of findings from situation to situation, country to country, and social setting to social setting.

SUMMARY

At this point, you are likely asking yourself: As a social worker, what do I stand to gain most from a careful examination of country-based examples of social work practice and policy? A number of benefits and disadvantages have already been explored. It also is important to note that international practice does not necessarily loom in every professional's future. However, regardless of your plans to practice abroad, Healy (2001) notes: "A related 'domestic' professional responsibility requires the capacity and willingness of the profession to develop and promulgate positions on social aspects of their own country's foreign policy and aspects of national policy that affect peoples in others countries, such as legislation on immigration" (p. 9).

Practitioners can use professional experiences in other nations to improve and refine practice activities and policy development in their home country. Innovation in service delivery and policy development often occurs as a result of seeing or hearing about policies, practices, and procedures in other, sometimes very different, venues. As helping professionals, social workers have a responsibility to stay abreast of and exchange information and experiences in a multitude of ways. Whether advocating for specific language for inclusiveness in an organization's policy manual or lobbying for legislative reform to ensure the dignity of all humans, the ability to cite a concrete example and provide related reasoning for change is a valuable and powerful instrument in interpersonal persuasion.

Examples and stories have a unique way of resonating with policy makers and leaders—often evoking this question: If an organization or community in Country X is capable of accomplishing or promoting these opportunities for consumers of social services, why can't we do the same?

Social work is a profession dedicated to finding ways to strengthen the voices and advance the interests of vulnerable and at-risk population groups. Identifying and using a variety of means to increase professional and public awareness concerning global as well as country-specific issues and problems should be a shared commitment for social workers. When we advocate for change, Wilson (1999) reminds us to utilize modes of communication that allow a broad range of people to relate to and comprehend human strife and societal response to need. Clearly, the purposeful use of examples falls into this domain.

REFERENCES

Bacon, F. (1970). On the interpretation of nature and the empire of man. In J. E. Curtis & J. W. Petras (Eds.), *The sociology of knowledge: A reader* (pp. 89–96). New York: Praeger.

Baker, T. (1999). *Doing social research.* Boston: McGraw-Hill College.

Belenky, M. G., Clinchy, B. M., Goldberger, N. R., & Tarule, J. M. (1986). *Women's ways of knowing: The development of self, voice, and mind.* New York: Basic Books.

Burn, S. M. (2005). *Women across cultures: A global perspective.* New York: McGraw-Hill.

Chetkow-Yannov, B. (1992). *Social work practice: A systems approach.* Binghamton, NY: Haworth Press.

Enns, C. Z. (1993). Integrating separate and connected knowing: The experiential learning model. *Teaching in Psychology, 20,* 7–13.

Freire, P. (1970). *Pedagogy of the oppressed.* New York: Seabury Press.

Healy, L. M. (2001). *International social work: Professional action in an interdependent world.* New York: Oxford University Press.

Hurdle, D. E. (2002). Native Hawaiian traditional healing: Culturally based interventions for social work practice. *Social Work, 47,* 183–192.

Lindsey, E. W. (2005). Study abroad and values development in social work students. *Journal of Social Work Education, 41,* 229–249.

Mandelbaum, M. (1938). *The problem of historical knowledge: An answer to relativism*. New York: Liveright.

O'Hare, T. (2005). *Evidence-based practices for social workers*. Chicago: Lyceum.

Payne, M. (2005). *Modern social work theory*. Chicago: Lyceum.

Powers, G., Meenaghan, T., & Toomey, B. (1985). *Practice focused research: Integrating human service practice and research*. Englewood Cliffs, NJ: Prentice-Hall.

Speier, H. (1970). The social determination of ideas. In J. E. Curtis & J. W. Petras (Eds.), *The sociology of knowledge: A reader* (pp. 263–281). New York: Praeger.

Towle, C. (1945). *Common human need*. New York: National Association of Social Workers.

Wilson, W. J. (1999). A coalition of power and hope. *Sojourners, 28*, 24.

Wolff, K. H. (1970). A methodological note on the empirical establishment of culture patterns. In J. E. Curtis & J. W. Petras (Eds.), *The sociology of knowledge: A reader* (pp. 320–341). New York: Praeger.

CHAPTER

3

Ethical Principles and Processes

Carolyn J. Tice

[S]ocial workers should promote the general welfare of society
from local to global levels . . . [including] social, economic, political, and cultural values and institutions that are compatible with
the realization of social justice.

—NASW (2000, pp. 26–27)

E thical decision making is an integral component of social work practice and policy. The formal education of social workers provides a
foundation of knowledge, values, and skills for problem solving, strength
assessment, and decision making. However, research indicates that con-
flicting demands for additional national and international services com-
bined with decreased funding challenge social workers to resolve ethical
dilemmas in an increasingly complex context (Dodd, 2007; Linzer, 1999;
Loewenberg, Dolgoff, & Harrington, 2000).

Classroom role-plays, case studies, professional readings, and assignments are designed to prepare students for ethical decision making.
However, despite extensive course content and case or example application, ethical deliberations in the classroom cannot ensure the preparation

needed to confront ethical issues that emerge in national or international practice (Anderson, 2000). For example, during a field experience in India, a woman living in a rural village described to a social work student what seemed to be an episode of domestic violence. What was the student to do with this information? What ethical and cultural elements were involved in the situation? What was the student's role?

This chapter defines ethics, ethical dilemmas, and ethical decision making in the context of international social work. Designed for social work students and practitioners, the chapter creates common language relevant to various cultures and professionals. The chapter's content provides insight into the tension or discomfort social workers might experience on foreign soil but are unable to identify as a particular ethical issue (Dodd, 2007).

WHAT ARE ETHICS?

Take a moment to think about the term "ethics." Does the definition of "ethics" reflect values and beliefs? What is the role of morality in ethical issues? Throughout this book, "ethics" refer to the values, norms, and moral judgments that guide the professional behavior of social workers with consumers and as a collective profession (Levy, 1984). Social work ethics, as stated in the National Association of Social Workers (NASW) *Code of Ethics* (NASW, 2000), reflect Judeo-Christian beliefs and the rules of acceptable conduct in society. This ethical system includes moral imperatives such as nonjudgmental assessment, acceptance, confidentiality, individualization, respect for colleagues, and loyalty to agencies (Walz & Ritchie, 2000).

Understanding the types of ethical issues that social workers might encounter in an international setting is good preparation for practicing social work in new and exciting locations. While many of the ethical issues that emerge in an international agency will be experienced by other professionals as well, social workers are often in the position to use resources and practice skills to resolve the dilemmas.

Resolving ethical dilemmas requires social workers and other professionals to go beyond "I" and "you" to the application of more universal laws. Thus, formal codes of ethics for doctors, nurses, and social workers have been created to guide ethical thinking and behavior related to practice. The Belmont Report (1974) is one of the most widely used frameworks in professional codes of ethics (http://ohsr.od.nih.gov/guide lines/belmont.html). An overview of the three principles from this framework provides an important backdrop for examining ethical considerations in greater detail.

THE BELMONT REPORT

Ethics provide a structure for analysis and decision making. Equally as important, ethics remind social workers and their colleagues of the need to protect consumers from harm, support social justice, and act to improve quality-of-life conditions. In the aftermath of major historical events, as described in Table 3.1, the United States Congress held hearings titled "Quality of Health Care—Human Experimentation" (http://ohsr .od.nih.gov/guidelines/belmont.html). The hearings led to the National Research Act of 1974, which established the National Commission for the

Table 3.1   History of Ethical Concerns

Date	Event
1947	26 Nazi physicians are tried at Nuremberg, Germany, for research atrocities performed on prisoners of war.
1940s	A series of research abuses starts in Tuskegee, Alabama.
1962	The Kefauver-Harris Bill is passed to ensure greater drug safety in the United States after thalidomide (a new sleeping pill) was found to cause birth defects.
1964	The 18th World Medical Assembly meets in Helsinki, Finland.
1974	The National Research Act prompted the establishment of Internal Review Boards (IRBs) at the local level. Such boards are designed to review, approve, and monitor all research done with human subjects.
1979	The National Commission for the Protection of Human Subjects was created.
1993	The *Albuquerque Tribune* publicizes 1940s experiments involving plutonium injections of human research subjects and secret radiation experiments.
1994	President Clinton creates the National Bioethics Advisory Commission (NBAC).
1995	The President's Advisory Committee on Human Radiation Experiments concludes that some of the radiation experiments from the 1940s were unethical.
1997	President Clinton issues a formal apology to the subjects of the Tuskegee syphilis experiments.

Source: Adapted from http:www.ethox.org.uk/reading/Guide/SectionC/section.htm

Protection of Human Subjects of Biomedical and Behavioral Research. The National Commission published the Belmont Report, a summary of basic ethical principles identified over the course of its four years of deliberations.

The Belmont Report identifies three ethical principles. These principles, commonly called the Belmont Principles, include autonomy or respect for persons, beneficence, and justice. The National Commission intended that each of the three principles should have equal moral force; consequently, one principle does not always outweigh another. Rather, professionals are required to consider each case separately and on its own merits in light of all three principles.

As indicated by the Belmont Report, ethical conduct is not considered intuitive. Rather, social workers must understand the principles of the Belmont Report and know how to apply them in order to engage in ethical national or international practice across consumer systems.

Autonomy

Autonomy is the most significant value contained in contemporary codes of ethics (Rajput & Bekes, 2002). This principle can be divided into two separate moral requirements:

1. Individuals should be treated with respect as autonomous agents.
2. Persons with diminished autonomy are entitled to protection.

Respecting the decisions, dignity, integrity, and preferences of persons is often referred to as self-determination in social work and other social science disciplines. The principle of autonomy requires all professionals to treat individuals as autonomous human beings, capable of making their own decisions/choices. The acknowledgment of autonomy has served to discredit paternalism and has led to the switch from "patient" to "consumer" and from being a recipient of treatment to being the partner in a program plan (Rajput & Bekes, 2002).

Autonomy or self-determination provides extra protection to those with challenging physical, mental, and/or life conditions. Consider the aging Kenyan woman who is experiencing visual problems due to bilateral cataracts. Brian, a social work student volunteering with an international medical relief team, recognizes cataract surgery as a viable option to the woman's condition, which is affecting her ability to participate in village activities, such as farming and cooking. Much to Brian's surprise, the woman refuses all treatment because it would require travel from her village, a short hospital stay, and a level of medical intervention unfamiliar to her and her family. Brian struggles to understand the woman's decision and is perplexed as to his next step.

This example highlights the fact that obtaining informed consent is an essential part of the principle of autonomy and consequently self-determination. The concept of informed consent has been a central topic in social work and other disciplines, such as psychology, health law, and bioethics. In requiring that consent is given before services, the laws support the value of self determination. Social workers often feel a strong obligation to make decisions to intervene, protect interests, and improve circumstances. Informed consent gives pause and consideration to ethical deliberations to ensure unnecessary interference in another person's life. Stated another way, Rajput and Bekes (2002, p. 871) conclude that informed consent protects consumer rights within international, organizational, and multidisciplinary environments by:

- Stating the nature of the decision and/or procedure
- Exploring reasonable alternatives to the proposed intervention
- Listing the relevant risks, benefits, and uncertainties related to each alternative
- Assessing the consumer's understanding of decisions made
- Accepting the consumer's position regarding the intervention

Beneficence

The principle of beneficence involves social workers, as well as other professionals, doing what is best for consumers and their communities. It highlights the moral importance of doing good to others while raising the question of who should be the judge of what is best. Beneficence necessitates that decisions pertaining to social work interventions must be agreed on by all those involved, including the consumer, family members, and other service providers. In this complex decision-making process, social workers must take seriously the ethical dimensions of decisions and must be prepared to justify publicly the decisions made and subsequent actions taken.

The justification of decisions in the context of beneficence turns attention to both the grounds and the process on which any social work decision is made (Parker & Gray, 2001). Some relevant questions to consider are:

- Were the right people consulted or involved in the decision?
- Was there adequate discussion of the issues and concerns?
- Was the consumer considered the expert in the situation?
- Were the unique strengths of the consumer and her/his community considered in the decision making?
- Was there a proper system for review of the decision?

As an example of the beneficence principle, consider the parents of a special needs child, Louisa, age 7 years. The family lives in Guatemala. The family was seen by Jeanne, a social work intern completing an independent research study at a community center. Jeanne knew of a residential school approximately 70 miles from the family's village that offered comprehensive services to children with educational needs similar to those of Louisa, who was not attending school and had little social interaction outside of the family. Jeanne, with her supervisor, spoke to the parents about the school, but the parents concluded that the academic advantages would not outweigh the anxiety Louisa would likely experience living so far away from her family and the community. Much to Jeanne's dismay, Louisa remained at home with few formal educational or social opportunities.

This example speaks to the need for research and/or program evaluation to ensure the potential benefits of interventions. In this example, the risks Louisa's family associated with a residential placement, such as separation from the family unit and all that is familiar, outweighed the perceived benefits of enhanced educational opportunities. As illustrated by this example, beneficence involves not only the avoidance of physical harm but also negative psychological, legal, social, and/or economic consequences (Leiby, 1978).

Embedded in the beneficence principle is the promise of confidentiality. Respect for confidentiality is firmly established in the code of ethics for social workers and many other helping professions. Social workers have a duty to respect a consumer's trust and keep information private. This action, in turn, encourages consumers to be as honest and straightforward as possible when discussing their situations and needs.

Justice

Jorge, completing a social work field education internship in Vietnam, quickly realized that adequate time and resources are not always available to every consumer. Specifically, Jorge witnessed a family of four receiving only minimal food rations and little sanitary water at a rural United Nations (UN) feeding station. Although the UN worker attempted to allocate limited resources in an equitable manner, the lack of food and water negatively impacted the delivery of outreach emergency health services to the Vietnamese community. Further, the resource distribution caused tension between the UN workers and community members.

The international situation Jorge experienced attests to the primary elements of the principle of justice: (1) consumers in similar situations normally should have access to similar services; and (2) when determining the level of services that should be available to one group of individuals or a community, social workers must take into account the effect of such a use of resources on others. Hayes (1997) argues that the principle of justice is about attempts to answer how burdens and benefits ought to be distributed among the members of a given society.

Another way of thinking about the principle of justice is that equals ought to be treated equally. However, this statement requires explication. Who is equal, and who is unequal? What considerations justify departure from equal distribution? Several widely accepted formulations of just ways to distribute burdens and benefits exist. Each formulation mentions some relevant property on the basis of which burdens and benefits should be distributed. These formulations are:

- To each person an equal share
- To each person according to individual need

- To each person according to individual effort
- To each person according to societal contribution
- To each person according to merit (http://www.hhs.gov/ohrp/humansubjects/guidance/belmont.htm)

APPLICATIONS OF ETHICAL PRINCIPLES

Examining the elements of ethics is an important step toward ethical practice. The next step is critically thinking about the application of the general principles to life situations. Review http://www.hhs.gov/ohrp/humansubjects/guidance/belmont.htm before considering the following material.

Informed Consent

Consumers should always be given the right to select what shall or shall not happen to them. As presented in the discussion on autonomy, the issue of informed consent is unquestioned (http://www.hhs.gov/ohrp/humansubjects/guidance/belmont.htm). What social workers must ensure is that consumers are capable of understanding the full nature of what they are agreeing to and how an intervention will affect their life in both the short and the long term.

Paulo, a Brazilian 22-year-old with a significant auditory challenge, was assigned to work with Stacey, a social work intern from a small midwestern state university. Although Stacey was keenly interested in services to people with auditory challenges, she had little actual experience in this specialized area of practice. Stacey realized she must secure a signed informed consent from Paulo before implementing any program plan, but she had minimal Portuguese language skills and was just becoming familiar with the technical system designed for those with auditory challenges.

If you were in Stacey's position, what steps would you take to secure an informed consent document that addresses the ethical principles of autonomy and beneficence? How would you explain the situation to Paulo? Describe how you would present Paulo with the necessary information so as to enable his participation in the service plan while ensuring that he understands the impact his decision will have on his life and the lives of those close to him.

Information

Codes of ethics usually specify items for disclosure intended to ensure that consumers are well informed and active members of their service or treatment plan. Examples of items or procedures include:

- A clear explanation of the program plan with goals and intended outcomes defined in measurable and observable terms
- An exploration of all possible alternatives to the presenting issues
- A detailed account of any possible negative outcomes or possible unintended consequences
- An opportunity to ask questions in a confidential manner
- The option to revise or withdraw from the program plan without any form of punishment or retribution

As a student in a large urban university social work program, Hector was accustomed to a wide range of service alternatives for people with persistent mental illness. However, during his international experience in Ulaanbaatar, the capital of Mongolia, Hector came to realize the global disparity of mental health services. Case in point is Zola, who was diagnosed with schizophrenia at 19 years and was institutionalized throughout most of the last decade. Currently Zola faces the possibility of transferring to a community-based congregate living facility, but a medication regime has not been established that ensures her stability. Hector knows of psychotropic medications available to Americans with a diagnosis similar to Zola's. Should he share this information? If so, to whom, and in what fashion? What cultural issues are involved in this situation? How does the dilemma that Hector faces correspond to other disparities between medical and mental health–related conditions?

Comprehension

The way in which information is presented to consumers is critical to ethical considerations. Specifically, all verbal and written information should be presented in an organized, concise, and logical fashion. Consumers' developmental stage, overall intelligence, educational status, maturity level, language, and cultural aspects must be assessed to ensure a fair and effective presentation of information.

On occasion, special provisions must be made if consumers' comprehension capabilities are limited. Thus, social workers must be respectful of and sensitive to people's capabilities, challenges, and resilience. If necessary, a third party should be invited to act on behalf of the consumer. This designated person should be available and encouraged to review, observe, and monitor the consumer's participation in the service or treatment plan on a regular basis.

Mary Kate, placed with a multidisciplinary team of healthcare providers, has been assigned the task of securing informed consent from a young mother in order for her 3-year-old son to undergo surgery. The woman and child reside in Lhasa, China, where education, especially for women from rural communities, is scarce. Mary Kate recognizes she is faced with a dilemma:

1. She does not know the mother's level of literacy.
2. The surgery is complex, so the risk and benefits must be clearly defined.
3. The medical procedure does not include any form of traditional medicine, which the mother is familiar and comfortable with.
4. The young mother has an involved extended family who is supportive of the child.

Describe a process that will help assure Mary Kate that the mother understands the medical complexities of the surgery, including the likely prognosis and subsequent risks for her son.

Voluntariness

Social workers should never place pressure on consumers to comply with a service or treatment plan. Further, any form of coercion or an overt threat of harm or disapproval is unwarranted under any circumstance. On the continuum of such influencing factors are other actions, such as monetary incentives, family member subversion, and withholding services.

As a research assistant on a child welfare grant, Juan is working at a daycare center in Peru for the summer. His role on the grant is to recruit participants from the daycare center for a child care training program that lasts 6 weeks, 1 evening per week. Outline how Juan will recruit and retain program participants. What ethical issues must he be mindful of when recruiting training participants?

Nature of Scope of Risks and Benefits

Services, treatments, and research require an assessment of relevant data in relation to risk and benefits. In this context, "risk" refers to a possibility that harm may occur. The term "benefit" connotes a positive value related to health, mental health, and/or general welfare conditions. Thus, a risk/benefit assessment is concerned with the probabilities and magnitudes of possible harm and anticipated benefits. It should be noted that risk and benefits, especially in the sense of research, may affect individuals, their families, and society at large. Relevant risks and benefits must be thoroughly discussed in documents and procedures used in the informed consent process.

Hannah plans to be a geriatric social worker, so she is thrilled to be an intern in a long-term care facility in Henderson, West Virginia. In conjunction with admissions procedures, Hannah stresses the benefits of facility placement, highlighting the medical care, social activities, therapeutic interventions, and social work services. To be ethical, she should also state possible risks. What are some of those risks, and how could they possibly impact family systems and communities?

IMPORTANCE OF LOCAL CONTEXT

It is essential that social workers have sufficient knowledge of the local, national, and international environment in which they are working to be able to implement services and address ethical dilemmas that honor the culture and values of the clients.

The local environment includes the social-economic, political, and cultural factors that influence the service delivery system and research opportunities. For example, mental health diagnosis and services require an understanding of family dynamics, religious beliefs, cultural norms, and community expectations.

Questions that may be innocuous in the United States could be offensive elsewhere. For example, medical histories, sexual preferences and practices, religious beliefs, and interpersonal relationships could be inappropriate topics even in the professional context. Further, the political aspects of a country and different authority structures may dictate the parameters of social services, professional responsibilities, and research potentials.

The framework described in Table 3.2 provides a framework that may be useful in national and international discussions of consumer-related cases. The questions can be revised to reflect local knowledge while the overall framework adherence to the ethical principles remains constant.

Cameron's (2002) ethical listening skills contribute to the ethics framework by enhancing communication techniques that cut across cultural and ethical domains and add to the notion of universal social work skills. These skills were derived from a study on ethical problems involving the health conditions of older people. The goal of ethical listening is to help

Table 3.2   Ethical Framework for Assessment

1. What are the relevant clinical and other facts (e.g., family dynamics, support availability)?
2. What would constitute an appropriate decision-making process?
   • Who is to be held responsible?
   • When does the decision have to be made?
   • Who should be involved?
   • What are the procedural rules (e.g., confidentiality)?
3. List the available options.
4. What are the morally significant features of each option; for example:
   • What does the consumer want to happen?
   • Is the consumer competent?
   • If the consumer is not competent, what is in his or her "best interests"?
   • What are the foreseeable consequences of each option?
5. What does the law/guidance say about each of these options?
6. For each realistic option, identify the moral arguments in favor and against.
7. Choose an option based on your judgment of the relative merits of these arguments using these questions:
   • Are there any key terms the meaning of which need to be agreed?
   • Are the arguments valid?
   • What are the foreseeable consequences (local and more broad)?
   • Do the options "respect persons"?
   • What would be the implications of this decision applied as a general rule?
   • How does this case compare with other cases?
8. Identify the strongest counterargument to the option you have chosen.
9. Can you rebut this argument? What are your reasons?
10. Make a decision.
11. Review this decision in light of what actually happens, and learn from it.

Source: Adapted from http://www.ethox.org.uk/reading/Guide/SectionC/section.htm

the individual thwart or resolve conflict and reshape or reframe the past (Cameron, 2002, p. 548). Ethical listening skills include:

- Establishing a nonjudgmental, caring rapport by behaving with compassion
- Maintaining culturally appropriate eye contact and body language
- Being fully present with the consumer even if a translator is involved
- Using open-ended questions as well as nonverbal and verbal probes
- Encouraging the consumer to focus on ethical conflict and what she/he thinks is the appropriate way to resolve it
- Uncovering hidden conflict that may be even more difficult to resolve than the presenting issues
- Listening carefully, without giving advice, lecturing or criticizing, or appealing to political or religious dogma
- Supporting the consumer in what he/she thinks is the right service, treatment, or approach

Reflection Exercise

While reading the next example, consider how you would approach the healthcare issue using both the ethical decision framework and ethical listening techniques. Keep in mind what ethical principles are involved in the international healthcare example.

With German maternal and paternal lineage, Hank enthusiastically enrolled in an urban university located in Germany to complete one semester of his undergraduate degree in social work. As part of an independent study in social work, Hank was placed in a hospital setting where he engaged in social work service 12 hours each week. Since he understood only an elementary level of German, Hank depended on a translator when working directly with consumers. One consumer, Gotlieb, was an 80-year-old retired railroad engineer who lived with his wife of 60 years, Gertrude. Recently Gotlieb had been experiencing "episodes" with symptoms ranging from numbing of the face, mental confusion, and slurred speech. Initially, Gotlieb ignored the symptoms, but his daughter witnessed one episode and contacted emergency services. Gotlieb was admitted to the hospital for extensive testing under the social work care of Hank.

Gotlieb made it clear to Hank, through the translator, that he wanted no part of the hospitalization or the scheduled battery of tests. He demanded to return home with limited home healthcare. However, Gotlieb's daughter, Karoline, refused to discuss any discharge plans and insisted that her father was not capable of determining his healthcare plan. Gotlieb's wife, Gertrude, expressed little verbally, but her frail condition and hesitation to engage her daughter and husband in conversation gave Hank pause.

Hank was to participate in Gotlieb's treatment planning session. He felt self-conscious about his German-language skills, the conflict between Gotlieb and Karoline, and Gertrude's passive position and general health status.

Given the situation Hank faces, take time to consider the next questions. Do not hesitate to discuss the questions and your responses with your classmates and colleagues.

1. How would you apply the ethical assessment framework to Gotlieb's presenting situation? What ethical principles are integral to his situation?
2. What are some ways you would highlight aspects of the decision-making process and the available options for Gotlieb and his family members?
3. What are the ethically significant features of the case?
4. How would you describe the unique strengths of Gotlieb and his family?
5. What cultural elements should Hank be mindful of when working with Gotlieb and his family?
6. How would you design a treatment plan for Gotlieb? Please justify your judgments and decisions.

CODES OF ETHICS

Balancing autonomy, benevolence, and justice while considering an ethical framework for assessment and ethical listening skills requires knowledge of professional codes of ethics. Codes provide a conceptual structure or guidelines to frame practitioners' thinking "that establish criteria for selecting goals and that influences how information is interpreted and understood" (Netting, Kettner, & McMurtry, 1998, p. 22).

National Association of Social Workers Code of Ethics

In 1955, the National Association of Social Workers was formed through the merger of seven social work organizations. The NASW has these three primary responsibilities:

1. To strengthen and unify the profession
2. To promote the development of social work practice
3. To advance sound social policies (www.socialworkers.org/pubs/code/code.asp)

Currently the organization has approximately 160,000 members in 55 chapters throughout the United States, Puerto Rico, the Virgin Islands, and abroad.

According to the NASW, the primary mission of the social work profession is to "enhance human well being and help meet the basic human needs of all people, with particular attention to the needs and empowerment of people who are vulnerable, oppressed, and living in poverty" (*NASW Code of Ethics*, 2000). NASW operationalizes this mission through six general purposes that:

1. Identify core values on which social work's mission is based.
2. Summarize broad ethical principles that reflect the profession's core values and establish a set of specific ethical standards that should be used to guide social work practice.
3. Identify relevant consideration when professional obligations conflict or ethical uncertainties arise.
4. Provide ethical standards to which the general public can hold the social work professional accountable.
5. Socialize practitioners new to the field to social work's mission, values, ethical principles, and ethical standards.
6. Articulate standards that the social work profession itself can use to assess whether social workers have engaged in unethical conduct. NASW has formal procedures to adjudicate ethics complaints filed against its members.

Table 3.3   National Association of Social Workers Ethical Principles

Value	Ethical Principle
Service	Social workers' primary goal is to help people in need and to address social problems.
Social justice	Social workers challenge social injustice.
Dignity and worth of the Person	Social workers respect the inherent dignity and worth of the person.
Importance of human relationships	Social workers recognize the central importance of human relationships.
Integrity	Social workers behave in a trustworthy manner.
Competence	Social workers practice within their areas of competence and develop and enhance their professional expertise.

Source: National Association of Social Workers, (2000). *Code of ethics of the National Association of Social Workers* (Washington, DC: Author).

In subscribing to this code, social workers are required to cooperate in its implementation, participate in NASW adjudication proceedings, and abide by any NASW disciplinary rulings or sanctions based on it.

It is important to note that the *Code of Ethics* does not set forth rules by which social workers must practice. Rather, it offers a guide for decision making and resolving ethical issues that emerge in practice and research. Table 3.3 summarizes the principles that underpin the code.

Besides recognizing that a unified code of ethics is important for the social work profession, it is equally as important that students and practitioners understand the NASW code and feel competent to use it resolving ethical issues. Thus, class instruction and field experiences must prepare students not only for ethical practice but for ethical deliberations.

International Federation of Social Workers

The International Federation of Social Workers (IFSW; http://www.ifsw .org/en/p38000324.html) is a worldwide organization committed to social justice, human rights, and social development through collaborative social work practice and partnerships. It is a successor to the International Permanent Secretariat of Social Workers, which was founded in Paris in 1928 and active until the beginning of World War II.

Founded on the principles of humanitarian, religious, and democratic ideals, IFSW strives to address human needs and to develop human potential. The IFSW constitution provides structure to the global organization by promoting:

- Social work through international cooperation
- The establishment of national organizations
- Training and professional standards

IFSW maintains numerous partnerships with international organizations, such as Amnesty International, the Council of Europe, the European Union, and Public Services International.

International Association of Schools of Social Work

The International Association of Schools of Social Work (IASSW; http://www.apss.polyu.edu.hk/iassw/) is the worldwide association of schools of social work, other tertiary-level social work educational programs, and social work educators. The IASSW promotes the development of education throughout the world by developing standards to enhance the quality of social work education and encouraging international exchange. Further, IASSW provides forums for sharing social work research and promotes human rights and social development through policy and advocacy activities.

International Federation of Social Workers and International Association of Schools of Social Work Principles of Ethics

The collaboration of IFSW and IASSW resulted in a statement, Principle of Ethics, promoting ethical debate and reflecting on ethical challenges confronting the international community (www.ifsw.org/en/p38000324 .html). Table 3.4 summarizes the IFSW/IASSW ethical principles. The principles have several distinguishing points, namely, the integral role that human rights and social justice play in social work practice and the responsibility social work has to challenge discrimination and recognize the value of diversity.

The ethical principles of the IFSW/IASSW express a commitment to and education in professional conduct. Both organizations speak to the need for social workers to follow ethical and practice guidelines in

Table 3.4   International Federation of Social Workers/International Association of Schools of Social Work Statement of Ethical Principles

4.1	**Human Rights and Human Dignity** Social work is based on respect for the inherent worth and dignity of all people, and the rights that follow from this. This means: Respecting the right to self-determination Promoting the right to participation Treating each person as a whole Identifying and developing strengths
4.2	**Social Justice** Social workers have a responsibility to promote social justice, in relation to society generally and in relation to the people with whom they work. This means: Challenging negative discrimination Recognizing diversity Distributing resources equitably Challenging unjust policies and practices Working in solidarity

Source: Adapted from www.ifsw.org/en/p38000324.html

accordance to their countries. IFSW/IASSW concludes that social workers are obligated to:

- Develop and maintain a competent skill set.
- Act in accordance with integrity.
- Focus on the needs of others rather than self-interest.
- Be prepared to defend their ethical decisions and practice-related judgments.

Reflection Exercise

A thorough examination of the NASW *Code of Ethics* and the IFSW/IASSW Principle of Ethics provides interesting points for comparison. With the information of both documents close at hand, respond to the next questions, keeping any international field experiences in mind.

1. What are the common elements between NASW *Code of Ethics* and the IFSW/IASSW Principle of Ethics?
2. Describe the major differences between the two documents regarding professional ethics and practice principles.

3. What does the IFSW/IASSW Principle of Ethics imply about the political environments in some countries?
4. What are some of the points of the NASW *Code of Ethics* and the IFSW/ IASSW Principle of Ethics that you consider especially helpful in guiding your practice?
5. Do you think any points should be added to the documents on ethics? Explain those points and why they should be added.
6. Describe a situation in which you would use the NASW *Code of Ethics* or the IFSW/ IASSW Principle of Ethics to guide your practice in an international social work experience.

SUMMARY

How should social workers handle ethical deliberations during international social work experiences? The material included in this chapter provides a broad base of knowledge for understanding and resolving ethical dilemmas according to principles and codes. Essential components of the chapter's content include: a consumer-centered approach; attending to culture, ethnicity, and issues of diversity; involving consumers as informed participants; establishing a system of accountability and a commitment to social justice (Gambrill, 2005).

The ethical problems that challenge consumers and social workers involve multidimensional issues and evoke strong feelings that defy concrete guidelines. No straightforward approach to analysis or resolution is available. An international social work setting often adds more complicated variables associated with culture, socialization patterns, and the political environment. Consequently, it is not uncommon for social workers to feel perplexed or unsure when confronted with the plethora of factors that must be assessed before deciding on a course of action. Supported by ethical principles and codes, the social work profession has cultivated a range of methods, structured learning opportunities, and resources required for informed and mature judgments.

When addressing ethical dilemmas, social workers need to remember the importance of colleagues, faculty, and supervisors with whom positions, judgments, and perspectives can be discussed in confidence.

Especially in the context of international social work practice, consumers of social work services can be vulnerable to specific forms of manipulation and exploitation endemic to a country and its level of social-economic development. For example, in Nepal, impoverished families afflicted by disease and living in dire circumstances can be easy and susceptible prey for medical companies and research groups to test products and unload inferior goods. At face value, such practices would appear to be outrageous. However, a thorough and multidimensional consideration and understanding of ethical dilemmas associated with this kind of country-based exploitation relies on the development of reflective practitioner skills, or learning from shared experience, as a critical form of knowledge (Schon, 1983).

REFERENCES

Anderson, D. (2000). Facing ethical dilemmas in the field. *New Social Worker, 7*, 17–18.

Cameron, M. (2002). Older persons' ethical problems involving their health care. *Nursing Ethics, 9*, no. 5, 537–556.

Dodd, S.J. (2007). Identifying the discomfort: An examination of ethical issues encountered by MSW students during field placement. *Journal of Teaching in Social Work, 27*, 1–19.

Gambrill, G. (2005). *Critical thinking clinical practice* (2nd ed.). Hoboken, NJ: John Wiley & Sons.

Hayes, H. M. (1997). Ethics of care work. In S. Bjorneby & A. van Berlo (Eds.), *Ethical issues in the use of technology in dementia care* (pp. 73–86) (The Akon Series, vol. 13). Knegsel: Akontes Publishing.

Leiby, J. (1978). *A history of social welfare and social work in the United States*. New York: Columbia University Press.

Levy, C. (1984). Values and ethics: Foundation of social work. In S. Dillick (Ed.), *Value foundations of social work: Ethical basis for a human service profession.* (pp. 17–30). Detroit, MI: Wayne State University.

Linzer, N. (1999). *Resolving ethical decisions in social work practice*. Boston: Allyn & Bacon.

Loewenberg, F., Dolgoff, R., & Harrington, D. (2000). *Ethical decisions for social work practice* (6th ed.). Itasca, IL: Peacock.

National Association of Social Workers. (2000). *Code of ethics of the National Association of Social Workers.* Washington, DC: Author.

Netting, F. E., Kettner, P. M., & McMurtry, S. L. (1998). *Social work macro practice.* New York: Longman.

Parker, M., & Gray, J. A. (2001). What is the role of clinical ethics support in the era of e-medicine? *Journal of Medical Ethics, 27,* 33–35.

Rajput, V., & Bekes, C. E. (2002). Ethical issues in hospital medicine. *Medical Clinics of North America, 86,* 869–886.

Schon, D. A. (1983). *The reflective practitioner: How professionals think in action.* London: Temple Smith.

Walz, T., & Ritchie, H. (2000). Gandhian principles in social work practice: Ethics revisited. *Social Work, 45,* 213–222.

4

Portugal: An International Field Education Experience

CAROLYN J. TICE

Midday

A corner of the deserted beach.
The huge, deep, open sun on high
Has chased all the gods from the sky.
The harsh light falls like a punishment.
There are no ghosts and no souls,
And the vast, ancient, solitary sea
Loudly claps its hands.

—de Mello Breyner Andresen (1990)

Sophia de Mello Breyner Andresen, considered one of Portugal's most important 20th-century poets, describes the coastline in a country where she has won numerous literary prizes, Portugal. What comes to your mind when the country of Portugal is mentioned? Although Portugal is one of Europe's oldest countries, most people have few images or knowledge of this country comprised of diverse landscapes, expansive coastlines, and distinct cultures within its relatively small area of 34,361 square miles (Porter & Prince, 2004). This chapter will acquaint you with the culture of Portugal by exploring a field placement in a social service organization and practice situations faced by a student. Rich in cultural details and facts on Portugal, the chapter highlights relationships, organizational settings, and ethical considerations.

PORTUGAL'S HISTORY, SOCIAL SYSTEMS, AND CULTURE

Uncovering the History

Take a moment to find Portugal on a world map, note its location on the west side of the Iberian Peninsula. The northern and central regions are heavily populated and characterized by rivers, valleys, forests, and mountains (http://www.portugal.org/tourism/index.html). The south is less populated and, apart from the rocky backdrop of the Algarve, much flatter and drier. Also, look to the west and south west of the country and discover the islands of Portugal, the Azores, and Madeira island, far out in the Atlantic Ocean.

It might surprise you that Portugal has been an independent country since 1143. Its rich history can be traced to the Celts, who settled in the Iberian Peninsula around 700 BC (Steves, 2005). The region, with its natural advantages of sun with diverse geographic features, attracted colonization by the Phoenicians, Greeks, Romans, and Visigoths. In the 8th century, the Moors migrated across the Strait of Gibraltar and commenced a long occupation that influenced the culture, architecture, and agricultural aspects of Portugal (http://www.lonelyplanet.com/destinations/europe/portugal/history.htm). However, resistance to the Moors eventually grew, and they were expelled from Portugal in the 13th century.

Thanks in part to Prince Henry the Navigator, Portugal engaged in significant oversea expansion during the 15th century. Mariners explored and developed ports of call in exotic locations in India, South America, and Africa. Portuguese commerce thrived, as did the exchange of ideas and culture that marked the apogee of Portuguese power and wealth. Within a few decades in the 16th century, the momentum of Portugal's growth and global presence dwindled under Spanish rule. Along with the empire's decline came an invasion in the 18th century by Napoleon, which the Portuguese successfully thwarted through an Anglo-Portuguese alliance (Steves, 2005).

The 19th century saw Portugal's economy falter, and republicanism eventually took hold. By 1910, national turmoil led to the abolition of the monarchy and the subsequent founding of a democratic republic. This democratic phase of Portuguese history was relatively short-lived; a 1926 military coup ushered in a long period of dictatorship under António de Oliveira Salazar (http://www.infoplease.com/ipa/A0107895.html). When Salazar succumbed to a stroke in 1968, a nationalistic movement defeated anachronistic attempts to maintain power. On April 24, 1974, a nearly bloodless coup, the Revolution of Carnations, resulted in the establishment of a parliamentary democracy, the Portuguese Republic (http://www.historyworld. net/wrldhis/PlainTextHistories.asp?groupid=1709&HistoryID=ab46).

Portugal experienced political and economic adjustments in the 1970s and 1980s while shifting from control by the central government to a system of private enterprise. The granting of independence to Portugal's colonies in 1974–75 resulted in over 500,000 refugees in the country (http://www.child policyintl.org/countries/portugal.html). Entering the European Community in 1986 restored some measure of stability. Portugal's acceptance as a full member of the European Monetary Union in 1999 supported this stability, and the euro became the nation's common currency.

The country's economy reflects a vigorous policy of development. Service sector employment comprises approximately 60% of Portugal's labor force followed by 30% in industry and 20% in agriculture (Steves, 2005). The northern portion of the country is a mountainous, rainy region, populated by many small farms. Vineyards are everywhere; Portugal is among the world's leading producers of wine with perhaps the most famous being Port and Madeira. However, over the last few decades, industry has taken precedence over agriculture in the nation's economy and the development of its urban centers, such as Lisbon and Oporto, where the majority of the country's production takes place.

Social Systems

Knowing the basic history and economic structure of Portugal helps in understanding its social service system. Portugal is less urban and less economically modernized than most of Europe. Of the approximately 20 million people who live in Portugal, approximately 17.5% of the citizens are under age 15 and almost 15% are over the age of 65 years (http://www.childpolicyintl.org/countries/portugal.html). As Wall (2003) of the EU Family Observatory reported:

> Recent data from the 2001 Population Census confirm long-term changes in the family that have taken place since 1960. The marriage rate has declined (to 5.7 in 2001) and is now similar to the average value for the EU countries (5.1). Cohabitation has increased, but the percentage of cohabitating couples is still much lower in Portugal than in Northern European countries. Finally the divorce rate has increased sharply since the 1970s (to 1.8, the same as the average value for the EU countries). (p. 8)

Portugal is profoundly Roman Catholic. According to a common saying, "to be Portuguese is to be Catholic," and approximately 97 percent of the population considers itself Roman Catholic—the highest percentage in Western Europe (http://www.photius.com/countries/portugal/society/por tugal_society_religion_and_the_rol~1083.html). However, over the last few decades, statistics indicate a departure from strong Catholic doctrine. Specifically, the fertility rate has declined, as have births outside of marriage. The average Portuguese family is comprised of 2.8 children with an increase in single-headed households. Further, labor statistics indicate that women's rates in the workplace have changed from 18% in 1960 to 65% in 2008, supported by policies to protect females from discrimination in employment (http://www.indexmundi.com/portugal/demographics_profile .html). Family planning has been available in the healthcare system since the mid-1970s, but there are strict limits on abortion (Amaro, 1994).

Through the years, Portugal has developed institutions and a continuum of services to support families and children, beginning with universal healthcare and maternal benefits. Other family policies include family and child allowances under the Child and Young People's Family Benefit Program, which provides coverage to the age of 24 for those still in school and for disabled youths, who also receive a supplement. Eligibility is restricted to the children of employed parents with social security coverage (Bradshaw, Ditch, Holmes, & Whiteford, 1993).

According to Pinto (1997), inequities in professional staffing and social service facilities exist between the poorer North and the remainder of the country. Another issue of concern is the lack of child care facilities, which corresponds to an increasing need for nurseries for children below the age of 3 and relatively low coverage for children between the ages of 3 and 6 years of age (Wall, 2003).

Literacy rates in Portugal have been historically low when compared to Europe. In response, Portugal has implemented compulsory schooling for children 6 to 14 years of age, and over 90% of this group are enrolled (Wall, 2003). High dropout rates are thought to reflect parental illiteracy and inadequate school facilities.

Unique Cultural Features

The street scenes of Portugal are marked by spontaneity and tradition. Images of fish sellers, stalls of flowers, curving alleyways, women carrying pitchers of water on their heads leave a lasting impression on tourists, as do windmills, which are more prevalent in Portugal than in any other country in Europe. The number of windmills is explained by the tradition that the Portuguese ground their own maize (corn). Today the mills are used mostly for irrigation.

Nearly every village in Portugal has its own pillory standing in the village square near the council hall. The column structure, invented by Romans who constructed them in Gaul, reached Portugal in the 12th century (Porter & Prince, 2004). These eye-catching monuments were used as a symbol of municipal power and often supported cages where criminals were placed for public display. In time, pillories became more decorative with ornamental ironwork or human or animals forms. They continued to be constructed until the 18th century.

Craftspersons offer a variety of objects including intricate basketwork, carved wooden objects, and lace. Perhaps most unique are village potters, who create decorative earthenware that varies according to the region of origin. For example, in Barcelos, pots are glazed colors vivid in yellows and reds, and ornaments consist of leaves, stems, and flowers; around Coimbra, green with yellow and brown overtones predominates, and the ornamentation is more geometric (Steves, 2005).

Much like ceramics, the music, folksongs, and dances of Portugal reflect provincial differences among regions. Fados, taken from the Latin word *fatum*, meaning "destiny," are sad and monotonous chants derived from the troubadour songs of the Middle Ages and usually are about the forces of destiny or human passions (Porter & Prince, 2004). The fado first appeared in Portugal at the end of the 18th century in the form of sailors' songs. It took on its present popular form in the 1830s with usually a *fadista*, a woman singer accompanied by one or two players and the Portuguese guitar (Steves, 2005).

Portugal abounds with *romarios* (religious pilgrimages), *festas* (festivals), and *ferias* (fairs) that bring towns to a standstill and, in part, reflect the nation's strong Catholic heritage. The farther north you go, the more traditional and less touristy these celebrations seem. Carnival, which takes place about 6 weeks before Easter, is one of the biggest events, featuring partying, parading, and painted faces. There are vast and colorful processions during the Easter of Holy Week Festival in the city of Braga, called the "Portuguese Rome" for its concentration of religious architecture. The Feira de Sao Martinho that takes place in Golega in November showcases all manner of horse, riding contests, and bullfights (Hole & Beech, 2005).

Portuguese meals are ample, wholesome, and tasty, and mealtimes are a relaxing pause in the day's events. The typical menu consists of several dishes, usually prepared with olive oil and flavored with aromatic herbs, such as rosemary and bay leaf. Although Portuguese cuisine has little international recognition, the meals definitely reflect local produce and customs. Soup, a staple served at most meals, is accompanied with bread made at local bakeries. Since seafood is so plentiful, it is an element in many entrees, including such traditional dishes as grilled sardines, fish stew and crayfish casserole. Pork is cooked in a variety of ways, and ham and sausage are often used to garnish dishes. Each locality has its own pastry; however, a custard cream, *pudim de fian*, is most frequently seen on menus (Porter & Prince, 2004). Meals are often accompanied by good-quality wine *vinhos* or Port, the drink that is synonymous with Portugal.

Agency and Its Culture

The Associação Portuguesa de Paralisia Cerebral (APPC), or the Portuguese Association for Cerebral Palsy, was founded in 1960, with its headquarters in Lisbon. It was established as a nonprofit organization to ensure rehabilitative services and opportunities for social integration for

⮡ Reflection Exercsises

Before moving on with the example of a field placement, consider the information presented on Portugal and complete the next exercises in a small group with other students in your course.

1. Find Portugal on a map and explore Internet sites on Portugal tourism. List at least 10 historical, cultural, and/or recreational sites of interest to you, and describe why.
2. Portugal is a homogenous country, largely Catholic, and Portuguese speaking. How do these characteristics complement or contrast with your background and familiarities? What are the advantages to homogeneity? What are the disadvantages?
3. As students preparing for an international exchange in Portugal, use your research skills and examine the period of dictatorship under António de Oliveira Salazar and the bloodless coup, the Revolution of Carnations. Discuss how this portion of Portugal's history would influence social policy development. Compare Portugal's path to democracy with that of the United States.
4. Using your knowledge on culture and diversity, what would you do to further understand the unique features of Portuguese culture?
5. Organize a Portuguese potluck meal by preparing traditional Portuguese recipes. What do you notice about the ingredients and tastes?

---

people with cerebral palsy. The overarching goal of the association is to enhance the quality of life for those with cerebral palsy through a variety of interventions and multidisciplinary partnerships. Other goals are:

- To arouse public awareness of the problem of cerebral palsy and its prevention
- To enhance rehabilitation and inclusion for children, young people and adults with cerebral palsy, by maximizing their development
- To protect disabled people's right to education, professional training, and work as well as to emotional and social fulfillment
- To promote the creation of support units for severely disabled and dependent people
- To foster research on cerebral palsy
- To promote the APPC's membership in national and international associations

To facilitate goal achievement, the APPC (2001) bases its organizational strategy "on inclusive development by benefiting from synergies . . . along with good resource management."

In 1975, in order to meet the need of people with cerebral palsy living in central Portugal, a group of parents and professionals founded a center in the city of Coimbra, which developed a unique partnership with Portugal's Social Security Administration to provide services to all people with disabilities. In response to the needs of children and their parents, the Coimbra site created a rehabilitation center for children, which became a public institution in 1977.

Coimbra and its environs offer APPC several advantages. Nestled on a hillside, the medieval city is overlooked by the tall tower of Velha Universidade (Old University) founded in Lisbon in 1290 and then permanently transferred to Coimbra in 1537. The city, peaceful throughout the summer, awakens at the start of the academic year. The 13,000 students retain traditions, which in some cases go back 400 years, like singing fados and dressing in traditional academic regalia, including caps.

Approximately 5 miles from Coimbra is Conraria Farm, the location of the most recent service associated with APPC of Coimbra. In a pastoral setting, this innovative component of APPC offers people with significant physical and intellectual challenges occupational services that promote personal autonomy. The program is based on educational training accredited by the Ministry of Education and individually designed according to a student's capabilities. Integral to the educational program are complementary activities including physical education, hydrotherapy, hippotherapy (therapeutic riding program), and Snoezelen stimulation.

Two of these complementary activities are especially noteworthy: hippotherapy and Snoezelen stimulation. To ensure program sustainability, the Conraria Farm boards privately owned horses and provides a riding ring and other exercise courses for consumers who pay a fee for service. This income-producing service coincides with a hippotherapy program for people with an array of physical challenges. Enhancing physical strength and condition, promoting self-esteem and demonstrated confidence, and enhancing caregiving skills are the goals of this program. Activities associated with these goals included walking, feeding, and grooming horses as well as riding and exercising the horses owned by the farm.

Snoezelen stimulation originated in Sweden and applies the theories of empowerment and self-determination to simulation conditions. More precisely, Snoezelen stimulation involves a room in which the lighting, music, colors, positioning, and textures as well as the duration of stimulation can be controlled by a consumer through multisensory devices applicable for use with people experiencing a wide continuum of challenges. Thus, even the most physically or mentally challenged individual learns to control the environment in a satisfying fashion.

Multidisciplinary staff and a strong team spirit are integral to the programs provided at the Coimbra Rehabilitation Center and the Conraria Farm. To a large degree this is due to the work of Luís Francisco Aguiar-Conraria, the executive director, who is administratively responsible for both programs. Conraria, the father of a son with cerebral palsy, created the entire APPC network in response to gaps in services. With diligent advocacy, a strong belief in the strengths of all people, creative programming, and national and international partnerships, the APPC network has recruited and trained talented people who share its values and vision of social inclusion.

Social workers play a critical role in service provision as do social work students. They work one on one with consumers and their families on issues ranging from initial intake to service referral and program termination. At the group level, social workers conduct consumer groups on skill development and offer a variety of group sessions for families based on their desires and needs. Social workers engage in local development, advocacy activities, and program administration. At the community and organization level, social workers have formed task forces to improve service for people with cerebral palsy.

The significance of collaboration is essential not only to social workers but to the APPC, as evidenced by the organization's long-standing relationships with national and regional ministries, including the Solidarity and Social Security Ministry and the Education Ministry. Further, the APPC maintains program coordination with local, regional, and national employment centers to ensure that agency curricula is current and in compliance with established norms and criteria. Physicians, employers, and representatives from nonprofit agencies are also program partners.

The agency is sponsored by elected officials, university professors, researchers, staff, parents of consumers, and consumers. The Board of

Advisors, per its adopted by-laws, meets quarterly, elects officers for specific terms of office, and operates via a committee structure in relationship to programming, program development, public relations, and finance. Decisions are made by consensus, and all decisions are recorded in meeting minutes. APPC's executive director is an ex officio of the board, as is the associate director. The agency's chief financial officer attends all board meetings and provides a comprehensive financial report. All meetings are open to the public, although executive sessions occur as needed.

APPC has a newsletter that is published on a quarterly basis and circulated to all consumers, their family members, program partners, board members, and all other collaborators and interested parties. The newsletter also contains a report from the executive director and a list of educational session and events sponsored by APPC. This publication also solicits financial donations and/or service contributions to the agency.

Financial issues represent ongoing challenges to the APPC. The organization's primary funding stream derives from annual appropriations granted by the national government. Local revenues are received from services rendered. Although government funding has been consistent and stable, increasing costs associated with staff recruitment, transportation and travel, consultation fees, and the conversion to the euro currency have plagued operational budgeting. Another underlying feature associated with finances is the aging nature of consumers with cerebral palsy. Although research is limited, the life expectancy of people with a variety of disabilities, including cerebral palsy, is increasing. With longer life comes extensive, complex, and subsequently costly service needs. To add to the complexities, the parents and care providers of consumers are also aging and consequently require greater assistance and additional service support to provide for their family members. The fee mechanisms for these kinds of supportive services are not well defined and were not considered at the inception of APPC.

Exploring Organizational Culture

The APPC center in Coimbra is located in a modern brick and stucco two-story building surrounded by cultivated gardens, a spacious parking lot with designated parking for senior administrators, a van drop-off, and entrance ramps. The building's signage is clear, uniform, and complements the building's contemporary architecture. Under large trees and to the left of the building are picnic tables used by consumers and staff. Behind the picnic area is a huge playground complete with a sand box, balance bar, and swings.

A close examination of the picnic and playground area reveals the names of donors, tagged on trees and pieces of equipment. On the far side of the picnic area is a small shady space with a perennial flowerbed, two iron benches, and a stone monument with the names of deceased consumers of services.

The organization's ambiance is influenced by its physical design and features. The center's entryway is covered and shaded by an awning. Upon entering the building, the initial impression of the organization is shaped by an abundance of light and appealing plants. Offices are located on the first and second floor, facing outward toward an atrium, giving the appearance of an upscale shopping mall. Suspended from the second-floor railing are large plants that extend down toward the first floor. The slate flooring that runs throughout the building is neat and clean as are the brick and beige-painted walls.

A receptionist dressed in casual, professional clothing greets all who enter the center. People known to the receptionist are called by their formal title, such as Mr. or Ms., along with their surnames. Children are welcomed with a cheery word and gesture. People are required to sign a register. The receptionist has a computer, a small vase of flowers, and family photos neatly arranged on her desk. Information stands, with brochures describing the center and other relevant services and programs, are conveniently located near the receptionist's area. Consumers of services are afforded a number of comfortable chairs and end tables containing recent magazines on parenting, travel, and current events. The reception area displays a free-standing marquee listing the names and office locations of various staff members.

When social work students begin work in the agency for field education, service learning activities, or voluntary service, they attend a two-day in-service training to learn about cerebral palsy, the service system, and established policies and procedures. During the training opportunity, students are asked to sign a statement pertaining to consumer rights and

✍ Reflection Exercises

In the preceding paragraphs, you learned some details about an agency, its environment, service system, and culture. Consider the next questions as a student preparing to participate in an international field placement at this agency.

1. Research the current literature on cerebral palsy. What evidence-based practice is available for practice with people with cerebral palsy and their families?
2. In light of your literature review, what research topics would you expect the agency to be considering?
3. Review the literature on the strengths perspective in practice. Does Associação Portuguesa de Paralisia Cerebral (APPC) use this perspective? Support you answer with details from the chapter.
4. Identify at least five cultural features of the agency. How do these unique features correspond or conflict with Portugal's culture? What do the features tell you about how consumers and their families are perceived and treated?
5. Considering Portugal's social systems described in this chapter, what are some possible challenges facing the agency and potentially Portugal's social service delivery system?

---

confidentiality. The training ends with a dinner, attended by administrators, service providers, and consumers and their family members.

Students engage in direct services. Some assist in the agency's research projects, commonly dedicated to aspects of community inclusion and the special needs of the population. The research function of the agency is viewed as significant and vital to practice. It is also an opportunity for the agency to interface with the two social work programs located in Coimbra. It is not unusual for students to participate in university-sponsored research conferences and poster sessions.

AN INTERNATIONAL FIELD EXPERIENCE

Using the history of Portugal and the description of the Associação Portuguesa de Paralisia Cerebral (APPC) as a backdrop, the next field education experience is designed to enhance critical thinking skills related to social work practice and processes, including ethical considerations and dilemmas. The goal is to consider various cultural aspects for learning across the social work curriculum.

Social Work Student

Pam, a 20-year-old undergraduate social work student at a midwestern public university, enjoys travel and adventure. As a junior, she decides to enroll in a summer international field placement in Portugal. Pam has several reasons for this choice. First, she has limited field experience and exposure to people with special needs. Second, she wants the chance to test her developing practice skills. Finally, she has visited England with her family and longs to visit another country "on her own." Pam's mother, father, and older married sister support her decision to participate in international travel, as does her maternal grandmother, with whom Pam has a close relationship.

Working with the assistant dean of Field Education, Pam learns of the APPC. Although she knows nothing about Portugal or cerebral palsy and does not speak Portuguese, Pam is intrigued by the university's long-standing relationship with the agency, the agency's geographic location, and its focus on community inclusion. Although the idea of 6 weeks alone in a foreign country is somewhat intimidating, Pam is up for the adventure. Further, the social work program has offered her limited funding, and the trip will fulfill her social work elective requirement. A faculty member from the social work program will accompany Pam to Portugal and remain in Coimbra for three days, after which time she will maintain contact with Pam via e-mail.

In preparation for her trip, Pam browses the agency's Web site, makes contact with her supervising social worker at the agency, and buys a tourist book on Portugal. She meets regularly with the faculty member who will serve as the international field liaison. They agree that Pam will maintain a journal of her experience.

Consumers

Pam arrived in Portugal without any difficulty and has spent 2 weeks shadowing Patrice, a master's-level social worker who speaks English as a second language. Both Pam and Patrice conclude that Pam should assume more responsibility in at least one consumer situation. The consumer assigned to Pam is described next.

Reflection Exercises

Imagine that you are Pam or another student preparing for an international field experience, and answer the next questions.

1. Make a list of tasks you would complete in preparation for the trip. What readings or research would you do? Remember to visit Web sites that will introduce you to a country's literature and art, such as the famous Portuguese poets described at http://www.ucp.org.

2. Given what you know about Portugal and the agency, what questions would you ask Pam about her expectations, values, and beliefs?

3. Describe at least five ways in which the social work foundation courses will enhance the knowledge base and practice skills Pam will need for a successful international experience.

4. What steps would you take to ensure the success of your trip? Discuss how you would address being away from home, friends, and family for a prolonged period of time.

5. How should Pam prepare to immerse herself in a country where she does not speak the language?

6. What do you see as the social work program's role in the international field experience?

7. Is Pam's motivation and decision to participate in this field education experience appropriate? Be sure to take into account her lack of experience with this population group, the language barrier, and resource allocation to support the placement.

Presenting problems. Joaquin is a 33-year-old man diagnosed at birth with cerebral palsy. For the last 10 years, Joaquin has attended day programming at APPC, where he participates in training sessions designed to enhance independence in activities of daily living, including self-feeding, computer-based communication, personal hygiene, and bowel and bladder control. Joaquin's process is slow but steady. His interactions with staff and other consumers are positive, as is his attitude toward learning.

Until 6 months ago, Joaquin lived with his mother, Mrs. Anna Abreu, who was 55 years old and divorced for the last 25 years. Unfortunately, Mrs. Abreu died suddenly as a result of a heart attack, leaving the immediate and long-term care of Joaquin in question. To date, Joaquin's 77-year-old maternal grandmother, Mrs. Rosa Ferreira, has assumed the role of care provider. Mrs. Ferreira had resided with her daughter, Anna, for 8 years, ever since the death of her husband; consequently, Mrs. Ferreira is quite familiar with Joaquin's routine service needs and day programming with APPC.

Since his mother's death, Joaquin has displayed occasional negative behavior in the form of opposition. For example, he repeatedly ignored the conversations of service providers and refused to move from one training session to another. When placed in group activities, he also appears withdrawn. The agency's nurse indicated that Joaquin lost 6 pounds over the last 5 months after maintaining optimal weight for several years. Joaquin shows little interest in food, even those foods that he thoroughly enjoyed in the past, such as potatoes, pork, and grapes. However, Joaquin's attendance at day programming has remained constant as has Mrs. Ferreira's participation in program planning meetings. Also, Joaquin remains focused in these training sessions once he gets to class; he tends to be receptive to assistance as needed.

Patrice relates Joaquin's social history and current situation to Pam. Together they conclude that Joaquin is likely experiencing grief over the death of his mother, although there are no mental health instruments to substantiate this assessment, and mental health services for people with cerebral palsy are not available.

Another issue that requires consideration is Joaquin's living situation. Mrs. Ferreira has done an outstanding job of maintaining Joaquin's living habits. And, while she is participating in program planning, there is increasing evidence that Mrs. Ferreira will need support to implement in-home programming in the fashion similar to her daughter. Perhaps the most pressing issue involves senescence, the natural aging process. Both Joaquin and Mrs. Ferreira are aging, and it shows in their energy levels, memory, and physical abilities and flexibility. More specifically, Mrs. Ferreira admits that it is difficult to provide Joaquin with the physical support he needs to bathe, transition from a sitting position, and ambulate.

Family system. Joaquin has two younger siblings. Antonio, an accountant, is 31 years old, married with one son, a 2-year-old named Luis. Antonio has traveled extensively, speaks fluent English and Spanish, and resides in Lisbon with his family. Antonio visits with Joaquin on major holidays but has had little contact with APPC and/or Joaquin's daily program. When Patrice spoke with him on the phone, Antonio made it clear that he had significant concern about his grandmother caring for Joaquin; however, he did not see himself or his spouse as a primary caregiver. During the conversation, it became apparent to Patrice that Antonio thought his mother's untimely death was connected to the demands of caring for Joaquin. "My mother dedicated her life to Joaquin's welfare. I understand this and admire my mother for her commitment to my brother. I learned much about caring and compassion from my mother, but there is no doubt in my mind that the strain and stress associated with Joaquin compromised her health."

Theresa, Joaquin's 29-year-old sister is married and the mother of two young children, Beatrice, 3 years old, and Sophia, 6 months. Trained as a teacher, Theresa works at home with her children while her spouse, Juan, is the owner of a retail store in Oporto. Much like her brother Antonio, Theresa has maintained contact with Joaquin through her mother and now her grandmother. Given her young family and her husband's irregular work hours, Theresa expresses being overwhelmed by household and child care demands. She also discloses that she misses her mother a great deal: "I miss my mother and her guidance. Throughout my life, my mother devoted much of her time to Joaquin, which I came to understand and accept as I matured but, I admit when I was a child, I was resentful of Joaquin and all the attentions he received."

Patrice noted that none of Joaquin's family members commented on Joaquin's father, Mr. Abreu, who was absent from the home for well over 25 years. There is no indication that Mr. Abreu ever participated in Joaquin's life and/or service provision. Further, no one disclosed information about Mr. Abreu's family or his current status.

Reflection Exercises

Patrice and Pam begin to prepare for an interdisciplinary program planning meeting with Joaquin and Mrs. Ferreira. Using the presenting situation and an understanding of the family, as described, consider how you would approach the next questions and why.

1. Construct a three-generation genogram to understand the Abreu family system. What additional information do you need to complete the diagram? What patterns are revealed through this graphical tool that will assist in the program planning meeting?
2. Write a short narrative of your assessment of Joaquin's situation, identifying both concerns and specific strengths.
3. Identify the theoretical model or approach that you would use to guide and evaluate the planning process.
4. How does Joaquin's and Mrs. Ferreira's situation reflect some of the issues facing Portugal's social service system? How can this be translated to a research question to support evidence-based practice?
5. What cultural aspects of Portugal and APPC do you think might influence the outcome of the program planning process? A helpful Web site for you to explore is http://www.portugal.com/news/culture.

6. What are Pam's advantages and disadvantages as a social work intern involved with Joaquin's situation? Consider how her self-awareness, values, and beliefs might affect her assessment and work with Joaquin and Mrs. Ferreira.

7. Pam's initial thought is that Joaquin is experiencing depression. Would other professionals agree? How is grief differentiated from depression in this culture? Is depression, especially for a person experiencing cerebral palsy, a diagnosis used in Portugal? If so, who would bestow such a diagnosis? What are the merits and disadvantages of diagnostic labeling in Portugal in comparison to the United States?

Planned Change

Pam attended the program planning session along with Patrice, Joaquin, Mrs. Ferreira, and the members of the interdisciplinary team. Prior to the actual meeting, Patrice and Pam met with Mrs. Ferreira to explain the meeting's process and to assure her that her opinions would be appreciated. Joaquin was also informed of the meeting process. Although Joaquin had limited speech, he made his wishes and ideas known through gestures. The resulting program follows.

Goal 1. Recognize the grief associated with the death of mother.

Objectives

1. Express grief with siblings in ways that nurture positive behavior and strengthen the family system.
2. Maintain eating and hygiene routines with appropriate reinforcement for positive behavior.
3. Refer grandmother and siblings to grief support groups.

Goal 2. Increase support at home and respite services.

Objectives

1. Refer to community home care provider service.
2. Investigate weekend respite services.
3. Contract with siblings to maintain phone contact with grandmother.

Goal 3. Prepare for eventual community placement.

Objectives
1. Explore options in proximity to family members.
2. Discuss options with grandmother and family members.

Pam, in conjunction with Patrice, was assigned several roles in the context of the plan. As a start, she was to monitor and record Joaquin's behavior and eating patterns. This data would be used with Goal 1, Objective 2. Since Antonio spoke English, it was Pam's responsibility to keep him informed of available grief (Goal 1, Objective 1) and respite services (Goal 2, Objective 2). Interestingly, Pam believed engaging with Mrs. Ferreira was relatively easy, even though language was a barrier. Thus, it was agreed that Pam would spend extra time with Mrs. Ferreira, including conducting a home visit.

Reflection Exercises

The APPC multidisciplinary team, along with Joaquin and Mrs. Ferreira, created the described program plan; however, the next exercises give you the opportunity to contribute to the effort.

1. How does the APPC interdisciplinary treatment team reflect the mission and goals of APPC? Consider how a strengths perspective, emphasizing the use of client abilities and capacities, is woven throughout the plan.
2. What roles would social workers assume on an interdisciplinary team? Considering Pam's background and educational foundation, consider what particular strengths she might offer the team, Joaquin, and Mrs. Ferreira? What challenges does Pam face as a team member?
3. How would you use your skills in assessment and direct practice to operationalize the proposed program plan? In other words, revise the objectives to be measurable and observable. In doing so, what cultural elements are critical to consider in Joaquin's plan?
4. What theoretical approach(es) did you use to expand the program plan?
5. Given your knowledge of APPC, what additional interventions would you recommend be considered? Use the literature and evidence-based research to support your suggestions.
6. Visit the United Cerebral Palsy homepage (http://www.ucp.org) and list at least three other Internet sites that might prove helpful to Pam when working with Joaquin.

Ethical Issues

In the weeks that followed, Patrice and Pam evaluated Joaquin's program plan by monitoring goal achievement via daily interaction with Joaquin while maintaining regular contact with Mrs. Ferreira. Initially, Pam was timid in Joaquin's company. She had a limited background in cerebral palsy and had little experience working with people with significant physical challenges. Noticing Pam's hesitancy in engagement, Patrice suggested that Pam play music for Joaquin after the noon meal. In response, Pam went to the Coimbra public library and selected an array of classical and contemporary compact discs. Patrice informed Mrs. Ferreira of Pam's activities. Mrs. Ferreira, a devout Roman Catholic, supported the musical activity and suggested that Pam include religious music in her repertoire.

Pam gave considerable thought to Mrs. Ferreira's suggestion in light of Joaquin's program plan. Religion and/or spirituality were clearly important elements for Mrs. Ferreira. Pam pondered if religiosity and spirituality were relevant considerations for Joaquin, Antonio, and Theresa. Frustrated by her limited use of Portuguese, Pam wondered what she should do in this situation. Further, since Pam was not Roman Catholic or especially religious, she felt pressured and personally intimidated by Mrs. Ferreira's firm request.

A positive consequence of working with Joaquin was the relationship Pam developed with Mrs. Ferreira, who reminded Pam of her own grandmother. Although Pam had not completed a course in gerontological social work practice, she was comfortable in the company of older people. Consequently, on occasion, Pam and Mrs. Ferreira would sit in the garden together or take Joaquin on long walks through the city. Mrs. Ferreira brought Pam homemade custard cream and gave her a piece of pottery in the green with yellow and brown overtones typical to Coimbra's earthenware.

Through gestures and diligent attempts to communicate in Portuguese, Pam asked that Mrs. Ferreira place a few pictures of her late daughter in Joaquin's room to help him with the grieving process. Mrs. Ferreira was pleased to accommodate the request, and Joaquin appeared to gain a sense of calm when viewing his mother's picture. Indeed, Joaquin began to display a decrease in oppositional behavior with service providers and improved in his transitioning from one programmatic area to another.

Reflection Exercises

The next questions focus on ethical issues and dilemmas. Before completing the questions, review the *Code of Ethics of the National Association of Social Workers* (http://www.naswdc.org).

1. Based on the NASW *Code of Ethics*, define the critical ethical terms associated with Joaquin's treatment plan and discuss at least two ethical concerns that Pam confronted in her interaction and work with Joaquin and family members. How do these concerns relate to cultural competence and belief systems?

2. How does the NASW *Code of Ethics* apply to interdisciplinary teams? What cultural considerations might impact the functions of the APPC team and Pam's role on the team and its decisions?

3. Identify research topics from Pam's field experience with APPC and in relationship to Joaquin, his family, and service delivery. Consider international codes for research (www.ifsw.org/en/p38000324.html). How might such codes guide or constrain a research agenda?

4. Pam had limited communication skills in the Portuguese language. As stated by the NASW *Code of Ethics*, what is she compelled to carry out with consumers who do not communicate in English?

5. Mrs. Ferreira brought Pam homemade custard cream and gave her a piece of Coimbra pottery. Given the NASW *Code of Ethics*, how should Pam respond to these acts of kindness? What is Patrice's role in helping Pam to judge the cultural relevance of such gifts?

Pam assumed that part of Joaquin's program plan evaluation would include periodic contact with his siblings, Antonio and Theresa. However, this did not occur. Given her position as a student in an international field placement, Pam was unclear how she should or could convey her ideas on evaluation and the need for specificity in measurement to Patrice and other members of the interdisciplinary team. Language barriers and cultural differences complicated Pam's ability to fully participate.

SUMMARY

As Pam's 6-week field experience comes to a conclusion, she reflects on the importance of understanding Joaquin and Mrs. Ferreira in the context of Portugal's geography, culture, and religious orientation. The cultural insight Pam developed in Portugal facilitated a beginning knowledge of how values and beliefs influence and shape the conceptualization of phenomenon, thinking, and actions toward others.

Pam's unique investigation of self in relation to people in a faraway land is especially important for undergraduate social work students. She went to Portugal, her self-selected "corner of the deserted beach," in search of an adventure with hopes of learning about another country, its people and culture. As an aspiring social worker, Pam soon began to contemplate her passion and abilities to approach and engage consumer systems from a generalist perspective. Given her minimal understanding of the values, culture, and people of Portugal, she found herself leaving the country with more questions than answers concerning social work, practice, and policy in Portugal. Most important, and Pam's personal "breakthrough" concerning skepticism, she has learned to question the efficacy and ethics of helping activities and intervention when one lacks a thorough grounding in and appreciation and understanding of language, culture, and cultural competency.

REFERENCES

Amaro, F. (1994). Portugal: Improvement of the quality of family life. In W. Dumon (Ed.), *Changing family policies in the member states of the European Union* (pp. 255–270). Brussels: Commission of the European Communities.

Associação Portuguesa de Paralisia Cerebral (APPC) [Portuguese Association for Cerebral Palsy]. (2001). *Centro de Reabilitacao de Paralisia Cerebral de Coimbra.* Coimbra, Portugal: Author.

Bradshaw, J., Ditch, J., Holmes, H., & Whiteford, P. (1993). *Support for children: A comparison of arrangements in fifteen countries.* Research report no. 21. London: Department of Social Security.

Clearinghouse on international developments in child, youth and family policies at Columbia University. Portugal. Retrieved June 17, 2005, from http://www.childpolicyintl.org/countries/portugal.html.

de mello Andersen Breyner, S. (1990). Midday. *Obra Poetica.* Lisbon: Caminho.

Facts about Portugal. Retrieved July 15, 2005, from http://worldfacts.us/Portugal.html.

History World. (n.d.). *History of Portugal*. Retrieved February 23, 2009 from http://www.historyworld.net/wrldhis/PlainTextHistories.asp?groupid=1709& HistoryID=ab46.

ICPE Portugal. (2005). *Travel & tourism*. Retrieved February 23, 2009 from http://www.portugal.org/tourism/index.html.

Index Mundi. (2008). *Portugal demographics profile 2008*. Retrieved February 24, 2009 from http://www.indexmundi.com/portugal/demographics_profile.html.

Lonely Planet. (2009). *Introducing Portugal*. Retrieved February 24, 2009 from http://www.lonelyplanet.com/destinations/europe/portugal/history.htm.

National Association of Social Workers. (2000). *Code of ethics of the National Association of Social Workers*. Washington, DC: Author.

Pinto, C. G. (1997). Health care systems, equity, and social welfare. In *MIRE, Comparing social welfare systems in Southern Europe* (pp. 141–154). Paris: Ministry of Labor and Social Affairs.

Photius Coutsoukis. (2004). *Portugal: Religion and the role of the Roman Catholic church*. Retrieved February 24, 2009 from http://www.photius.com/countries/portugal/society/portugal_society_religion_and_the_rol~1083.html.

Porter, D., & Prince, D. (2004). *Frommer's Portugal*. Hoboken, NJ: John Wiley & Sons.

Portugal. Retrieved February 24, 2009 from http://www.infoplease.com/ipa/A0107895.html.

Steves, R. (2005). *Portugal*. Emeryville, CA: Avalon Travel.

Wall, K. (2003). *The situations of families in Portugal—2001. European Observatory on the social situation, demography, and family*. Retrieved January 2009, from http://www.indexmundi.com/portugal/demographics_profile.html.

CHAPTER

5

Mongolia: A Focus on Community Practice

Carolyn J. Tice

> Before us lay Mongolia, a land of painted deserts dancing in mirage; of limitless grassy plains and nameless snow-capped peaks; of untracked forests and roaring streams! Mongolia, land of mystery, of paradox and promise. The hills swept away in the far-flung, graceful lines of panorama so endless that we seemed to have reached the very summit of the earth.
>
> —Andrews (1921)

This excerpt is taken from the American explorer Roy Chapman Andrews, who in 1918 drove across the unmapped Gobi desert of Mongolia and recorded his experience in a now-famous book, *Across the Mongolia Plains: On the Trail of Ancient Man*. Not only did Andrews

The contents of this chapter are taken from the author's 6-week experience in Mongolia. The agency name and all other identifying information have been changed to protect confidentiality. However, much of the description and incidences are firsthand, representing the experiences of the author. The travel to Mongolia was sponsored through a Senior Specialist Fulbright Award.

discover traces of early humans in Mongolia, he found dinosaur eggs, the first ever seen by humans. Travelers to Mongolia will be dazzled by the country's rich history and traditions, geographic diversity, sparse population, and political environment.

OVERVIEW OF MONGOLIA

History

The Mongolians, or Mongols as they were known previously, recorded their history for centuries in oral epics sung by bards, until writing was introduced approximately 800 years ago. Until the 12th century, the Mongols were little more than a loose confederation of rival clans. Until a Mongol who came to be known by the honorary name of Chinggis (Genghis) Khaan, meaning "oceanic (or universal) king," declared the formation of the Mongol empire and himself as supreme leader.

By the time of Chinggis's death in 1227, the Mongol empire stretched from Beijing, China, to the Caspian Sea. The grandeur of the Mongol empire lasted over a century. After Kublai Khaan, a grandson of Chinggis, died in 1294, the Mongols became increasingly dependent on, and influenced by, the people that ruled them (Sermier, 2002). Although demonized by foreign historians, Chinggis Khaan introduced a written script for the Mongolian language, instituted a tradition of religious tolerance, and initiated the first direct contact between the East and the West. He is attributed with the introduction of the *yasaq*, or the Mongolian legal code, which influenced the Mongolian government for centuries. There was however, a darker legacy. In portions of the Gobi desert, there exist plague foci such as rats and fleas. Although these places were isolated for most of history, by 1250, Mongol caravans on new trade routes, armies, and the "Mongol express" transported rats and their fleas to more populated areas, and facilitated the spread of the plague known as the Black Death (http://www.bukisa.com/articles/22152_the-black-death-and-its-route-to-europe).

Further, the fierce Mongolian warriors and their war machine destroyed great cultures of the Middle East and Central Asia, many of which were never to recover (http://www.infoplease.com/ipa).

A revival of sorts occurred under Altan Khaan (1507–83) via a conversion to Buddhism, despite warring with Tibet (Becker, 1992). Buddhism became the state religion for 200 years. Interestingly, it was the Buddhist monks who attempted to reunite the quarreling Mongol clans, but Mongolia's tendency to fragmentation persisted. In 1691, Mongolia submitted to Manchu rule, China's last ruling dynasty. The Mongol war machine, comprised of horses, compound bows, and the ability to shoot while riding forward and backward, was defeated by the Manchu's new form of weaponry: muskets and cannons.

The Russian Revolution of October 1917 came as a surprise to Mongolia's aristocracy, under the control of Bogd Khaan (Holy King) since 1915. Deciding that the Bolsheviks were their best hope for military assistance to expel the increasingly threatening Chinese warlords, the Mongolian People's Party came to power. It was the first political party in Mongolia's history, and the only one for the next 69 years. In 1924, the Mongolian People's Republic emerged to become the world's second communist country (Kohn, 2005).

Mongolia followed in the footsteps of the Soviet Union until 1990, when pro-democracy protests and widespread hunger strikes erupted. In response, the Mongolian constitution was amended to permit multiparty elections (Kohn, 2005). The communist Mongolian People's Revolutionary Party (MPRP) won the majority of the elected positions, and freedom of speech, religion, and assembly was granted. In 1996, the MPRP was defeated by the Mongolian Democratic Coalition, ending 75 years of communist rule.

The road to democracy has been challenged by corruption, economic hardship, and political turmoil. However, the June 29, 2008, elections brought with them the promise of power-sharing agreements. Universal suffrage for anyone 18 years or older is in place. There are two principal government officials: a president and a prime minister. The president is the head of state, commander in chief of the armed services, and the head of the National Security Council. He or she is popularly elected by a national majority for a 4-year term of office and is limited to two terms (http://www.mongolianembassy.us/eng_about_mongolia/social.php).

The prime minister is nominated by the president and has a 4-year term of office. The prime minister selects a cabinet, subject to approval by the State Great Hural, the legislative branch of the government comprised of 76 deputies. Local hurals are elected by the 21 *aimags* (provinces) plus the capital, Ulaanbaatar.

🖋 Reflection Exercises

1. Go online to locate Mongolia on http://www.lib.utexas.edu/maps/
mongolia.html. How does Mongolia's location help you to understand
its political history and current economic situation?
2. Review http://www.state.gov/r/pa/ei/bgn/2779.htm. What do the flag
and national seal of Mongolia look like? What do the various symbols
reveal about the country's heritage and culture?
3. Take some time to read about Chinggis (Genghis) Khaan or watch the
film *The Monguls*. A helpful Web site is http://www.fsmitha.com/h3/
h11mon.htm. Why do you think Chinggis Khaan was named the Man
of the Millennium?

AN OVERVIEW OF MONGOLIA

Mongolian People

With a population of 2.56 million (2007 estimate), Mongolia is sparsely
populated. Nearly half of its citizens live in Ulaanbaatar, the country's
capital (www.infoplease.com). A seminomadic life continues to dominate
the countryside; however, settled agricultural communities are becoming
more common. Currently, 50.4% of the population is comprised of women
with 49.6% of the population being male (http://www.mongolianembassy
.us/eng_about_mongolia/social.php). Interestingly, about two-thirds of
the total population is under 30 years of age, of whom 28.5% are under
14 years. Consequently, Mongolia has a relatively young population. The
average life expectancy for men is 62 years as compared to 69 years for
women (http://www.w-mongol.com/mongolia).

Mongolian women occupy a valued role in the household and are often
in charge of the family's daily affairs. Although economic hardship and
social unrest over the past 15 years have forced women to shoulder heavier
workloads to supplement the family income, few women hold positions of
power; administrators, company directors, and political leaders are usually
men (Kohn, 2005). Economic strain, including few stable employment
opportunities, has contributed to an increase in divorce among Mongolians

and discourages marriage among the younger generation. To combat this trend, the government has introduced stimulus packages to support newly married couples and their newborns.

With compulsory education to the ninth grade and a literacy rate of 83% (2002 estimate), one-third of Mongolians live below the poverty line, which means that they earn less than US$30 per month (http://www .w-mongol.com/mongolia). Even with this poverty, Mongolians tend to live in viable communities thanks to strong family networks. If one family member is employed, he or she has the responsibility of aiding all other family members in need.

Cultural Characteristics

Mongolia is slightly larger than Alaska. Almost 90% of its land is pasture or desert, of varying usefulness. In the north, Mongolia borders with Russia (central Siberia), sharing a frontier, and in the south with China. One of the largest and most landlocked countries of the world, Mongolia experiences extreme climate conditions. Specifically, from the middle of October until mid-April, the temperature rarely climbs above 32°F (0°C). During the coldest winter days, the temperatures can remain at −22°F (30°C) for days on end. Further, during winter, the sun sets by 4:00 P.M., creating a cold, dark, and long season.

Mongolia's geographic location, seasons, and harsh weather help to shape its unique cultural character. Called "Asian by ethnicity and Western by culture" (Kohn, 2005, p. 26), Mongolians use utensils rather than chopsticks, the Russian Cyrillic alphabet, and the togrog as their form of currency. However, perhaps most symbolic of the Mongolian culture and life is the *ger*, the one-room round felt tent. It might be hard to imagine, but nearly half of the Mongolian population lives in gers, which serve as sleeping, eating, and social spaces for entire families.

Gers are equipped with traditional furnishings painted bright orange with fanciful designs. The majority of gers are arranged in a similar manner, with three beds around the perimeter, a chest covered with Buddhist relics at the back wall, and a low table upon which food is set. Everything revolves around a central hearth, with the women's side to the right of the hearth and men's to the left. The head of the household sits at the northern end of the ger with honored guests sitting to the right. The area nearest the door is the place of lowest rank and the domain of the children.

At the top of all gers is a hole permitting light to enter and allowing the smoke of the hearth to escape (Myagmarbayer, 2007). Essential features of society and integral components of the Mongolian character include offering gracious welcome into gers and food to all visitors.

Nomadic Mongolians spend most of their time out of doors. Another unique characteristic of Mongolian life is that of riding hardy horses and moving gers from one pasture to the next, as the season or land conditions change. This nomadic feature makes the Mongolian culture probably the last of its kind in Asia (http://www.mongolianculture.com/Mongolia-Information.htm).

If the ger is the traditional home structure of Mongolia, a *deel* is the exotic and colorful traditional costume. This coatlike dress originated in the era of the Huns more than 1,000 years ago. Cut in a very simple pattern of a double T-shape, the deel is ideal for cold and hot seasons, for men and women of various ages (Tsolmon, 2004). The deel's combination of colors, decorative ornamentation, and design depicts the wearer's ethnic membership. Moreover, the deel is designed to provide the freedom of movement necessary for herders to ride horses and perform daily tasks. For example, inside the deel is a large pocket to keep small items, including a cup or knife.

In terms of religious practices, traditionally Mongolians are Tibetan Buddhist Lamaists; however, religion was suppressed under the communist regime until 1990, with only a few showcase monasteries permitted to remain. Since 1990, as the government began its transformation, Buddhism has enjoyed resurgence; however, there is a lack of trained Buddhist lamas. Additionally, two or three generations of Mongolians were raised without any Buddhist training or adherence to religious rituals and customs. Thus, to varying degrees, Mongolians have become dependent on theologians from Tibet, India, and the West for religious training.

Over the ages, two musical features evolved that are purely Mongolian. The first is the *moriin khuur*, or horsehead fiddle. This wooden instrument has a trapezoidal sound box and two strings of horsehair and is played with a bow made of horsehair. Its scrolled head generally ends in a carved

Reflection Exercises

1. Diane, a social worker employed in Mongolia with a nongovernmental agency for people with visual challenges, was alarmed to learn that some backpackers and other travelers took advantage of people living in gers by accepting food and lodging without giving anything in return. Discuss what some international rules to follow would be for people visiting not only people in the Mongolian countryside but also the homes of strangers in general.

2. Tibetan Buddhism is the predominant religion of Mongolia, influencing a way of life and habits of the mind. Examine some of these Web sites on Buddhism, or others sites that interest you, and connect aspects of Mongolian character and culture to the practice of Buddhism.

   www.tibet.com/Buddhism/index.html
   www.buddhism.org
   www.fundamentalbuddhism.com
   www.writespirit.net/religious_traditions/buddhism

3. Mongolians are said to be natural singers and dancers. Listen to moriin khuur music and khoomi (http://www.greenkiwi.co.nz/footprints/mon golia/mong_music.htm). Even without understanding the Mongolian language, what are your impressions of the music and lyrics?

---

horse's head, symbolic of the horse ridden by the poet-musician on his mystic travels (Sermier, 2002). The second musical feature is *khoomi*, or throat singing, which produces a whole harmonic range from deep in the larynx, throat, stomach, and palate (Kohn, 2005). Remarkably, khoomi has the effect of producing two notes and melodies simultaneously.

Mongolians eat a simple diet of meat, rice, flour, and potatoes. They tend to be big tea drinkers; most meals start with tea, which is thought to aid digestion. *Buuz*, steamed mutton dumplings, and *khuushuur*, fried mutton pancakes, are two of the most popular menu options found in local restaurants (Kohn, 2005).

SOCIAL WORK IN MONGOLIA

The profession of social work is new to Mongolia. In fact, only in the last 10 years have social workers been trained in the country's university system at the baccalaureate and master's level. Many master's-level practitioners traveled to other countries, including the United States, to complete their graduate work, most often on scholarships or supported by an international fund or foundation.

A review of the social work curriculum across the majority of Mongolia's private and public schools and universities reveals several interesting features. Perhaps most obvious is the long-standing Soviet influence on the curriculum. For example, social work students are required to take a significant number of science courses, including physics, while most of the social work sources use Russian political and theoretical frameworks. Due to a lack of textbooks, social work instructors prepare reading packets, including the course syllabus and a description of assignments.

As social work students graduate, they are gaining employment in Mongolia's developing social service network, which includes programs across consumer systems and social welfare needs. In particular, there is a focus on domestic violence, child welfare, mental health, and substance abuse, primarily alcoholism. Many of the programs are supported by Mongolia's central government; however, internationally funded nongovernmental organizations (NGOs) have a significant presence throughout the country.

Social work services in rural areas are limited, challenged by fragmented or nonexistent public transportation, few roads, and dispersed populations who for centuries have been self-reliant. Although the Mongolian government is aware of the social needs of rural people, such as herders, NGOs often provided immediate services, especially in times of crisis.

A significant strength of the emerging social work network is the Mongolian Association of Social Work Educators. Comprised of both educators and practitioners, the association was formed in 2002 and has a current membership of approximately 40 social workers who meet at least annually at a summer institute. The institute brings together social workers from across the country to attend a series of workshops on interventions, emerging social issues, relevant book publications, and educational developments, such as accreditation standards for social work programs. During the course of the four-day event, information is shared, program collaborations are negotiated, and curriculum suggestions are discussed.

Agency Setting

The agency setting highlights a social work–related project sponsored by an NGO under the direction of a humanitarian association that works with international partners, including faith-based and government entities. The humanitarian association, which began in 1995, provides assistance to countries through a grant funding process. Its mission is "to help our neighbors, especially children in need, regardless of their race, nationality or religion."

In 2000, a development aid department was added to the association, which shifted its focus from emergency or crisis relief to long-term development programs, requiring sustainability and cooperative agreements with countries receiving funds. It was through such funding that a social work project designed to address Mongolia's street children was funded for three years. During that time, the project was designed to train social workers in child welfare, who in turn would establish and work in services for children. Equally as important, the project would support advocacy efforts for funding increases and expanded government involvement in child welfare. Thus, from its inception, the social work project defined a targeted population, worked across consumer systems, and involved both direct and policy practice.

Since its inception, the social work project worked closely with a leading Mongolian university and its undergraduate social work program, comprised of 400 students and 8 faculty members. Some faculty members have a MSW but the majority hold master's degrees in related areas, such as public health or political science. There are no doctoral-level social workers in the university system and no social work doctoral programs in Mongolia.

The lack of attention to social work as a profession makes sense when placed in a political context. Since 1996 and the introduction of a parliamentary democracy, the Mongolian social service system has gone through considerable change. In December 2005, Mongolia passed three hallmark pieces of legislation that gave shape to the social service system: the Social Systems Act, Disabled Persons Social Act, and Old People Social Security Act. At the same time the status and work of social work were defined by the National Accreditation Council of Mongolia.

Mongolia's limited social service system is reflected in field education, a persistent challenge for social work programs. More precisely, none of the social work programs has designated field education directors, and only a few have a written field manual or any sort of informal or formal learning contract. Trained field instructors or faculty field liaisons are also limited in number as are actual agency-based field placements. Further, the lack of university resources and considerable teaching effort requirements thwart the advancement of field education. Equally as significant is university administrators' unfamiliarity with the profession of social work and its educational standards.

The social work project operates in an office complex adjacent to a state university in Ulaanbaatar, the capital and largest city of Mongolia. The office space is expansive with windows on all four walls and plants on the windowsills. The grant pays the office rent and salaries for three staff members: project director, project assistant, and accountant. The project director holds an MSW from a large American East Coast university, where she studied for two years via a scholarship. The project assistant has an undergraduate degree in social work from a Mongolian university.

The office contains six movable conference tables with chairs used for various trainings and meetings. Six computer stations for use by social work students are also part of the office's decorum, along with a phone and one printer/copier. The office's hours of operation are from 9:00 AM and to 6:00 PM, Monday through Saturday. Always busy with students and faculty members, the atmosphere is welcoming and casual with lemon tea, a traditional drink of Mongolia, served throughout the day. Posters on various child welfare issues hang on the wall along with notices of student events.

Student Role

Since there are few trained social workers in Mongolia, the social work project recruited international social work faculty and students to volunteer for 4 to 6 weeks in support of its efforts. While in Mongolia, the volunteers were given housing in a college dormitory and a small allowance with which to buy food and basic supplies. At the project office, volunteers shared a desk, computer, and copier. They were expected to maintain a daily work schedule and complete assigned tasks in a timely manner. In general, all volunteers were assigned to one of these project areas:

- *Early childhood care.* Assisting parents and caregivers in providing services to children under 5 years of age experiencing either mental or physical developmental challenges.
- *Social and recreational activities.* Providing events and activities for school-age children at area agencies or community centers.
- *Street children shelters.* Serving lunch at one of Ulaanbaatar's 20 shelters for street children and conducting group sessions on health and hygiene issues with the children.
- *Sex workers' relief.* Working with a child welfare agency and assessing the extent to which the street children living in Ulaanbaatar were involved in sexual exploitation and/or forced labor.

Volunteers were expected to arrange and pay for their travel to Mongolia. Upon arrival in Ulaanbaatar, the volunteers designed an activities schedule with the project director that specified tasks and roles. All volunteers work closely with the assistant project director, who served as a translator and provided other assistance, such as facilitating money exchange, navigating directions, making telephone calls, and helping with food purchases and preparation.

Reflection Exercises

1. Social work as a profession is in the initial phase of development in Mongolia. Based on your social work education, compile a list of 10 readings that you would recommend to help Mongolian social workers implement a social service network.
2. The Mongolian Association of Social Work Educators was established in 2002 to promote quality social work education throughout Mongolia. Visit the Web sites of similar organizations in your country and note their mission statement and objectives. What do the organizations have in common, and what are their differences?

3. What are nongovernmental organizations (NGO), and how do they complement the social work profession? To answer this question, search online under "nongovernmental organizations" and locate a NGO site that addresses an interest of yours. When you have located an NGO site, examine its mission, objectives, projects, project locations, and funding sources. What did you learn that was surprising?
4. With an understanding of NGOs, search online for agencies that address child welfare issues, such as poverty, health or education. What did you learn about the global state of affairs for children? How does the position of children in various parts of the world compare to the conditions of children in your state and/or country?

CONSIDERATIONS BEFORE ARRIVING IN MONGOLIA

Anticipating Consumer and Service Needs

Given what you have read thus far, how would you imagine the consumer and services needs of Mongolia? It seems three points are essential considerations. The first is that Mongolia is in a transitional period of development. As was described, Mongolia was under Soviet domination for 70 years and operated almost like a colony; any form of dissent was impossible. During this time, the country was virtually closed to Western exposure. Only Russian was spoken in schools. Important cultural elements in Mongolia (e.g., the practice of Buddhism) were forbidden, as were statues and pictures of Mongolia's historic figures, including Chinggis Khaan. The transition to a parliamentary democracy began only in 1990, when the ancient battle cry, "Mongols! To your horses!" was heard once again in Ulaanbaatar.

A second consideration is that Mongolians are not accustomed to social services or social workers. Under communist rule, services were institutional and centralized with an ideological foundation that did not include social work as a profession. Since 1990, some services remain institutional; however, the ideological foundation has been eliminated. Further, there is a growing base of community services funded by NGOs and private funds that recognize the need for social workers and value the contributions of the social work profession.

Finally, social need is evident in Mongolia. The economy is converting to a market system with help from the European Union, Japan, South Korea, and the United States. But the conversion is slow, and the needs of

Reflection Exercises

1. Visit the Web site for the National Center for Preparedness, Detection, and Control of Infectious Diseases (NCPDCID) to learn what inoculations are needed prior to traveling to Mongolia (http://wwwn.cdc.gov/travel/default.aspx).
2. Visit the Web site for the Mongolian embassy or your country's embassy to learn of the visa regulations (www.mongolianembassy.us).
3. Take time to read accounts of Mongolia. A vivid picture of medieval Mongolians and their empire is provided in David Morgan's classic *The Mongols* (1986). *Mongolia: Empire of the Steppes* (Sermier, 2002) is an informative guide to Mongolia's developing national identity. With precise descriptions and excellent use of practical examples and narratives, the book is highly readable, comprehensive in scope, and offers an abundance of lively cultural information on Mongolian music, food, and customs. In a similar fashion, *The Lost Country: Mongolia Revealed* (Becker, 1992) captures the personality of Mongolia through the travel tales of the author.

---

people, ranging from adequate housing to medical care are obvious. This is especially true for children, some of whom have left situations of extreme poverty or families where alcohol was abused for street life in Ulaanbaatar. The sight of children roaming city streets, begging for food or money and engaging in work-related tasks, is difficult to witness, especially in light of Mongolia's harsh weather conditions.

Taken together, the political history of Mongolia, the newness of social services and the social work profession, and the needs of people require social workers to remain flexible with expectations, patient with understanding, and generous with time and energy. Mongolia represents a level of poverty and living conditions unfamiliar to many Westerners and residents in industrialized societies.

EXAMPLE OF COMMUNITY PRACTICE

Diane, a third-year undergraduate social work student from a large mid-Atlantic university, was interested in Asian affairs, primarily because of Chinese art and literature. When the opportunity to spend 6 weeks in Mongolia working with children was presented to her through the Field

Reflection Exercises

1. Diane has an important decision to make regarding an international experience in a distant and unfamiliar place. Given the information Diane has available, how would you proceed? What would be some of your next steps before you make the commitment to travel to Mongolia? How big of a personal and professional leap would this type of experience be for you and your comfort zone?

2. Review the next links and make a list of the strengths associated with a social work experience in Mongolia as well as some of the challenges or barriers.

   http://userpage.fu-berlin.de/~corff/mf.html
   http://www.lib.utexas.edu/maps/mongolia.html
   http://www.mol.mn/
   http://www.mongolianembassy.us
   http://www.pmis.gov.mn/

Education Office, Diane thought about the experience long and hard. Her primary concern was being so far from home for such a long time. Undoubtedly, she would miss her parents and younger brother. Also, since Diane had no international travel experience, she wondered how she would do with languages. Diane spoke a little Spanish but that was the extent of dabbling in a language other than English.

To learn more about Mongolia, Diane visited the campus International Student Organization to see if any Mongolian students were attending her university. Unfortunately, there was none, but Diane was encouraged to contact another school of social work that routinely recruited at least two Mongolian students each academic year and had regularly trained faculty from Mongolia. Diane was given a number of online resources that would acquaint her with the country and its people.

Making the Transition

Over a period of 3 weeks, Diane decides to move forward with her plans to spend 6 weeks in Mongolia and work with children and community-based child welfare agencies in the capital, Ulaanbaatar. She had already obtained a passport, so with flight tickets in hand, Diane began the 29-hour trip to Mongolia, which includes a layover in Seoul, Korea. The stop and change of planes in Seoul, originally scheduled for 3 hours, became an 8-hour ordeal, primarily a result of wind conditions in Ulaanbaatar. The lack of clear communication from the airlines, the difficulty in understanding the language, and Diane's realization that she was traveling alone gave her pause and made her wonder whether she had made a wise decision.

Eventually, Diane reached the airport in Mongolia to be greeted by two women from her social work project, holding a sign with Diane's name. Their jubilant faces eased Diane's worry and concerns. Without much delay, the three women piled into a car and headed to the apartment that would be Diane's home for the next 6 weeks. What Diane immediately noticed was the small size of the airport, how dark the area seemed, and the poor condition of the roads.

Eventually, the car drove into a dirt parking lot surrounded by a five-story cinderblock-like structure. Diane recognized the bland architectural design from old movies filmed in Soviet state countries. Compared to back home, Diane thought the buildings were foreboding, almost frightening. The apartment itself was located on the second floor and had three large rooms with 12-foot ceilings and large windows, a small kitchen, and a bath. The furniture was sparse and drab as were the appliances and light fixtures. The presence of a television brought a huge smile to Diane's face. Surrounded by unfamiliar physical features and living conditions, a television was a familiar and recognizable feature that somehow provided a sense of comfort for Diane.

If the apartment left Diane feeling rather depressed, the office environment and warm welcome from her new Mongolian colleagues served to boost her emotional well-being. The office was bright, modern, and equipped with computers. Diane had a space of her own with a comfortable desk and chair. Perhaps most exciting, she had access to a phone and an international calling card, so she could hear the voices of her family and friends.

Working with Street Children

At one time, approximately 5,000 children lived on the roads and sidewalks of Ulaanbaatar. Some were sent to the streets to panhandle by relatives from the countryside; other children left alcohol-plagued families

Reflection Exercises

1. Describe how Diane's first impression of Mongolia reflects the idea of "person in the environment." Identify environmental factors (e.g., societal and community) that contributed to Diane's initial impressions and perceptions of her new living situation, and explain how they did so.
2. As you think about an international experience, list your specific creature comforts—items deemed essential for your sense of comfort and safety. Consider how these needs and wants are grounded in and shaped by your social-economic status and the conveniences found in one's country of residence. For example, how do commercialism and the possession of nonessential material goods and services contribute to a person's almost never-ending passion to obtain more?

(Kohn, 2005). Although the number has decreased over the last few years, children wandering the streets asking for money, engaging in a variety of work, and sitting on a corner with an infant in their hands are a common component of the urban scene. In the harsh winter months, when they often live in the sewer and water system beneath Ulaanbaatar, the boys and girls suffer from high rates of malnutrition, scabies, and body lice.

Within a week of arriving to Mongolia, Diane was assigned to work at a shelter that provided a daily lunch and weekly lessons for street children. Along with a Mongolian social worker, Oyut, who served as a translator, Diane discovered that walking to the agency—or any place in Ulaanbaatar for that matter—was no easy feat. Hectic traffic patterns and blaring horns with no apparent rules of the road made the life of pedestrians a dangerous game of dodging and zigzagging to cross poorly-surfaced and unpaved roads.

The shelter was sponsored by an international nongovernmental organization that Diane was familiar with from advertisements and newscasts in the United States. The agency was simple in design but welcoming with an artsy décor. Its primary purpose was to provide health and educational services to street children. The children came to the center voluntarily or were brought by social workers, interested people, and sometimes family members. The soup kitchen, open Monday through Saturday, was a particular draw to the children, who otherwise were dependent on the kindness of strangers or trash heaps for food. It was in the soup kitchen that Diane began her work and became familiar with street children. For Diane, the notion of street children was truly a foreign concept. She struggled to even say the words.

Coming from an urban center in the United States, Diane had seen poverty and the plight of children firsthand, but nothing quite prepared her for the street children of Ulaanbaatar. Boys at the tender age of 7, 8, or 9 walked and talked with bravado well beyond their years while both girls and boys, no taller than Diane's waist, smoked cigarettes and sometimes smelled of alcohol. All the children were dirty with ragged clothing. High-spirited and humorous, the children playfully interacted with one another and the agency staff. Several said "hello" to Diane, although in general, no special attention was given to her.

It surprised Diane that after lunch and a training session on dental hygiene, the children scattered to the streets. Through a series of questions, she learned that Mongolia had few social policies protecting the rights of and ensuring services to children, and social workers were not mandated to report situations of abuse and neglect. However, Save the Children, a United Kingdom–based international program dedicated to helping children worldwide, had been working in Mongolia since 1994 and operated two offices, one of which was in Ulaanbaatar. Save the Children launched a research project entitled "Children Protection System of Mongolia" in 2006 in cooperation with a Mongolian lobby group for child development and protection (http://www.savethechildren.org). An integrated national child system was designed, creating a legal environment to prevent and protect children from violence and abuse. However, national policy had yet to be approved, and the child protection system was clearly in the planning stage.

Ethical Considerations

Diane kept a daily journal of her activities. Reading her notes, she realized that she had become comfortable with her role with the project and various staff people. Diane developed a routine of spending time in the children's agency, visiting tourist sites in Ulaanbaatar, and reading about Mongolian history and culture. Often she was invited to meetings with government dignitaries or university faculty, where issues related to child welfare were discussed. Diane was always made to feel welcome and useful.

Reflection Exercises

1. Given Diane's description of Mongolia's street children, how would you assess the children and community from a strengths perspective? What qualities have served the children well, and how could a community program or service system build on these qualities?
2. Visit the online sites for listed child welfare programs and discuss what you perceive are the international issues facing children. In what capacities can social workers offer support to these organizations and the children they serve?
   www.savethechildren.org
   www.lotuschild.org
   www.cncf.org
   www.ilo.org/childlabour
3. As Diane learned, social workers are not mandated to report suspected incidents of child abuse and neglect. How would you explain Mongolia's current position on this issue? What do you consider to be Diane's ethical role with respect to advocacy under these circumstances?
4. When considering available resources and expertise, what is the prospect for conducting research to better describe the plight of street children? Would social research be a good use of time and money?

However, it did occur to her that meetings usually started late and were scheduled for one day and quickly changed to another. To Diane's surprise, people used their cell phones throughout the gatherings. Furthermore, meetings lacked agendas and recording procedures and processes (e.g., minutes). Diane found meetings to be informal and disorganized.

Overall, lack of documentation was a persistent theme in Diane's journal. It was obvious at the children's shelter. Social histories, assessments, and planning documents (individual and planning) were nowhere to be found. Diane wondered about issues of accountability but did not believe it was her place to question the shelter's policies and procedures or impose administrative oversight and structure that could easily be interpreted as mere paperwork. She did observe that workers appeared to share consumer information freely with people inside and outside of the shelter and project.

Perhaps the most intriguing account in Diane's journal involved her trip to the countryside, where she was part of a team providing food, bags of powdered milk, and baked goods to people suffering from the effects of a late-season snowstorm. The relief effort was sponsored by several NGOs and involved 6 hours of travel, primarily over unpaved roads, in an old Soviet jeep. Diane observed that along the way, money had to be exchanged to the driver of the jeep, an interpreter, a guard at a toll gate, a government agent, the owner of the jeep, and his brother-in-law, a local official.

Diane made detailed notes about visiting families living in gers, describing the hospitality of parents in the face of undernourished children and underfed livestock. Diane had never experienced a nomadic lifestyle firsthand. She marveled at the people's closeness to and dependency on nature. With no physical address and appreciable distances between them, the people of the countryside appeared self-reliant while demonstrating a connectedness to others via warmth and outgoing personalities. Families invited Diane into their gers, offering her milk tea with salt, boiled mutton, and unleavened bread, although it was obvious that supplies, particularly food, were limited.

Based on Diane's observations, the country women did an extraordinary amount of work under very difficult situations. Since there was no running water, fuel, or sewers in the gers, women carried water long distances; gathered anything they could find to burn in their stoves, which were used for both heating and cooking; washed clothes by hand in buckets; prepared all the family's food from basic ingredients; cared for the children; tended the garden; and cleaned the ger and its surrounding area. And yet the women stopped their work, extending Diane their time graciously and without hesitation. In her writings, Diane reflected on the ironic position in which she found herself; bringing food to people in obvious need while generously offered precious food and time.

Language barriers prohibited Diane from exploring her thoughts and ideas with others in an in-depth manner. Nevertheless, she felt the need to talk with someone about how she struggled to refuse street children money or how disgusting it seemed that people would spit anywhere at anytime. The inebriated people sleeping on the street and in trash heaps bothered Diane, as did the abandoned dogs that survived on unwanted scraps and garbage. Throughout her experience in Mongolia, Diane considered her social work roles as an advocate, educator, counselor, and

Reflection Exercises

1. Journaling is a long-standing means to record not only international adventures but daily life events. Diane used a journal to process her thoughts about people in very specific cultural contexts. If you do not already keep a journal, do so for at least 3 days and see what you learn about your talents for observation, ability to reflect, and recording skills.
2. Some of the very best writing and literature results from personal experiences. Conduct an online search of famous personal journals and list at least 3 journals of interest. What appeals to you (e.g., format, content, writing style, depth in reflection)?
3. The profession of social work is unlike other academic disciplines in that it builds on a liberal arts base for understanding. Examine your program's definition of "liberal arts," and use content from your liberal arts courses (e.g., history, language, economics, political science, geography, and environmental studies) to derive a more thorough understanding of Mongolia's herding people as individuals and as groups.
4. Review both the National Association of Social Workers *Code of Ethics* (www.socialworkers.org/pubs/code/code.asp) and the International Federation of Social Workers (IFSW) and International Association of Schools of Social Work (IASSW) Principles of Ethics (www.ifsw.org/en/p38000324.html). Consider at least 3 ethical deliberations Diane entertained as part of her reflection about relief efforts, program delivery, and her countryside excursions. Based on ethical premises, how would you have acted under similar circumstances?

---

researcher, feeling derelict in not taking some form of concrete action in the face of such apparent and dire need. Diane faced people experiencing vital needs involving food, shelter, and medical care in a cultural context well beyond imagination. Diane experienced a wide range of emotions involving privilege, sorrow, gratefulness, concern, humility, and helplessness.

SUMMARY

As Diane prepares to leave Mongolia, she realizes that she received much more than she contributed to colleagues, children, families, and the community during her 6-week stay. She appreciates the diligence of social

Reflection Exercises

1. Diane's adventures in Mongolia highlight the significant need for undergraduate- and graduate-level social workers to assist with a transitional government and the emerging social service system as a function of community development. To consider what grants and funds might be available to support Mongolia, visit the Web site of the Open Society Institute and Soros Foundation Network (www.soros.org). What did you find that could be useful to Diane and her colleagues in Mongolia?
2. The Fulbright Program is a source for faculty and students to exchange scholarships and research possibilities (www.cies.org). Review the various Fulbright programs, and identify opportunities to support Mongolia's effort to establish social work as a profession.

---

work students and their faculty, all of whom were focused on developing a profession during a period of change in the nation. Diane considers the resilience of the street children remarkable and their situation one that cannot be ignored or forgotten, etched in her mind forever.

In an effort to sustain her commitment to community development and the people of Mongolia, Diane decides to earmark an annual pledge to an NGO for community development efforts in Mongolia and to arrange for her student organization to collect and send social work books to Mongolia's schools of social work. In addition, with e-mail addresses in hand, Diane makes a promise to keep in touch with new colleagues and friends in the days and years to come.

REFERENCES

Andrews, R. C. (1921). *Across the Mongolia plains: On the trail of ancient man.* New York: D. Appleton.

Becker, J. (1992). *The lost country: Mongolia revealed.* London: Hodder and Stoughton.

Embassy of Mongolia, Washington DC. (n.d.). *Health and social welfare.* Retrieved February 23, 2009 from http://www.mongolianembassy.us/eng_about_mongo lia/social.php.

Kohn, M. (2005). *Mongolia* (4th ed.). Oakland, CA: Lonely Planet.

Mongolia. (n.d.). Retrieved February 24, 2009 from http://www.mongoliancul
ture.com/Mongolia-Information.htm.

Morgan, D. (1990). *The Mongols: People of Europe*. Oxford: Blackwell.

Myagmarbayer, B. (2007). *History of Mongolian ger*. Ulaanbaatar, Mongolia: Ashmon Art.

Save the Children. (2006). *A child protection system in Mongolia*. Retrieved June 25, 2008, from http://www.savethechildren.mn/data/file/1160071677.pdf.

Sermier, S. (2002). *Mongolia: Empire of the steppes*. New York: W. W. Norton.

Tsolmon, T. S. (2004). Deel forever: Elegance and color harmony. *Mongolian Magazine*, no. 1, 21–23.

Webika Ltd. (2009). *The Black Death and its route to Europe*. Retrieved February 24, 2009 from http://www.bukisa.com/articles/22152_the-black-death-and-its-route-to-europe.

CHAPTER

6

South Africa: Conducting Research with a Population at Risk

ANN DINAN

I have cherished the ideal of a democratic and free society in which all persons live together in harmony and with equal opportunities. . . .
—Mandela (1964, p. 2)

Social workers must demonstrate proficiency and competency in nine professional areas, of which research is one. The term "research," in the context of this chapter, is defined as "informed criticism and a spirit

The research that is referred to in this chapter was supported in part by the University of Missouri–University of the Western Cape (South Africa) Linkage, a Tertiary Education Linkage Project (TELP) funded by the College Fund/UNCF from a grant awarded by the United States Agency for International Development. Acknowledgment must go to George McCall and Diana Gibson for their grant-writing ability and great vision for this research project. Sarah Thornton proved to be a tremendous asset as our graduate research assistant. Acknowledgments must go as well to Nomvo Dwanda-Henda and Mary Siajunza for their valuable contributions as interviewers. Finally, gratitude must also be expressed to the New World Foundation, a nongovernmental organization in Lavender Hill (Cape Town, South Africa) that provides a variety of community, development, and counseling programs in the surrounding area and to the Vrygrond Community Development Trust.

of inquiry are the basis of scientific thinking and of systematic approaches to the acquisition of knowledge and the application of it to practice." The content in research classes should include information about scientific methods of building knowledge for practice and also should include information about evaluating service delivery (www.socialworkers.org/ swportal/ssw1/details.asp?pVal=%7BB86E9514-0127-4228-AA2A-49A EB983463F%7D&pType=3).

Although Research Methods is often a dreaded required junior-year class, when directly applied to an area of interest, it can prove to be interesting and informative. In the case considered in this chapter, both quantitative and qualitative research methods ask important questions that ultimately helped not only to inform the situation regarding violence against women in certain South African townships but also to provide information regarding the construct of posttraumatic stress disorder (PTSD) itself.

Social science research often is conducted within the boundaries of a specific country. This chapter, however, takes research methods on the road. Some may ask: Why international research? Aren't there a plethora of social issues in any one country that can be researched and better understood? The short answer is yes, of course. But given today's global society, it is necessary to understand and appreciate not only different cultures but the environments that are influencing the thoughts and behaviors of people. Furthermore, it would be ethnocentric to believe that the answers to social issues cannot be found by looking outside the boundaries of one country or another. In this chapter, by considering situations of extreme violence, we examine PTSD in such a way as to inform practice worldwide.

OVERVIEW OF SOUTH AFRICA

South Africa is a country that is diverse and ever evolving. According to the Central Intelligence Agency (CIA) *World Factbook* on South Africa, in terms of diversity, 11 languages are recognized as official languages, and housing can range from mud huts or tin-roofed shacks to palatial multimillion-dollar homes (www.cia.gov/library/publications/the-world-factbook/geos/sf.html). Ethnic groups range from 79% black to 9.6%

white, 8.9% coloured (a term still largely used for people of mixed race descended from slaves brought in from East and Central Africa), and 2.5% Indian/Asian. There is a similar level of religious diversity: Zion Christian 11.1%, Pentecostal/Charismatic 8.2%, Catholic 7.1%, Methodist 6.8%, Dutch Reformed 6.7%, Anglican 3.8%, Muslim 1.5%, other Christian 36%, other 2.3%, unspecified 1.4%, none 12.1%, according to the 2001 census as reported by the CIA.

Although many of these diverse characteristics remain relatively unchanged, as the country goes through the growing pains of postapartheid, new and different social problems present themselves. Unfortunately, due to the often extreme economic and social situation, the corresponding violence is also extreme. This chapter examines the domestic and community violence and corresponding mental health issue of PTSD experienced by women in certain South African townships.

History

It is impossible to understand the current plight of the clients who were part of our research study unless one has a working knowledge of the country's history. In terms of background, the CIA *World Factbook* states:

> Dutch traders landed at the southern tip of what is known today as South Africa in 1652. The idea was to establish a stopping point on the spice trade route between the Netherlands and the East. Thus, the city of Cape Town was founded. The British subsequently seized the Cape of Good Hope area in 1806. When this happened, many Dutch settlers, also known as Boers, moved north. To make a long story short, the Boers resisted the British but were ultimately defeated in the Boer War (1899–1902). However, the British and the Afrikaners (as the Boers became known) ruled together under the Union of South Africa. In 1948, the National Party was voted into power and instituted a policy of apartheid which resulted in the separation of the races.

In a country profile of South Africa, the BBC (British Broadcasting Corporation) states that this separation of the races dictated that black and white communities should live in separate areas, travel in different buses, and stand in their own lines. This government introduced social engineering schemes, according to the BBC, to resettle hundreds of thousands of people. Purportedly, this government poisoned and bombed opponents and encouraged trouble in neighboring countries. (http://news.bbc.co.uk/2/hi/africa/country_profiles/1071886.stm)

In 1994, the first multiracial elections brought a resounding end to apartheid and began a time of black majority rule. While a democratic culture does seem to be taking hold, the BBC profile delineates some major problems that South Africa is currently facing:

- Many South African citizens remain quite poor, and unemployment is very high although South Africa is developing into an economic power within Africa. In fact, high unemployment currently is blamed for the recent wave of violent attacks against migrant workers who hail from neighboring countries.
- The government has stated that land redistribution is an objective. The aim is that by 2014, 30% of farmland will be transferred to black South Africans. This represents a considerable shift in power and wealth.
- South Africa has the second-highest number of HIV/AIDS patients in the world. One in 7 of its citizens is infected with HIV.

It is also imperative to understand that South Africa is still a patriarchal society characterized by gender oppression and the legacy of its previous apartheid regime (Dangor, Hoff, & Scott, 1998). Gibson and Hardon (2005) state that in South Africa, domestic violence and the battering of women are often understood as the embodiment of South African society's most fundamental inequalities, problems, and conflicts (p. 149). This violence is contextualized against the legacy of an oppressive patriarchal and apartheid system and the ensuing inequality and normalization of violence outside and within family relations, especially since black women had the least power and were the most oppressed and exploited. It is widely assumed that the institution of violence under apartheid led to many black men experiencing a sense of powerlessness and perceived emasculation (Park et al., 2000).

Thus, one can easily see how understanding history is a critical contextual backdrop for undertaking research. In terms of the current situation in South Africa, the women interviewed regarding community and domestic violence described their neighborhoods as quite violent. This finding is consistent with Vogelman and Simpson's (1990) conclusions that South Africa's pervasive culture of violence translates into a society that endorses and accepts violence as an acceptable and legitimate means to resolve problems and achieve goals.

Social Service System

The social service agency highlighted in this chapter, the New World Foundation (NWF), is located in Lavender Hill, situated in Cape Flats, outside of Cape Town. NWF was founded in 1980 as an umbrella body unifying a wide range of local churches and communities (http://www.surefish.co.uk/news/southafrica/010604_partners.htm). As a community, Lavender Hill lacks economic security, public services, and political power. NWF addresses the needs of Lavender Hill and its residents through a broad network of services that support individual and community growth and development. Perhaps NWF is best known for its commitment to women. On a regular basis, the agency sponsors health education and personal safety training for women along with other services that enhance the economic stability of women and their families. Issues of domestic violence are also addressed by NWF. The agency shelters women as needed and refers them to report to the Lavender Hill Clinic, Retreat Day Hospital, and the Steenberg Police Station.

Anecdotal evidence seems to indicate that many women experience double victimization as a result of "blaming the victim" whereby they are held responsible for the violence they sustain because of their dress, attitude, appearance, or some other behavior or particular characteristic. Although double victimization does not occur all that often at the New World Foundation, women are understandably nervous about being seen going into the facility and receiving services. The foundation is located in a residential neighborhood; women clients express fear that if they were seen and their husbands were informed, the likely consequence would be an act of violence. Gibson and Hardon (2005) captured the words of those who experienced domestic violence firsthand:

- Husbands beat their wives every day, they fight, and there are shootings, rapes. You can't trust anybody, your father, brother, cousin, friend, nobody, no men. (p. 150)
- I hit her sometimes, but she will not listen, she talks back, she looks for it. . . . she takes me for soft if not . . . other [men] can also [see me as weak] . . . if they think I cannot/will not do [violence]. (p. 150)
- At night, they fire shots in the street, I hear it. He is in jail now, I keep everything dark, because the men out there, you never know what they can do . . . it is not safe . . . I have not been here so long and I am still afraid, but many people [who are] used to it, they do not thought [sic] about it, they do not even scare. (p. 155)
- I had sex against my will, but it was not rape. He is my man and loves me a lot. I gave birth to his children. (p. 157)
- My father used to beat my mother and all of us. I am the oldest, you know. It was like this . . . Fridays, Saturdays, and Sundays, he abused us and Monday up to Thursday, he bought us everything we needed. I saw my mother was not going to do anything, so I ran away. I have lived here in Lavender Hill many years now. (p. 160)

Cultural Features

In addition to the culture of violence that is often in homes and communities, it is also important to note that the New World Foundation of Lavender Hill is a "Coloured" area. This designation reflects an earlier apartheid state intervention to forcibly remove certain population groups from the center of the city to outlying areas (Unterlander, 1987). "Coloureds" were defined in contrast to "Whites" and "Blacks" as a "mixed race" group, usually having some Khoisan ancestry (Carter, 1958). The Khoisan language family is the smallest of the language families of Africa. The name is derived *Khoisan* from the Khoi-Khoi group of South Africa and the San (Bushmen) group of Namibia. Currently, Khoisan is used for several ethnic groups who were the original inhabitants of southern Africa. The community of Vrygrond came into being much later, as a mainly black squatter area of Lavender Hill. Squatter areas, or informal settlements, emerged as unauthorized shack communities in unclaimed or unsupervised crannies of South African urban regions (Cole, 1987; Silk, 1981).

South African townships have a culture of "masculinity" that impacts both domestic and community violence. Specifically, South African researchers have found a strong association between homosexuality and violent/coercive male sexuality (Shefer, Ratele, Strebel, & Shabalala, 2005). The violent sexuality includes date rape, stranger rape, and economically coercive practices. Male sexuality is constructed as central, dominant, and privileged, while female sexuality is constructed as responsive to the needs

Reflection Exercises

1. Locate South Africa on a map (http://www.sa-venues.com/maps). What countries are South Africa's neighbors? What are its borders? How has the geographic location of South Africa influenced its history and culture?

2. What is the African National Congress Youth League, and what role did Nelson Rolihlahla Mandela have in this organization (http://www.anc.org.za/people/mandela.html)? Write an overview of the major contributions Mr. Mandela offered to South Africa. How does the life of Mr. Mandela reflect the values and principles of social work?

3. Review the history of apartheid in South Africa (http://www-cs-students.stanford.edu/~cale/cs201/apartheid.hist). How has the policy of apartheid achieved preferential treatment for whites? Support your response with data, including economic and educational status.

4. Human rights organizations have investigated violence against South African women (http://hrw.org/doc/?t=women_domesticviolence&c=safric). Contrast and compare the information you find with that on the incidence of violence against women in your country. What research topics emerge from the various human rights reports?

5. Eleven languages are spoken in South Africa (http://www.sa-venues.com/sa_languages_and_culture.htm). What influence does a multilingual society have on culture? How many languages are spoken in your country, and how many languages do you speak?

of males (Gibson & Hardon, 2005). Further, there is a prevailing myth that engaging in sex relations with virgins will cure or protect men from contracting HIV/AIDS. This belief has led to an increase in male sexually coercive practices against young girls and infants (Lovelife, 2000; Vetten & Bhana, 2001). The enmeshment of violence does not end here. As the divide between wealth and poverty continues, more and more young men are drawn into violence through the gang culture (Gibson & Hardon, 2005). One South African study found that men involved with gangs were twice as likely to abuse women (Abrahams, Jewkes, & Laubscher, 1999).

AGENCY SETTING

The New World Foundation (NWF) is a strengths-based organization in which women are viewed as strong and empowered. Specifically, NWF embraces a mission statement that works toward the transformation of the South African society so that all people will have a rightful place, free from oppression, violence, and poverty (De Waal & Argenti, 2004).

The organizational structure is horizontal rather than hierarchical; consequently, collaboration and cooperation among people are apparent. According to De Waal & Argenti (2004), the international humanitarian group Christian Aid has supported NWF since 1998, when the organization provided a unifying force to local churches and community organizations. Initially, NWF functioned primarily as an antiapartheid organization that worked directly with individuals combating issues associated with discrimination. Over time, NWF developed a network to assist with community empowerment and capacity building through training and education.

As mentioned, NWF is situated in Lavender Hill, a geographic area estimated to be 76% black, 15% coloured, and 9% white. It is characterized by high levels of alcohol and drug abuse as well as increasingly high rates of unemployment and gang violence. The gang violence is not limited to residents of Lavender Hill. Rather, the violence is widespread and random, since the area's residents view all white people as oppressors. Over the years, safety reasons have prevented international researchers from working in the area.

NWF's main building is nondescript and easily overlooked in the neighborhood. Once inside, the facilities are quite modern and adequate to meet organizational needs. More specifically, there are offices with computers, large meeting rooms, and smaller counseling offices. The overall atmosphere is comfortable, welcoming, and secure, in sharp contrast to Lavender Hill itself.

Over time, NWF developed a positive reputation throughout the community. The women served by the organization seek assistance because they trust the staff and feel safe within the confines of the agency. The menu of services available to women is comprehensive, ranging from counseling to courses in microeconomics. This holistic approach to service provision addresses personal needs while recognizing that women must acquire marketable skills to better their economic situation.

Research Project

The objective of the quantitative research project was to examine the frequency and type of domestic and community-based violence occurring in Lavender Hill. An ancillary feature of the project explored mental health issues associated with posttraumatic stress disorder and experienced by women.

The project's sample included 90 women who sought services from the NWF and 40 women from the Lavender Hill community. The dean of the University of Western Cape provided the internal review and granted permission for the use of human subjects.

Reflection Exercises

1. What does the term "organizational culture" mean to you? What are some cultural markers in an agency that would clue you in to its method of operation and attitude toward consumers?

2. Review information on posttraumatic shock disorder (http://www .ncptsd.va.gov/ncmain/index.jsp). What events can cause PSTD, and how does the disorder develop? Describe some of the primary symptoms used to diagnose this disorder.

3. Explore the treatments for PTSD, including cognitive therapy, exposure therapy, eye movement desensitization and reprocessing, medication, and group therapy. Given what you know of women in South Africa, the Lavender Hill community, and the New World Foundation, what treatments seem appropriate, and why? How do cultural factors intersect the choice of treatment modalities?

4. Review Chapter 3, "Ethical Principles and Processes," when considering the next questions:
    a. What are the relevant clinical factors to consider when working with the women who seek services at the NWF?
    b. What are the procedural rules to maintain confidentiality in the community-based agency?
    c. What are some of the anticipated local and broad consequences for women who seek services and for the service providers?
    d. Consider at least three ways in which a research project could contact practice to policy initiatives.

Role of the Student Research Assistant

The role of the social work student research assistant was to support the project's researchers in an array of capacities, including scheduling interviews with women at NWF, offering assistance to translators, and assisting in training sessions. Once the interviews were completed, the student research assistant was expected to enter data and assist with coding the transcribed interview sessions.

RESEARCH EXAMPLE

Anna, a social work student enrolled at a large urban university, had volunteer experience working at a women's resource center, where she made consumer referrals for healthcare services. She found the volunteer commitment demanding but gratifying in that the women displayed remarkable resilience and resourcefulness, given their dire situations. To complement her volunteer service, Anna completed three courses in women and gender studies and attended various events and seminars that focused on the mental health and health issues of women.

It was during one of the women studies seminars that Anna learned of the research assistant position with marginalized women (NWF) in South Africa. Anecdotally, she learned that the experience required a 6-week summer placement; all travel and living costs would be included in the student stipend. In terms of academic requirements, Anna learned that the minimal requirements were a course in statistics and research along with courses in human behavior in the social environment, social welfare policy, and introductory social work practice. Although Anna met all the qualifications, she had some qualms about participating.

Anna's family background was white working class. In fact, she was the first person in her extended family to attend college. She has been raised in a homogenous community and attended schools that offered little diversity. Although she had limited knowledge of South Africa, she understood the impact of apartheid policies and knew of Nelson Mandela, his contribution to the country and his long imprisonment.

Intrigued by the opportunity for international travel and recognizing the need to explore her values and beliefs in a new environment with unfamiliar people, Anna applied for the position of student research assistant. After an extensive interview process, she was informed that she received the position.

In preparation for her travel, Anna reviewed her research course content and read two books, *Long Walk to Freedom* (Mandela, 1994) and *A History of South Africa* (Welsh, 2000). She also reviewed Amnesty International's report on violence (http://afp.google.com/article/ALeqM5jqDCg_4mTC d2OnzaC8dH0MI67WPA), which outlines incidences of violence, South Africa's response, and the United Nations position toward violence in general and in South Africa specifically.

Time passed quickly. Before she knew it, Anna found herself and two social work researchers landing in Cape Town, where they were greeted by staff from the NWF. Cape Town is the second most populous city in South Africa and the provincial capital of the Western Cape as well as the country's legislative capital. The National Parliament and many government offices are located there. Off in the distance, Anna saw the city's famous harbor as well as its well-known landmark, Table Mountain. However, perhaps most striking were the variations in language Anna heard. She thought back to her home and how she took communication for granted.

At the NWF agency, Anna was introduced to staff members and some consumers. She tried not to show her shock at the neighborhood's dilapidated conditions, the staff's minimal and outdated office equipment, and the physical appearance of women whose difficult lives were etched on their faces. Although the women seeking services were not much older than she, their faces and body language made them seem much older.

Within a short period of time, Anna was working with the researchers by scheduling interviews, assisting with consent forms and data entry, and discussing general impressions of daily happenings. Although the days passed quickly, Anna missed the interactions with people more her age and with whom she had more in common. Language, written and spoken, proved challenging, as were the limited opportunities for social interaction and reaction. For example, Anna, a competitive runner, was hesitant to run through the neighborhood because of community violence and the fact that she appeared so "different" from the vast majority of residents. Staff members warned Anna that she could be targeted because of her gender, age, nationality, and race. Thus, for the first time in her life, Anna felt marginalized and confronted with discrimination and stereotypic images. Clearly she was perceived as "other," an outsider.

If there was a place of comfort for Anna, it came by way of the women who came to the NWF agency. Through their struggles and unspeakable trauma and tragedies, they saw in Anna the hope of forward thinking that comes with education, economic security, and nurturing relationships. In turn, Anna found the women's willingness to work through life's difficulties remarkable, especially given the lack of family and societal support. No matter what the state of their mental and/or physical health, the

Reflection Exercises

1. Anna had volunteer experiences with women in crisis. How did this experience help to prepare her for the international research project? What has been your volunteer experience, and what have you gained from such activities? What offices or departments in your community or university campus will assist you with finding volunteer opportunities?

2. Describe Anna's background and family of origin. What does it mean to come from a "homogenous community"? How would you describe your background and family influences?

3. Apartheid is an integral part of South Africa's background. Define this term and consider the influence apartheid has had on people in their environments, social welfare policies, social interactions, and service delivery systems.

4. Anna spent time in preparing for her international research internship by reading books. What additional books would you consider reading to become acquainted with South Africa and its people? Be sure to become familiar with the author J. M. Coetzee, and ask yourself the question: What contribution did Coetzee's writing offer South Africa and the world? A helpful starting point for your literature review is www.southafrica.info/about/arts/music.htm.

5. Many people have routines in their lives, such as an exercise or running schedule. Anna is a runner, but her routine was disrupted. What could Anna do to maintain this routine and minimize the sense of isolation she was experiencing? What daily routines are especially important to you? How would you feel if such habits were compromised?

6. Anna describes feelings of being "marginalized" in the area of Lavender Hill. Give some thought to the term "marginalized" and what that meant to Anna in the context of South Africa. Have you experienced being marginalized? When, where, and why? What groups or people within your country are marginalized? What are often the roles of social workers who practice with marginalized groups?

---

women seeking services displayed a commitment to their children and respect for the dignity of themselves and others.

ETHICAL CONSIDERATIONS

Anna works on the research project throughout the day. At lunch she sometimes joins staff members, and together they take a walk and enjoy a shared meal. During these times, there is joking and a relaxed atmosphere; however, on numerous occasions, some of the staff began to question Anna about the details of the project, information she has gathered, and her impressions of certain people. To date, Anna has brushed off such questions politely, but she is becoming increasingly uncomfortable with the interactions.

On a weekly basis, Anna meets with the two social work researchers for supervision and a briefing on the project's progress. A recurring topic of the meetings is the need to be mindful of unintended bias in the survey process. At this point in the meeting, the social workers usually discuss the need to be sensitive to the backgrounds of consumers while evaluating their own conditioned values and assumptions (Sue & Sue, 1990).

Although Anna is not part of the actual interviewing process, she wants to learn good research designs and procedures. Further, she does not want to influence consumers in any way; consequently, she diligently observes and records particular aspects of the research project. For example, as part of the informed consent procedures, consumers are given the details of the research project, including its rationale. Anna also observes the nonverbal behavior and body language of the social workers and concludes that they strive not to give consumers indications of how they are being affected by the information they receive. Indeed, Anna recognizes that subtle messages can be powerful influences on consumers' behavior (Corey, Corey, & Callanan, 1998).

The longer Anna lived in the Lavender Hill area and interned at NWF, the more certain she became that the research project could foster real and lasting change only if it impacted the milieu of people's lives. Anna saw that the aspirations and difficulties of consumers were intertwined with those of many other people, the community, and ultimately South Africa at large. It was amazing for Anna to realize that she was questioning who the consumer was. Was the consumer a woman who sought services from NWF, or was the larger community the consumer? Anna could not ignore community needs and challenges if the situations of consumers

Reflection Exercises

1. What do you think of the way Anna handled the situation with the causal conversation the staff wanted to have regarding consumer information? If you are faced with a similar circumstance, how do you think you might relate to staff?
2. Define the term "unintended bias" as it relates to research. Why are the social workers concerned about unintended biases in their research project? What are some unintended biases that could occur in their project or in other international research projects?
3. What values and beliefs do you owe primarily to your culture? Have any of your values and beliefs changed over time, and if so, how? How might your values influence your work with consumers who are culturally different from you?
4. Regular supervision is part of Anna's international internship. Consider the value of supervision and how you would use supervision sessions to improve your understanding and practice of social work.

5. What do you think consumers involved in a research project must be told about the project? How might you implement informed consent procedures, given the agency setting and consumers' needs?
6. Anna realizes that she cannot play a major role in changing negative environmental or community conditions for consumers, but what actions could she take? Would it be appropriate for the social workers and Anna to assist consumers in understanding the forces in the environment that are causing or contributing to their distress? Explain the reasons behind your response.

---

were to be addressed in a meaningful fashion. Thus, slowly Anna came to believe that as a social worker, she had a broader responsibility to address the conditions that create problems for individuals.

RESEARCH FINDINGS

The New World Foundation research project generated some findings for consideration:

- In the help-seeking sample, two-thirds of respondents reported having experienced several traumatic events outside the home. Respondents displayed a median of 9 PTSD symptoms, with nearly half of the respondents meeting all criteria for PTSD (Dinan, McCall, & Gibson, 2004).
- In the community sample, two-thirds of respondents reported having experienced several traumatic events outside of the house. These respondents displayed a median of 8.8 PTSD symptoms, with none meeting all criteria for PTSD (Dinan, McCall, & Gibson, 2004).

A question Anna and the social work researchers had was: Why is there such a difference between the samples who experienced roughly the same number of PTSD symptoms but had diametrically opposite reactions to developing PTSD? In response to the question, project members concluded that PTSD has long been associated with acts of war and warlike violence. Although service providers in South Africa were aware of PTSD, some

Reflection Exercises

1. Bronfenbrenner (1979) developed the ecological systems theory commonly used in social work theory and comprised of four systems: *microsystem:* the immediate family, school, peer, neighborhood environments; *mesosystem:* the system that connects between two immediate environments, such as home and school; *exosystem:* the external environmental settings that indirectly affect one's development, such as a parent's workplace; and *macrosystem:* the larger cultural context. Apply the ecological systems theory to the research findings. For example, in terms of the macrosystem, the economic and political policies of South Africa affected women. More specifically, for many years, the president of South Africa denied a link between sexual activity and HIV/AIDS. The result was a major delay in the distribution of antiretroviral drugs. The policy implication was significant for the women in the research project, many of whom were raped and subsequently concerned about HIV infection.
2. Define the terms "reliability" and "validity" as they apply to research. Then consider what issues of reliability and validity could challenge the research findings.
3. Given the findings, what roles do you think Anna and the researchers might play when working with the NWF: consultant, researcher, advocate, educator, change agent, clinician, and/or policy analyst? Explain your response, and provide a definition of the role and expected actions.

---

were not aware that PTSD could be brought on by living in dangerous communities and by experiences of domestic violence.

Given the epidemic of violence that is claiming South African townships, the research finding is significant and clearly informed practice suggests that screening for PTSD should be routinely conducted at the time of intake. Furthermore, ensuring that staff is trained in the delivery of PTSD amelioration techniques is also imperative in terms of best practices.

SUMMARY

Learning about culture and becoming aware of how your own culture affects your social work practice with others who are culturally different is a unique feature of international experience. From a research perspective, social workers need to anchor their practice in theory and connect their findings to action in a way that is culturally relevant. Thus, issues in theory, research, policy, and practice are necessarily connected to one's vision of the world.

We can increase our awareness of various cultural and ethnic experiences by the direct contact that derives from an international experience. Reading, special course work, workshops, and volunteer service can also increase our ability to conduct research and provide services appropriate for consumers. As social workers, examining assumptions, attitudes, and values must become a lifelong task so we can determine and modify how they influence our practice.

REFERENCES

AFP. (2008). *UN rights chief, Amnesty, criticise SAfrica over xenophobia.* Retrieved October 7, 2008 from, http://afp.google.com/article/ALeqM5jqDCg_4mTCd2 OnzaC8dH0MI67WPA

Abrahams, N., Jewkes, & Laubscher, R. (1999). "I don't believe in democracy in the home." Men's relationships with and abuse of women. MRC Technical Report: Cape Town. Reprinted in D. Gibson & A. Hardon (2006) (eds.), *Rethinking masculinities, violence and AIDS* (pp. 223–256). Amsterdam: Het Spinhuis.

Bronfenbrenner, U. (1979). *The ecology of human development: Experiments by nature and design.* Cambridge, MA: Harvard University Press.

Carter, G. (1958). *The politics of inequality.* London: Oxford University Press.

Central Intelligence Agency. (2009). *The World Factbook: South Africa.* Retrieved January 2009 from https://www.cia.gov/library/publications/the-world-factbook/ geos/sf.html.

Cole, J. (1987). *The politics of reform and repression 1976–1986.* Johannesburg, South Africa: Raven Press.

Corey, G., Corey, S. M., & Callanan, P. (1998). *Issues of ethics in the helping professions.* Pacifica Grove, CA: Brooks/Cole.

Dangor, Z., Hoff, L., & Scott, R. (1988). Woman abuse in South Africa. *Violence Against Women, 4,* 125–152.

De Waal, A., & Argenti, N. (2004) (eds). *Young Africa: Realising the rights of children and youth.* South Africa: Africa World Press.

Dinan, B., McCall, G., & Gibson, D. (2004). Community violence and PTSD in select South African townships. *Journal of Interpersonal Violence*, *19*, 727–742.

Gibson, D., & Hardon, A. (2005). *Rethinking masculinities, violence and AIDS*. Amsterdam: Het Spinhuis.

Jung Park, Y., Fedler, J., & Dangor, A. (Eds.). (2000). *Reclaiming women's spaces. New perspectives on violence against women and sheltering in South Africa*. Johannesburg: Nisaa Institute for Women's Development.

Lavender Hill. (2009). Retrieved January 2009 from http://www.surefish.co.uk/news/southafrica/010604_partners.htm.

Lovelife. (2000). *Hot prospects, cold facts: Portrait of Young South Africa*. Cape Town, South Africa: Colorpress/Henry J. Kaiser Foundation.

Mandela, N. (1994). *Long walk to freedom*. London: Abacus.

Profile of South Africa (2008). Profile of South Africa. Retrieved January 2009 from http://news.bbc.co.uk/2/hi/africa/country_profiles/1071886.stm.

Shefer, T., Ratele, K., Strebel, A., & Shabalala, N. (2005). Masculinities in South Africa: A cultural review of contemporary literature on men's sexuality. In D. Gibson & A. Hardon (Eds.), *Rethinking masculinities, violence and AIDS* (pp. 74–87). Amsterdam: Het Spinhuis.

Silk, A. (1981). *A shantytown in South Africa: The story of Modderdam*. Johannesburg, South Africa: Raven Press.

Sue, D. W., & Sue, D. (1990). *Counseling the culturally different: Theory and practice* (2nd ed.). New York: John Wiley & Sons.

Unterlander, E. (1987). *Forced removal: The division, segregation and control of the people of South Africa*. London: International Defense and Aid Fund.

Vetten, L., & Bhana, K. (2001). *Violence, vengeance and gender: A preliminary investigation into the links between HIV/AIDS and violence against women in South Africa*. Johannesburg, South Africa: Centre for the Study of Violence & Reconciliation.

Vogelman, L., & Simpson, G. (1990, June 17). Current violence in South Africa. *Sunday Star Review*. Retrieved May 2008 from http://www.thestar.co.za/.

Welsh, F. (2000). *A history of South Africa*. New York: HarperCollins.

Western, J. (1981). *Outcast Cape Town*. Minneapolis: University of Minnesota Press.

CHAPTER

7

Costa Rica: A Cultural Study Tour

LISA E. COX

Peace is a never ending process. . . . It cannot ignore our differences or overlook our common interests. It requires us to work and live together.

—Sánchez (2005)

Human behavior is multidimensional, yet students may appear rather "unidimensional" in their outlooks if they have not been exposed to other cultures and people. While thematically oriented courses in Human Behavior and the Social Environment (HBSE) teach social work students how to be prepared to practice on micro, mezzo, and macro levels and how to understand personal, environmental, and time dimensions (Hutchison, 1999), merely reading about theory and people in their environments is different from actually immersing oneself in another's timeframe, space and place. Being exposed to theories—whether ecological, psychodynamic, cognitive-behavioral, sociological, ethnic-sensitive perspective and others—is not the same as seeing the constructs come alive amid everyday living.

Adventuresome educators who decide to develop and offer cultural study tours must be prepared for the immense workload involved in coordinating such efforts and for the toll it takes on students, who are rarely prepared for the culture shock they experience. When students are exposed to poverty and the mores of a developing Central American country, for example, they realize how entangled their lives are in the world's geopolitical and socioeconomic context. Such exposure to new, scary, and exciting experiences helps them be more understanding of other cultures and better informed decision-makers and citizens of the world. Successful study tour leaders will be calm, caring, and creative as they help students cope with foreign food, perplexing communication, and ever-present homesickness.

Grounded in the author's experience of designing and implementing study tours since 2001, this chapter highlights the use of experiential learning during a Costa Rican social work study tour to enhance student's learning about how human behavior actually functions in a culturally diverse social environment. You will gain a glimpse of Costa Rica. You will also learn how a cultural study tour can effectively provide international social work content and expose cultural and ethical realities to enhance understanding of human behavior in the social environment.

INTERNATIONAL CONTEXT OF THE CONTENT AREA

The Educational Policy and Accreditation Standards (EPAS) of the Council on Social Work Education (CSWE) place an emphasis on social work programs infusing and teaching global content in curriculums. However, social work educators must discern what "international social work" or "global practice" means and decide how best to teach it.

A certain level of maturity is required to maximize learning from a cultural immersion and study tour experience. Multiple majors on a cultural study tour can work; however, fundamental standards must be maintained. All group participants must understand that they are ambassadors, in a sense, who represent a particular country. When students embrace cultural immersion, they will learn the language and can become more culturally aware, competent, and sensitive.

Experiential learning can help students envision social and economic justice and perceive culture differently. While in language classes, in home-stays, and in painting murals in the center of a shantytown, students are privy to the norms, values, customs, symbols, thoughts, traditions, politics, religions, philosophies, material objects, and language of their teachers and hosts (*mama ticas*). Experiential learning can modify students' precon-ceived views of human behavior and social circumstances.

According to Pillari (1998), "views of human behavior range from a holistic approach to biological, intrapsychic and social/behavioral view-points" (p. 1). Also, "regarding social development and behavior, roles, transmission of norms, and how people, things and systems change are all part of an evolving process that varies culture to culture. . . . while develop-ment refers to change, not all changes are developmental" (pp. 1–3). When student learners who have taken the Costa Rica course are asked, "What impact do you think that this trip will have on your future?" these are some typical responses: "The trip reshaped the way I view the world"; "The trip expanded my horizons and gave me the hunger to travel more"; "I learned assumptions about myself, my classmates and my instructors"; and "I think I will stay more aware of global issues."

The understanding of human behavior and practice levels, for social work majors in particular, are broadened after traveling outside of their comfort zone and being immersed in another culture. On the micro level, they learn about the relevance of age, gender, income, health, language, spirituality, IQ, recreation, emotion, cognition, and self-esteem. Students note how proud Costa Ricans are despite their income level, and they become aware of the respect in people's actions through the use of formal language and gestures in communication. On the mezzo level, observant students notice aspects of the neighborhood, church, local economy, and resources when walking to language school or painting murals in school classrooms. Those with better language skills may hear their home-stay hosts discuss realities of work, government, and politics. Also on the macro level, in addition to government and politics, discerning students usually pick up on community cultural values and existing services and resources, as they exchange money at the bank, buy items at a local store or storefront, or watch children in their homes or on the soccer fields relate to elders and each other.

Such experiential learning helps students and teachers alike acquire an up-close-and-personal understanding of a developing country's educational and governmental infrastructures, as they experience the challenge of coping with another culture, language, and pride-filled yet impoverished people. Social work educators who accompany students also have time to reflect on global dynamics and HBSE ideas while traveling. Thoughts cross one's mind about why and how HBSE courses are taught and why the life span (from infancy through older age) and global content is important to today's students and tomorrow's citizens. Amid study tour zip line and rainforest excursion experiences, students and educators together sit to learn and study Spanish, cope with home-stay experiences, and work together on service learning projects.

One value of a cultural study tour is that it may be useful in teaching conflict resolution and better defining what one means by "culture"—the way of life of a group of people. During travel, students must get along with each other and be courteous to Latino strangers while they experience their own personal stress reactions, cognitive fatigue, role shock, and personal shock (Winkelman, 2005). A second value of immersion learning is that students in past study tour cohorts have seen how, from birth to death, people constantly face cultural messages that may make them feel bad or good about themselves.

Reflection Exercises

1. This chapter begins with a quotation by Oscar Arias Sánchez. Search the Internet to learn of Sánchez and why his comments are relevant to Costa Rica. Explain how the quotation supports human behavior in the social environment context.

2. As you begin thinking about participating in a cultural study tour, ask yourself what you would like to learn from the experience, especially in relation to human behavior and the social environment. Write at least three measurable and observable learning objectives that would guide your tour involvement.

3. Search the Internet and find information on various international educational experiences. A beginning point is to view http://www.ticotimes.net and http://www.socwel.ku.edu/academics/CostaRica/index.shtml. How do the tours meet your financial expectations? Take time to explore whether you are eligible for scholarships, grants, or other forms of support.

4. Although Costa Rica is often described as Central America's success story, 10% of Costa Ricans live in absolute poverty, 40% of young females do not attend school, and 28% of adolescents between the ages of 12 and 19 are employed for wages below the poverty level. Search the Internet on Costa Rica (http://www.nationsencyclopedia.com/econo mies/Americas/Costa-Rica-POVERTY-AND-WEALTH.html) and explore other challenging social issues confronting the country. What social work roles and skills could be used to address these issues?

5. Read the article "Single Mothers and Poverty in Costa Rica" (http://ideas.repec.org/p/iza/izadps/dp3286.html) and write a paragraph or two about the impact of poverty on women and children in Costa Rica.

Many facets of culture exist. These facets include beliefs and values, perceptions and emotions, aspirations and attitudes, norms and material possessions, and laws and symbols (Kabagarama, 1997, p. 21). Potentially, international travel can increase people's cultural competence and broaden their understanding of life span development. Witnessing students magically become more multidimensional in their global thinking and understanding of other humans and social environments is beautiful and satisfying.

OVERVIEW OF COSTA RICA

During the Costa Rican cultural study tour, students are responsible for meeting specified and multifold course objectives. For example, students are expected to enhance their ability to speak Spanish and to better understand another culture and how it affects people's views, assumptions, and individual, family, community, and societal behavior. Students also are expected to adapt to and function within a different environment, where they must try new foods, live with limited warm water, and appreciate others' living conditions, family life, religious customs, music, level of economic development, weather, and terrain, and try to respect differences.

The cultural study tour also endeavors to help students become more self-aware and self-efficacious; become more knowledgeable about Costa Rican culture(s), history, and environment(s); and have experiences to help both social work and non–social work students see the social work profession and social development issues from a global perspective.

As one former student noted (Thiel, 2003), living with a family from a different culture, and traveling in a group can evoke stress.

> Living in a place that speaks a language different from your native language, living with a strange family that speaks that language, and constantly studying and doing activities can all be sources of stress. However, traveling as part of a group can serve as a buffer from that stress by giving you social support and a group that keeps you connected to your country and language of origin.

History

Before physically landing in Costa Rica, students benefit from prior reading about the country's history, land, and people. Usually, students do not realize that Costa Rica lies at the heart of the Central American isthmus, nestled between Nicaragua to the north and Panama to the south. Although the country is about the size of our state of West Virginia, it is as complex and more diverse, perhaps, than any place of its size on our planet, and each of its regions looks like an entirely different environment. Costa Rica contains hot tropical zones with rolling wild grasses and palm and banana plantations as well as thickly forested coastlines and valleys, surrounded by beaches of every description imaginable. The beach called Playa Conchal, near Playa Flamingo and Tamarindo is a favorite of study tour alumni.

The country has a network of seemingly endless waterways that rise and fall through the mountains. The soil of the Central Valley is exceptionally fertile because of centuries of volcanic activity. This drainable rich soil is ideal for coffee production, and numerous coffee fincas with their deep-green foliage rise up incredibly high ridges and across the floor of huge alluvial valleys.

Groups of Indians with diverse languages and cultures settled in Costa Rica. Chortega, Bribri, Cacebar, Coctu, and Corobici were some of the names that Spanish colonists gave to the small chiefdoms. Influenced by other indigenous cultures of the Americas, the native people of Costa Rica acquired skills in ceramics, gold and metalwork, fine weaving, and stone carving. Photographic and narrative content from a small book entitled *Taking Care of Sibo's Gifts*, enlightens student travelers about the indigenous people of Costa Rica (Palmer, Sanchez, & Mayorga, 1993). Additionally, Molina and Palmer's (2000) history of the country traces how Costa Rica evolved from the time of Columbus.

On Columbus's fourth voyage in 1502, he discovered Costa Rica (literally meaning "rich coast"). Over the next 60 years, from his first landing in Limón, the Spanish explored both coastlines of Costa Rica. The Costa Rican colony grew very slowly. In 1573, only 50 families lived in Cartago (the country's first capitol) and in a fledgling community that evolved later into San José. Costa Ricans like to tell the story of how they received their independence from Spain by mail.

In 1889, Costa Rica drafted its liberal constitution and began to prosper and maintain political stability. Following economic difficulties in the 20th century and a civil war, Costa Rica reformed itself. To this day it is a symbolic peace broker in Central America, as it is a nation without a standing army. On occasion, study tours visit the Peace Pilgrim statue—erected as a tribute to peace—on the grounds of Costa Rica's University of Peace (Friends of Peace Pilgrim, 1994).

People of Costa Rica

Costa Ricans, or Ticos (as they have nicknamed themselves), come in all shapes, colors and sizes. People tend to be well-dressed, and the homeless are not readily visible. They are a proud people who may appear both narcissistic and chauvinistic, as they are quite skilled in being poor and not showing it. Shantytowns exist yet do not dominate the cityscape, as they do in other Latin American countries. Students who complete service projects in Shantytowns are brought to tears by the smells, sights and sounds of the place.

Ticos know that political corruption and problems abound; however, visitors will not hear them nag, complain, or be hopeless. Instead, Costa Ricans are generous people who are ardently patriotic and passionate in uttering their signature phrase, *pura vida*, meaning "great" or conveying other positive feelings.

Fewer than 5% of Costa Ricans are black. Although only a handful of Chinese came to Costa Rica in 1864, a sizeable Chinese community now exists in Puntarenas and San José. No data exist on the actual number of Chinese who are now thriving in the commercial sector. Ticos are quick to brag about their former NASA astronaut Franklin Chang-Diaz. While entire indigenous tribes have been obliterated by European diseases, Indian groups do remain today, such as the Bribri, who refer to their deity as Sibu and whose shamans have in-depth knowledge about the rain forest's resources.

In comparison to other Latin American countries, the health and education standards in Costa Rica are very good. Because Ticos are not burdened by supporting an army, they invest approximately 10% of their gross national product in healthcare. The quality is so exceptional that supposedly some Beverly Hills residents go to Costa Rica for plastic surgery.

Costa Rica boasts a 93% literacy rate for the population age 10 and older. While in home-stays, however, students learn that many families cannot afford to buy school uniforms, which prohibits some children from continuing their education. The nation has long been progressive in electing teachers and physicians to high political posts. For example, a recent President's educational background was in psychiatry.

Social Service System

Study tour participants hear local Costa Rican social workers speak about social services and resources that exist in Costa Rica. For example, Lidia, a social worker who is with the Patronato Nacional de la Infancia (PANI), the Costa Rican child welfare authority (Costa Rica Adoption Agency), speaks to groups. Listeners quickly learn how PANI is in charge of any matters related to child protection, which allows for comparisons to be made insofar as how families and children are advocated for in Costa Rica versus the United States.

Essentially, PANI is the national office for children. This organization is comparable to the Division of Youth and Family Services in the United States. Costa Rican social workers, or social workers who work in Costa Rica and are employed by PANI, help families seek child support and intervene in cases of abuse and neglect. Extensive biopsychosocial assessments are completed on children. Protective measures in the form of housing a child with another family member or in an orphanage are available. Assessment and intervention processes used by Costa Rican social workers mirror those embraced by North American–trained social workers, who typically have access to more tangible resources.

A typical case example, which PANI social worker Lidia shared with our study tour members, describes an incident in which PANI was involved:

> A mother attacked her two children, ages 3 and 5, then fled the home and left them inside. Police searched for the woman. PANI sought protective placement for the children. In Costa Rica a children's shelter is called *el hogarcito*, and children who are physically or sexually abused or abandoned are taken care of here. PANI is financially supported by donations and fundraisers as well as the government.

During the study tours, a PANI worker informs students of the human trafficking, child labor, and child prostitution issues that Costa Rican social workers confront and must handle. The PANI social worker discusses *el día del niño* (the day of the child), and alerts students about the child protection law that contains strong penalties for murder, simple kidnapping, and aggravated kidnapping. Further, information is provided about the *hospital nacional de niños* (national hospital for children) and its prevention programs, security issues, and the realities of drug use.

Government

Wilson's (1998) compilation roundly educates students about politics and government. Readers learn that Costa Rica is a democracy governed by a president who is elected every four years. There are two vice presidents, many of whom have been women, and a cabinet of 12 ministers. Members of the Legislative Assembly are elected every four years. Costa Rica's constitution was adopted in 1949, after a civil war abolished the military. Not having to support an active military complex translates into more funding for social and governmental health programs. A very humane society, Costa Rica has no capital punishment.

Climate

Two seasons exist in Costa Rica: the rainy or green season (*invierno*) and the dry season or summer (*verano*). In the Central Valley, the rainy season spans from May to November; the dry season runs from December through April. Most mornings, no matter the season, are bright and sunny and rain can fall at any time on the Caribbean coast. The low tourist season is around May/June, and this is an excellent time for a college study tour. In May and June, travel is more affordable and language classes can be scheduled during the rainy part of the day.

Economy

Tourism, coffee, and bananas boost Costa Rica's economy; and Ticos enjoy one of the highest standards of living in the Americas. They have free healthcare and public education, and one of the highest literacy rates (93%) in Central, South, or North America. Study tour participants are surprised at the low cost and personal attention they get when they fall ill and require clinic services in Costa Rica. Likewise, when students' service projects involve painting elementary school classrooms and exteriors, they observe both the poor quality of the paint and how grateful the uni-formed schoolchildren and teachers are despite the fact that they know such painting will be required again quite soon.

Tico Cooking

Oatmeal and pancakes are not the typical fare in Costa Rica. The classic Costa Rican dish is *gallo pinto* (literally, painted rooster). Basically, this dish consists of rice and black or red beans mixed with seasonings that include onion, garlic, and finely chopped bell pepper. Although it is pre-dominantly a breakfast food, Ticos may eat *gallo pinto* three times a day with corn tortillas. For lunch, professionals, businesspeople, students, and farmers alike usually have a *casado* (meaning "married man"), a hearty combination including rice, beans, cabbage salad, fried plantains, and chicken, fish or beef. The curious student will learn that this term, *casado*, exemplifies Tico macho humor; it connotes that this is the ordinary daily fare a man will likely get after he is married.

Fruits of Costa Rica

Home-stay hosts provide delicious fruits distinctive to Costa Rica. The rainbow of fruits found in Costa Rica are a delight to the senses: *anona* (scaly custard apple), breadfruit, *caimitos* and other star fruits, cashew fruit, *granadilla* (passion fruit), *guanabana* (prickly custard apple from the Soursop tree), guava, loquat, mango, nanzi, paw-paw, *pejibaye*, rambutan, rose-apple, and *zapote* (mambey). Refrescos are refreshing fruit drinks that accompany almost every Costa Rican meal. A *mora* (blackberry) refresco is very nourishing, and *casa*, a type of guava, is very thirst-quenching. Home-stay hosts often mix these wonderful fruits with milk or water and serve the treats at breakfast and dinner.

Reflection Exercises

1. A way to learn about a country is to read its literature, including both prose and poetry. Review http://www.infocostarica.com/culture/prose .html and http://www.infocostarica.com/culture/poetry.html. Select a book to read about the land and people of Costa Rica. What unique information did you discover about Costa Rica that would be of assistance to you on a cultural study tour?

2. Culture involves values and beliefs, both of which are reflected in religious practices. Go to http://www.infocostarica.com/culture/religion .html and read about religion in Costa Rica. What do the religious affiliations of Costa Ricans suggest to you in terms of holiday celebrations, Holy Week, marriage, and funerals?

3. Read the information at http://ticotimes.com/costa-rica-government or another site that describes the elected officials of Costa Rica. Who are the country's current president and two vice presidents? What parties do they represent? Identify the country's other political parties. To what degree are women and minority groups represented in the government?

4. Find and follow a recipe that is considered "typically Costa Rican" in terms of preparation and ingredients. A good place to begin is http://www.globalgourmet.com/destinations/costarica/costcuis.html. What did you notice about the dish that was different from your usual fare?

5. Locate Costa Rica on a map (http://www.costaricamap-online.com). As you explore the country's location and natural resources, explain why you believe tourism is an economic boom for the country. On which country(s) is Costa Rica's economy dependent? Using ecological

theory, how might the 2009 economic downturn in the United States impact everyday life?

6. Review material on a state or federal child welfare agency department in your country. What does the department have in common with the Patronato Nacional de la Infancia (PANI), the Costa Rican child welfare authority? What are the differences between the departments (e.g., structure, programs, and services)?

7. Costa Rica's high literacy rate offers many possibilities for social workers. Explain how social work services can build on the strengths of people with strong reading and writing skills. How will such skills impact consumer-based advocacy and efforts at community planning and development and the advancement of research?

AGENCY OR SOCIAL SERVICE SETTING

Too often, social work students engage in various forms of field education with a limited educational foundation (e.g. have taken only an introductory social work and/or single HBSE course). And non–social work undergraduates may not have had an opportunity to experience field education or enroll in HBSE coursework. Despite a mix of majors and variation in field-oriented exposure, experiential-based immersion/study tour experiences can serve as a viable mechanism for participants to understand the organizational culture of a community-based language school dedicated to giving back to its citizens.

The culture of the Centro Panamericano de Idiomas (CPI) language school involves being Spanish-student centered, community oriented, enjoyable, and supportive. Dance and cooking classes and games of Scrabble played in Spanish facilitate language acquisition. Teachers are extremely accommodating of *gringos*, and they are quite prepared and willing to administer pre- and posttests of Spanish class learning. Students soon realize that because so many community members serve as home-stay hosts, CPI is almost a family name. CPI administrators make sure that the female home-stay hosts receive payment. These hosts perform household chores for the student: cooking, cleaning, and laundering.

Costa Rica constitutes a developing country. Central American Ticos, even the CPI teachers, earn little compared to North Americans. Therefore, Ticos purchase few sweets for dessert and are early to bed and quick to rise. Over time, students tend to pick up on these cultural subtleties. As an adaptive mechanism, students often adopt their own subculture within the study tour group, wherein they may nitpick, form cliques, or become homesick. Such human behavior is understandable. The wise student will learn from introspection concerning these behaviors.

Evaluation of the international study tour experience occurs via multiple methods. First, an objective multiple-choice and short-answer examination is given at the end of the pre-study tour preparatory course. Content is mostly derived from the Biesanz, Biesanz, and Biesanz (1999) book and lecture materials involving culture shock, awareness, competency and sensitivity. Second, the CPI language school administers before and after language tests to evaluate students' increased ability to speak Spanish. As one might expect, participants with the least Spanish knowledge tend to demonstrate greater improvement than those starting classes with some modicum of Spanish-language proficiency. However, even native speakers who tend to speak Spanglish, experience advancement.

Third, a quantitative measure concerning cultural awareness is administered before the preparatory course begins and after the study tour ends. This cross-cultural development self-assessment by Winkelman (2005) has limited utility, given the length of time of the course and study tour. Nevertheless, this self-assessment scale is designed to measure these concepts: ethnocentrism, universalism, acceptance, adaptation, marginalized, bicultural, integrated, cultural competence, and cultural proficiency.

Reflection Exercises

1. Consider how Hank, a social work student enrolled in a cultural study tour, experienced the next home-stay host situation:

   Hank was assigned to reside with a home-stay host comprised of four children under the age of 6 and their parents, Roberto and Flora. The family home was comprised of four rooms; two bedrooms, a living room, and a kitchen. Neat and well organized, the home was decorated with colorful, comfortable furniture and adorned with family photos and religious ornaments. The family's bathroom was located outside near the rear of the home.

   Upon arrival, Hank was given one bedroom all to himself. He greatly appreciated the room's easy chair and window that faced the family's well-tended garden. When Hank realized he was to have one of the two bedrooms while the rest of the family moved into the other bedroom and living room, he felt uncomfortable but grateful for the family's graciousness.

Raised as an only child, Hank was unaccustomed to small children and their level of activity. Try as he might, Hank had difficulty interacting with the children since their language, much like his Spanish, was somewhat limited. Further, he was unfamiliar with their play, songs, and toys. It was obvious that the children wanted his attention and were eager to please him, but Hank felt inept. Roberto and Flora perceived Hank's hesitancy to become engaged with the children as rejection or aloofness. Within days, they felt inadequate as home-stay hosts.

   a. Social workers possess the interpersonal skills to establish rapport with consumers and insight with regard to human interaction and family dynamics. Identify three reasons Hank experienced difficulty in establishing a relationship with the four small children. How would you suggest that Hank address this problem?

   b. Hank is surprised with the space that has been allocated to him by the home-stay hosts. What did Roberto and Flora convey to Hank by giving him one of the two bedrooms?

   c. Language skills appear to be a challenge for Hank. Consider some strategies Hank could embrace to build on the strengths of his native language skills in the host home. Are symbolic interactions and social constructivism helpful considerations? If so, how?

   d. What do you think is the role of the cultural study tour faculty in Hank's situation? How would you discuss this issue with faculty members, and what would you expect as resolutions?

2. The described cultural study tour includes elements of evidence-based research. What does this term mean, and how is this type of research integrated into international experience? How could evaluation be enhanced?

3. Dance, cooking classes, and games played in Spanish help to facilitate language acquisition. List at least five other activities that could be used to support language acquisition in this cultural context.

4. Music often serves as a bridge to various cultures around the world. Listen to the music of Costa Rica (http://www.vivacostarica.com/costa-rica-information/costa-rica-music.html). How does the music compare to what you are accustomed to? Consider the relationship between music and Costa Rican historical and political events. What genre of music is most appealing to you, and why?

Fourth, qualitative measures in the form of journals and reflection papers are culled for themes. These tools are intended to promote and evaluate the student's ability to function within a different culture, respect differences, obtain self-knowledge, and gain a global perspective on social work and social issues.

CONSIDERATIONS BEFORE ENTERING AN INTERNATIONAL EXPERIENCE

Pre–study tour meetings prepare students for the immersion/study tour experience. Preplanned service learning experiences are also coordinated to coincide with the study tour component.

The two main goals of the pre–study tour are to create cultural awareness and to convey information on Costa Rica. To create cultural awareness, lectures on culture shock and awareness are given, excerpts from previous student's reflection journals are shared, and experiential simulation exercises are practiced in small groups. These efforts attune students to cross-cultural and value dimensions that have to do with individualism versus collectivism, power distance, uncertainty avoidance, masculinity–femininity issues, and loose versus tight social structure issues. Small-group exercises also help students think through issues of space and touching and how nonverbal communication can differ across cultures (e.g., gender differences).

Insofar as conveying historical and background information about Costa Rica, lecture materials draw from textbooks and Web sites. *The Ticos* (Biesanz, Biesanz, & Biesanz, 1999) and other books (Kabagarama, 1997; Kohls & Knight, 1994; Seelye, 1996) highlight Costa Rican characteristics in relation to economics and politics, class and ethnicity, education, family, religion, and health.

Various methods are used to prepare students before they depart for Costa Rica. For example, group leaders tell stories about home-stay experiences and refer students to appropriate reading materials and Web sites. Students prepare and deliver short topical oral reports with handouts and learn Spanish-language fundamentals.

Specific cross-cultural concepts and value dimensions are incorporated into pre–study tour class discussions. For example, discussions ensue about how societies regard individualism versus collectivism; and participants examine and discuss the concepts of power distance, uncertainty avoidance, masculinity versus femininity, and loose versus tight social structures.

Intercultural awareness is fostered in class by experiential or simulation exercises addressing issues of space and touching; differences in nonverbal communication; and openness to trying something new/different. We define culture, talk about value orientations, and complete an activity to heighten awareness about the relevance of time and social relations.

The pre-study course is also intended to convey factual historical (e.g., pre-Columbian to modern-day internationalization), economic, and cultural information about Costa Rica. Therefore, students are required to read *The Ticos* (Biesanz et al., 1999), a comprehensive work with content about history, the land and people, economics and politics, class, ethnicity, education, family, religion, health, social economic development, and democracy.

While the main methods used to prepare students in the pre–study tour course involve stories about prior home-stays, short topical oral reports with handouts, and acquistion or review of Spanish-language fundamentals, reading Costa Rican online news items and other books about Costa Rica's indigenous population, the Bribri, (Palmer, Sanchez, & Mayorga, 1993) is also valuable.

Typically, from evaluations of study tour experiences, anticipation rises steeply as students prepare for international departure. Despite their reading and experiential learning preparation, students often become homesick. Yet upon returning to the United States, students report a sense of mastery, likely attributable to their successful completion of a living and learning experience in a faraway land.

Two to three weeks is a long time for many students to be away from their creature comforts and familiar environments. Distractions, as manifested in service learning experiences (Brasilito School, Habitat for Humanity, *asilos* or day centers for older adults, the shantytown project) are meaningful ways for students to observe human behavior, explore social issues,

Reflection Exercises

1. Using a group approach, try to reach a consensus in defining these terms and phrases: individualism versus collectivism, power distance, uncertainty avoidance, masculinity–femininity issues, and loose versus tight social structure issues. Then apply the concepts to Costa Rica. Why are shared definitions and application of key concepts to a specific country critical to social work practice and social welfare policy?
2. How would you describe your personal and professional strengths? Describe how you could use these strengths to facilitate your transition from home to a Costa Rican home-stay host.
3. Define "evidence-based research." Discuss how the profiled cultural study tour uses this type of research. How can the findings from such research be used to improve the quality of international tours?

---

confront limited resources, and receive sincere appreciation and gratefulness from a pride-filled, generously giving people. In addition to classes, students participate in service learning, scholarly lectures, and excursions (e.g., to Guanacaste, Playa Flamingo, Manuel Antonio National Park). These activities contribute to students' learning and analytical thought, facilitating the change from tourist to traveler and learner.

CONSIDERATIONS FOR PRACTICE

Study tour/experiential learning can enhance students' knowledge of human behavior and social-cultural context in environments. When traveling in a Spanish-speaking country like Costa Rica, students also benefit from acquiring language to enhance communication and to promote new and different ways of thinking. For students who may already know some Spanish, participation in a Costa Rican study tour provides exposure to unique Costa Rican expressions (*Tiquismos*). Typically, the familiar *tu* ("you") is not used in Costa Rica, even with children; instead, the archaic form *vos* is often used.

Because this type of language usage is tricky and often idiosyncratic to a region, even advanced students of Spanish resort to *usted*. When walking in areas outside of San José, people who are passed on the street may greet one another with *Adiós* (good-bye, literally "go with God") or just *diós*. *Hasta luego* (until later) is used to say good-bye. Ticos love to use nicknames, often involving a person's physical attributes: *macho/macha* (pale-like) if they are slightly fair-skinned or blondish. *Gordito* (a little fat) is used for someone who is slightly overweight, and *moreno* and *negro* are used to refer to brownish or black skin color. *Pura vida* ("great"), *con toda la pata* (literally "with all the paw"—terrific), and *tranquilo* ("relaxed" or "be cool") are favorite Tico phrases students love to adopt and then wear on T-shirts. These examples illustrate how understanding language enhances one's appreciation for the cultural aspects of human behavior in a particular social environment.

Reflection Exercises

1. Notice how language is used in your community to educate, advertise, advocate, and solicit. Before leaving on an international experience, identify key terms and phrases you believe would be crucial to learn in the country's language and dialect.

2. An elementary understanding of language is needed to conduct commerce. Visit and http://www.vacationcity.com/costa-rica/informa tion/money. What is the monetary unit of Costa Rica? What are the denominations of the bills and coins? When are banks open, how is money exchanged, and what is the current exchange rate between Costa Rica and your country?

3. Buy a comprehensive Spanish dictionary and begin to keep a list of words you learn and use. Review http://www.infocostarica.com/cul ture/language.html and discuss what you have learned about the form of Spanish spoken in Costa Rica and its differences from Spanish spoken in other countries.

4. Read about Marcos, a bilingual social work student considering a cultural study tour in Costa Rica:

   Born in Madrid, Spain, Marcos is bilingual in Spanish and English. He is interested in a career as a social worker in an international relief organization. As a result, Marcos thought a cultural study tour made sense for him, especially since he could use his language abilities. Marcos spoke with his academic advisor about the idea and, with her encouragement, decided to learn more about the study tour.

When Marcos found out about the pre–study course, he met with the course's faculty member and read the course content. Since he already spoke fluent Spanish, Marcos saw no reason to spend additional time learning Spanish, plus he was quite familiar with Spanish culture. As required, Marcos enrolled in the pre–study course but made little effort to read the assigned articles, buy a Spanish dictionary, or engage with other applicants to the cultural study tour.

In short time, Mr. Rivera, the tour's faculty advisor, discovered Marcos's lack of involvement in the pre–study course and overall lackadaisical attitude regarding preparation for the tour.

Mr. Rivera soon met with Marcos to indicate that the pre–study course was a prerequisite for the international experience. During their meeting, Mr. Rivera took time to ensure that Marcos understood the relevance of human behavior (e.g., expectations, customs, prohibitions) in the social environment. Marcos left the meeting understanding Mr. Rivera's position but rethinking his commitment and involvement in the cultural study tour.

a. As described in this example, identify four of Marcos's personal and professional strengths. What should the social work faculty advisor involved in this tour include in working with Marcos?

b. Review your course text and class notes on human behavior in the social environment (HBSE). If you have not taken a HBSE course, ask to borrow a text from a social work faculty member or student. What did Mr. Rivera mean regarding the relevance of human behavior in the social environment (HBSE) to the cultural study tour? Specifically, how would HBSE prepare to practice on micro, mezzo and macro levels in Costa Rica? Consider how HBSE would facilitate students' understanding of the personal, environmental, and time dimensions (Hutchison, 1999).

c. Contemplate theoretical considerations (e.g., ecological, psycho-dynamic, cognitive-behavioral, symbolic interactionist, social constructivist, and the ethnic-sensitive perspective) and their applicability to HBSE in a cultural study tour of Costa Rica.

d. Costa Ricans do not use the same Castilian Spanish that is spoken in Spain. Spaniards lisp the letters *c* and *z* and use the *vosotros* pronoun, while Costa Ricans use the antiquated form of *vos* and the more formal *usted*. Explain why this information would be important for Marcos to know in contemplating his career in international social work.

e. Read http://www.infocostarica.com/culture/traditions.html and discuss how Costa Rica's cultural traditions reflect concepts intrinsic to human behavior in the social environment.

ETHICAL ISSUES AND DILEMMAS

In addition to university-based standards of conduct, a code for international travel and course work is highly recommended for anyone designing or participating in a cultural immersion or study tour experience. This type of code clearly outlines that students, faculty members, and staff are expected to abide by the customs and the laws of the host country and that respect for the country visited is absolutely mandatory. As an example, students will find it helpful to know that body piercing and tattooing in Costa Rica are prohibited by study tour leaders because of health risks. Additionally, participants need to be aware of immunization requirements and any stipulations for disclosing major health or mental health challenges. A code of ethics for international travel can delineate the appropriateness of actions while highlighting other important university or departmental policies regulating role expectations (e.g., student and professor) and behavior.

An ethical issue that may occur is how to handle free time. A code of conduct can specify that when time is available, students are permitted to move about (alone), as long as the faculty tour leaders are aware of individuals' plans and whereabouts. Pairing up with someone (e.g., a buddy system) is highly recommended, even when students become accustomed to the new geography.

Reflection Exercises

1. Use the Ethical Framework for Assessment described in Chapter 3 (Table 3.2) when answering the questions related to the next case example.

   Miriam is a nontraditional social work major from a small college. After raising her three children, working for over a decade in her home, and serving as a nurse's aide in a long-term facility, Miriam decided to return to college to complete her undergraduate degree. At college, where the majority of students are 20 years or more her junior, Miriam often assumes a parental role. Miriam tends to think that the fact that she is a mother, has had more life experiences, and has an employment history distinguishes her from other students.

   Since Miriam has never been outside of her country she thought a cultural study tour would be an outstanding opportunity to both travel and learn about a new culture. As required, Miriam attended the pre–study tour meetings, where she quickly assumed a leadership role and took it upon herself to organize a shopping trip to buy necessary travel items.

When Miriam arrived in Costa Rica, she was matched with a home-stay host family comprised of two teenage boys, their parents, and a maternal grandmother. Miriam felt comfortable in the home; however, within three days, she was convinced that the grandmother was in need of placement in an *asilo*. Miriam based her assessment on HBSE content on aging as well as her previous employment as a nurse's aide.

Miriam shared her assessment of the grandmother's needs and the idea of the older woman's involvement at a center with the tour's faculty advisor, who reminded Miriam that she was a visitor, had few details concerning the home situation and little understanding of cultural norms. However, Miriam could not abandon her position and, during an evening meal, shared her thoughts with her home-stay hosts.

The hosts were dismayed with Miriam's comments. Although they remained hospitable, they made it clear to the faculty advisor that Miriam was intruding in the family's affairs with little insight into family wishes and dynamics.

a. Imagine that you are the cultural study tour's faculty advisor; consequently, you have a responsibility to both the student, Miriam, and the host family. You recognize that something must be done to address the situation, but what? To answer this dilemma, consider:
   • What is your primary role and responsibilities as a faculty member?
   • What are the relevant expectations for the student?
   • Have cultural norms and/or mores been violated?
   • Should the student continue in the living situation?
b. In this example, whom should the faculty member consider to be the consumer? Explain your response.
c. What do you consider to be Miriam's personal and professional strengths and areas for improvement?
d. The ethical principles of the International Federation of Social Workers and the International Association of Schools of Social Work express a commitment for and education in professional conduct. Both organizations speak to the need for social workers to follow ethical and practice guidelines in accordance to country (www.ifsw.org/en/p38000324.html). Review the code of ethics and explain what you think of Miriam's actions in the context of the ethical principles.

Participants are expected to respect and abide by the lifestyle patterns and customs of their home-stay family. Often Ticos provide students with house keys so they can enter the home later in the evening (e.g., after returning from cultural events). Ticos rarely smoke cigarettes; therefore, students need to be courteous with regard to smoking.

Students are encouraged to participate in host-family activities, such as birthday parties and attending religious services or cultural activities. Such experiences serve to enhance the preplanned activities of the group and offer more opportunities for students to observe human behavior in various social environments.

SUMMARY

Rose-colored glasses in the form of worldviews will change after students experience poverty and cultural differences up close and personal. Perhaps the best way to truly remember and indelibly inscribe HBSE content on students' psyches is immerse them in another culture. A desired outcome of the Costa Rica Spanish immersion seminar/cultural study tour course is that upon their return, students will become committed to a lifetime journey toward cultural competence and global understanding. Thus far, desired outcomes have been achieved. "Survivors" of past Costa Rica cultural study tours have successfully garnered employment that confirms a beginning appreciation of and interest in Spanish and Latino culture. Students have also returned to the CPI language school for continuing independent study and have volunteered for leadership roles on campus and in the community.

A model of a cultural study tour is attached as an appendix for your review and consideration as well as for comparison with other tour models. A salient aspect of this chapter involves the experiential learning focus of the study tour, designed to enhance students' learning about how human behavior is rooted in and shaped by cultural components of a social environment (e.g., society and community). Integral to such learning is a commitment to and passion for viewing the world through cognitive lenses squarely focused on a desire for cultural understanding and competence.

REFERENCES

Biesanz, M. H., Biesanz, R., & Biesanz, K. Z. (1999). *The Ticos: Culture and social change in Costa Rica.* Boulder, CO: Lynn Rienner.

Brown, L. (1989). *State of the world: 1989.* New York: W.W. Norton.

Castillo, C., & Bond, O. F. (Compilers). (1987). *The University of Chicago Spanish Dictionary* (4th ed.). Chicago: University of Chicago Press.

Centro Panamericano de Idiomas. (2001). *Social work seminar 2001.* San Joaquin, Costa Rica. Author.

Cox, L. E., Falk, D. S., & Colon, M. (2006). Spanish language and cultural immersion for social work students. *The Journal of Baccalaureate Social Work Program Directors, 1,* 61–77.

Friends of Peace Pilgrim. (1994). *Peace Pilgrim: Her life and works in her own words.* Somerset, CA: Friends of Peace Pilgrim.

Geshke, N., Shanti L. A., & Salazar, J. C. (1998). *Essential Spanish for social services.* New York: Living Language/Random House.

Hutchison, E. D. (1999). *Dimensions of human behavior: The changing life course.* Thousand Oaks, CA: Pine Forge Press.

Johannesen, T. (1997). Social work as an international profession: Opportunities and challenges. In M. C. Hokenstad & J. Midgley (Eds.). *Issues in international social work: Global challenges for a new century.* Washington, DC: NASW Press.

Kabagarama, D. (1997). *Breaking the ice: A guide to understanding people from other cultures* (2nd ed.). Boston: Allyn & Bacon.

Kendris, C. (1996). *501 Spanish verbs: Fully conjugated in all the tenses in a new easy-to-learn format alphabetically arranged.* Hauppauge, NY: Barron's Educational Series, Inc.

Kohls, L. R., & Knight, J. M. (1994). *Developing intercultural awareness: A cross-cultural training handbook* (2nd edition). Yarmouth, ME: Intercultural Press, Inc.

Molina, I. & Palmer, S. (2000). *The history of Costa Rica.* San José, Costa Rica: Universidad de Costa Rica.

Murphy, P. (Project Editor) (2000). *Insight Guide: Costa Rica.* New York: APA Publications.

Palmer, P., Sanchez, J., & Mayorga, G. (1993). *Taking care of Sibo's gifts: An environmental treatise from Costa Rica's Kekoldi indigenous reserve.* San José, Costa Rica: Asociacion de Desarrollo, Integral de la Reserva, Indigena Cocles/Kekoldi.

Pillari, V. (1998). *Human behavior in the social environment.* Pacific Grove, CA: Thomson Brooks/Cole.

Rachowiecki, R., & Thompson, J. (2000). *Costa Rica* (4th ed.). Melbourne, Australia: Lonely Planet.

Richard, C. (2005). About face! A world without armies! Costa Rica's past president, Oscar Arias Sanchez. *New Internationalist, 381,* 21–32.

Sánchez, O. A. (2005). An interview with Costa Rica's Nobel laureate and tireless peacemaker. *Guernica.* Retrieved February 2008 from http://www.guernicamag.com/interviews/36/oscar_arias_snchez/.

Seelye, H. N. (1996). *Experiential activities for intercultural learning.* Yarmouth, ME: Intercultural Press.

Thiel, S. (2003). *The dynamics of traveling in a group.* Compendium of Final Papers of Participants of the May 24–June 14, 2003 Social Work Spanish Immersion Seminar in Costa Rica. (Assembled by Dr. Lisa Cox and Dr. Diane Falk, The Richard Stockton College of New Jersey Social Work Program, pages 18–19).

University of Kansas School of Social Welfare Web site. (2007). Office of Study Abroad. Retrieved from http://www.socwel.ku.edu/Academicx/costarica/index.shtml.

Winkelman, M. (2005). *Cultural awareness, sensitivity and competence.* Peosta, IA: Eddie Bowers.

APPENDIX A

THE RICHARD STOCKTON COLLEGE OF NEW JERSEY

GIS 47012-001: Spanish Immersion Seminar

Term: Fall
MW 8:00–9:50 P.M.; West Quad 104
Instructor: Dr. Lisa E. Cox
e-mail: Lisa.Cox@stockton.edu

Course Description and Purpose

This course will be divided into two segments. The first will occur in the Stockton classroom during the Fall Semester. The second will occur during Winter Break, when we travel to Costa Rica.* The purpose of

---

*Because the course will not be completed until after the Winter Break, all students will receive an "Incomplete" grade for the class at the end of the Fall Semester. Early in the Spring Semester, grades will be changed.

this advanced level, integrative course is to introduce students to the language, culture, and social issues in contemporary Costa Rica and to enhance their level of cultural competence. Students will meet during Fall Semester for a number of classes designed to prepare them for the immersion experience. On December 28, they will travel as a group to Costa Rica. There they will reside with Spanish-speaking families; spend over 50 hours in the classroom studying the Spanish language, with a focus on the specialized vocabulary of social work; attend lectures; visit social agencies; participate in volunteer community service; and meet with their instructors to reflect on and integrate their learning experiences. Throughout the course, students will examine the parallels between Costa Rican society and their own. They will examine their responses to the immersion experience. Students will also have an opportunity to travel to sites of natural beauty and to learn about the unique features of this biologically diverse region. As they do so, they will examine the relationships between sociodemographic and environmental changes.

Course Objectives

This course aims to enhance students':

1. Ability to comprehend, speak, read, and write the Spanish language
2. Intercultural awareness
3. Understanding of the origins and diversity of contemporary Costa Rican culture
4. Appreciation of Costa Rica's efforts in its creation of and commitment to one of the most extensive welfare states in Latin America—which has played a major role in reducing poverty, infant mortality, the incidence of major diseases, and illiteracy
5. Ability to understand Costa Rican social policies and social services in a cross-cultural perspective, including the roles that social workers play in addressing social problems
6. Understanding of the relationship between the people and the land

Method

This course involves both classroom and experiential learning. The primary method will be immersion in Spanish language and Costa Rican culture.

Required Readings and Course Resources

Students will attend all preparatory classes at Stockton. They will read assigned materials from the textbook other sources and complete assignments. They will attend Spanish-language classes at the language school, participate in group trips in Costa Rica, and give service to local community agencies.

Student Responsibilities

Students are expected to abide by the *Student Code of Conduct* included in this syllabus.

They are expected to attend, participate in, and be on time for all scheduled classes and other learning experiences. They are responsible for completing all homework assignments. They are expected to participate in all group activities, including service learning.

Required Texts

1. A good Spanish dictionary
2. Kendris, C. (1996). *501 Spanish verbs: Fully conjugated in all the tenses in a new easy-to-learn format alphabetically arranged*. Hauppauge, NY: Barron's Educational Series.
3. Biesanz, M. H., Biesanz, R., & Biesanz, K. Z. (1999). *The Ticos: Culture and social change in Costa Rica*. Boulder, CO: Lynn Rienner.

Assignments

1. All assigned readings.
2. Journal: Students are expected to keep a journal on their experiences. See detailed journal assignment included in this syllabus.
3. Participation in all group discussions and trips (with Stockton instructors).
4. Participation in all mandatory pre–study tour and Spanish-language classes.
5. Presentation and paper. See detailed presentation and paper assignment included in this syllabus.
6. Participation in service learning.

Grades Will Be Based On

1. Exam on assigned readings	20% of grade
2. Quality of journal	30% of grade
3. Quality of presentation and paper	20% of grade
4. Attendance and participation in class	10% of grade
5. Quality of participation in group discussions and service learning during trip	10% of grade
6. Effort and attendance in Spanish classes	10% of grade

Table 7.1   Segment 1 Calenda

Week	Topic	Assignments
September 8	Introductions, ice breaker Overview of course—its two segments Segment 1: • Schedule of classes • Required books • Assignments • How class sessions will be conducted Segment 2: • What to expect/slide show • How to prepare yourself • What is required • What to take	Homework assignment
September 20	Intercultural awareness Ticos and the country of Costa Rica Overview of geography, history, economy, government/politics, class/ethnicity, community, family, everyday life, culture/customs/religion, leisure, indigenous people	
October 18	Class presentations begin	Exam on assigned readings Payment for study tour due!!
November 15	Class presentations continue	
December 6	Class presentations conclude	

Course Web Site

http://loki.stockton.edu/~coxl/COSTARICA/welcome_CR.htm

Table 7.2   Segment 2 Calendar

Week	Topic	Assignments
Week 1 of tour Tuesday, December 28, 2004, through Sunday, January 2, 2005	Week 1: San Joaquin de Flores (Heredia) Overview of seminar Social work as an international profession Orientation to physical arrangements, routines, language school, transportation, eating arrangements Assignments Meeting schedule Introduction to Costa Rica Testing, orientation Spanish classes Dessert at Fresa's Restaurant Trip to Café Britt Cooking class (lunch) Ring in New Year with host families Trip to Arenal Volcano/Hot Springs	First week of journal entries to be turned in to Stockton course instructors by Sunday, January 2
Week 2 of tour Monday, January 3, through Sunday, January 9, 2005	Week 2: Monteverde Spanish-language classes 4 hrs. daily Lunch at Stella's Bakery, possible visit to Monteverde Institute Game night at CPI Service learning project Movie night at CPI Sky trek or sky walk Dance class Cooking class (lunch), Peace Pilgrim talk, and visit to Quaker meetinghouse Music night at CPI Lunch at CPI (Johnny's pizza), depart for Manuel Antonio National Park Manuel Antonio National Park (on the Pacific Ocean) Transfer to Flamingo Beach	Second week of journal entries to be turned in to Stockton course instructors by Sunday, January 9

Week	Topic	Assignments
Week 3 of tour Monday, January 10, through Saturday, January 15, 2005	Week 3: Playa Flamingo Spanish-language classes 4 hrs. daily Trip to Conchal Beach (picnic on the beach), snorkeling, swimming Service learning project at primary school Spanish classes, posttest	Completed journal to be turned in to course instructors by Saturday, January 15

Class Presentation and Paper Assignment

For class presentation (which is strictly limited to 15 minutes) and paper (which should be around 5 to 6 typewritten, double-spaced pages), choose one of 20 listed topics. To ensure that we cover the topics in the class presentations, no two students may choose the same topic. (A sign-up sheet will be provided.) Your presentation and paper should give evidence that you have done some research on the topic, using the library, Costa Rican newspapers, or other resources as approved by the instructors. You must include in-text citations and a bibliography that includes all your sources. For your presentation, consider the use of PowerPoint slides, overheads, and handouts.

Here are the topics:

1. Some aspect of the healthcare system in Costa Rica
2. Domestic violence in Costa Rica
3. Costa Rica's commitment to peace, its policy of no standing army
4. Community development in Costa Rica
5. Social work education in Costa Rica
6. Women's issues in Costa Rica
7. Child neglect and abuse in Costa Rica and the system of child protection
8. Costa Rican cuisine and cooking
9. Environmental issues in Costa Rica
10. Biodiversity in Costa Rica

11. The Costa Rican economy
12. Family life in Costa Rica
13. Religious life in Costa Rica
14. Recreation in Costa Rican communities
15. Substance abuse in Costa Rica
16. Costa Rican art and/or literature
17. Costa Rican government and politics
18. The national park system
19. Ethnic minorities in Costa Rica
20. Ecotourism

Journal Assignment: Guidelines for Writing Journal Reflections

Please keep your reflections in one notebook or binder. Entries should be dated and kept in chronological order. The journal is meant to be a reflective log of your activities and impressions as you have experiences and make observations at language school, in your home-stay, or during cultural tours and events. Make time (e.g., at least 20 minutes daily) to journal regularly. A lot of important process, developmental data, and feelings will be lost if you don't keep daily entries. You will also want to write descriptions of what you hear from other Stockton students and the members in your home-stay or people at the language school—wherever you're interacting. Consider writing about settings, learning or interaction objectives, and the ages and backgrounds and interactions of people around you.

You might focus on issues such as these examples:

- What are you learning? (Have you learned anything about the group's culture, behaviors, impressions of you, feelings about environmental issues, pride in the neighborhood, attitude toward Americans, social service systems, etc.?)
- Have you been surprised by anything you have experienced?
- What is the most surprising aspect to you concerning your language school experience?
- Have you been disappointed by any of your experiences? (Was there any part of the program that did not meet your expectations?

Why do you think things did not turn out the way you expected? Examine your expectations, and decide if they were realistic. Was the effort put into meeting that particular goal appropriate?)

- As you spend more time with people in your home-stay, are you learning more about their culture? Are they learning about yours?

Other more specific reflection points to consider and address include:

1. How does your home-stay experience compare to your U.S. home?
2. What is it like to learn Spanish at CPI, as compared to how you've previously learned another language (like Spanish) in the United States?
3. What have you observed about how people relate to one another in the Tico community/culture?
4. How effective are your language teachers in helping you learn? What do you need them or you to do differently to enhance learning?
5. What are your impressions about the land and people that you've encountered to date in Costa Rica?
6. How well have you managed to get your needs met, insofar as daily living in your home-stay? And how have your experiences changed from week to week?
7. What observations have you made about the importance of family, religion, and cultural traditions?
8. How have you handled introducing yourself to others?
9. What is it like to communicate in your own language versus communicating in a foreign language?
10. How is living in a Costa Rican family different from living in your own family?
11. How does your family's neighborhood compare to your own neighborhood?
12. How do your experiences getting from place to place in Costa Rica differ from what you are used to at home?
13. How do the interests of your Tico family members compare with those of your own family?

14. What is it like to study at the Centro Panamericano de Idiomas language school, as compared to studying at Stockton College?
15. What is it like to try to express your feelings in Spanish?

WHAT YOU SHOULD KNOW BEFORE DEPARTURE

Transportation

1. We will be flying to Costa Rica on US Airways, departing Philadelphia on Tuesday, December 28, 7:30 AM, on Flight 373, arriving at 2:45 PM in San José, Costa Rica. Our return flight will be departing San José on Saturday, January 15, 2:45 PM, on Flight 1498V, arriving Philadelphia at 8:39 PM. Please be aware that airlines can make last-minute changes in departure times, so it would be wise to check with your instructors prior to the departure date and also to check with the airlines.
2. The CPI Language school maintains their own vans, tour buses, etc. CPI provides ground transportation for students to and from the airport and to and from language school locations and cultural sites. CPI maintains appropriate documentation such as "certificates of insurance."

Insurance

Richard Stockton College has purchased group insurance for students and faculty participating in this study tour. This insurance is mandatory and covers emergency medical evacuation and related costs. It does not cover medical expenses. Students must provide proof of medical insurance prior to departure. Your student policy is sufficient.

Documents

Your travel documents include airline tickets, a detailed itinerary, and your travel insurance. No one is permitted to travel without a passport, and each of you must acquire a passport as soon as possible, if you do not already have one. Please carry a photocopy of your passport with you at all times, and leave a copy of same with someone at home in the United States.

Airport Check-In

Be sure to check your itinerary and airline tickets for departure times. You must be at the airport at least 2½ hours prior to departure, so that you can check in with our group, with the airlines, and clear security. Remember to check your luggage all the way through to your final destination. Please make certain that your luggage is clearly labeled with your name, address, and phone number.

Security

Airports have heightened security measures for our safety. It is not unusual for airport personnel to inquire about or search your luggage or any items you may be carrying on board. Please cooperate with security personnel. Be aware that you may not carry on anything that could remotely be perceived as a weapon, such as a nail file, scissors, penknife, and so on.

Baggage

Regardless of airline luggage limits, we must restrict all participants to only one piece of checked luggage and one carry-on. We strongly recommend that you bring no larger than a 26-inch suitcase, plus a small knapsack. We will be traveling around Costa Rica on a small bus, and luggage must be lifted onto the roof of the bus by the bus driver. Overweight, extra-large pieces will cause delays and potentially could cause injury to those hoisting the luggage onto the bus. Please be considerate!

Student Code of Conduct

1. It is essential that all members of our group travel and participate in all activities with mutual respect and understanding. In essence, we need to put aside our own ethnic/class differences and travel together in harmony.
2. Tour leaders expect students to be serious learners (e.g., complete all required homework and attend all classes) and be respectful houseguests.
3. No student is allowed to deviate from the study tour itinerary.

4. All students are expected to abide by the customs and the laws of the host country. Respect of the law of the nation visited is absolutely mandatory.

5. Anyone who is found in possession of illegal drugs is subject to severe reprimand or being sent home immediately, and the academic institution of *The Richard Stockton College of New Jersey* is NOT LIABLE for the cost the student incurred in signing up for the tour.

6. Body piercing and getting tattoos are *strictly prohibited* because of health risks.

7. When there is free time designated on the itinerary, students are permitted to move about alone, as long as the faculty tour leaders are aware of individuals' general plans during designated free time. Pairing up with another is highly recommended, because you are not accustomed to your new geography.

8. As we have planned this study tour, all students have been asked to disclose any major health or mental health problems and any medication(s) they use.

9. The faculty tour leaders expect that students will abide by the airline regulations with regard to weight and luggage limits. Any excess luggage is entirely the responsibility of the students and not the institution or the faculty members. Students also need to restrict the weight and bulk of their luggage even further, because we will be taking a small bus between locations in Costa Rica. The capacity of this bus is quite limited, and luggage needs to be lifted onto the roof of the bus. Please do not expect others to lift weights that you cannot lift yourself. Be considerate.

10. Students are expected to respect and abide by the lifestyle patterns and customs of their home-stay family. Typically, Costa Ricans are "early to bed and early to rise." Often Ticos (nickname for Costa Ricans) will provide students with house keys so they can enter the home later in the evening, when returning from cultural tours/events. Ticos rarely smoke cigarettes; therefore students need to be courteous with regard to smoking.

11. Because we represent a country that is considered to be a world leader, we are expected to be respectful, humble, and honest.

Moreover, we are expected to carry ourselves in public with dignity and restraint with regard to audible conflict, general noise, and other behaviors that call attention to ourselves. Binge drinking and drunken behavior is *strictly prohibited,* and anyone who is found or known to be drunk is subject to severe reprimand or being sent home immediately, and the academic institution of *The Richard Stockton College of New Jersey* is NOT LIABLE for the cost the student incurred in signing up for the study tour.

12. Costa Rica has big cities like San José and small towns like Grecia and Sarchi. Students who want to shop for food, necessities, or souvenirs should be prepared to pay for their purchases at all times. Faculty members will not be able to advance funds to students for unexpected purchases.

13. There will be times when the faculty tour leaders will require the total, undivided attention of the students. Students are expected to be quiet and to listen attentively whenever faculty tour guides call for their attention for any announcements.

Table 7.3   Provisional Itinerary

Date	Morning	Afternoon	Evening
Tuesday, Dec. 28	Leave from Philadelphia	Arrive San José/San Joaquín de Flores, meet host families	
Wed., Dec. 29	Testing, orientation, Spanish classes		Dessert at Fresa's Restaurant
Thurs., Dec. 30	Spanish classes	Trip to Café Britt	
Fri., Dec. 31	Spanish classes	Cooking class (lunch)	Ring in New Year with host families
Sat., Jan. 1	Trip to Arenal Volcano/ Hot Springs	Trip to Arenal Volcano/Hot Springs	Trip to Arenal Volcano/Hot Springs
Sun., Jan. 2	Trip to Arenal Volcano/ Hot Springs	Transfer to Monteverde	Meet Monteverde host families
Mon., Jan. 3	Spanish classes	Lunch at Stella's Bakery, possible visit to Monteverde Institute	Game night at CPI
Tues., Jan. 4	Spanish classes	Service learning project	Movie night at CPI

Table 7.3   (Continued)

Date	Morning	Afternoon	Evening
Wed., Jan. 5	Spanish classes	Sky trek or sky walk	Dance class
Thurs., Jan. 6	Spanish classes	Cooking class (lunch), Peace Pilgrim talk and visit to Quaker meetinghouse	Dance/karaoke
Fri., Jan. 7	Spanish classes Early-morning bird walk	Lunch at CPI (Johnny's pizza), Depart for Manuel Antonio National Park	
Sat., Jan. 8	Manuel Antonio National Park (on the Pacific Ocean)	Manuel Antonio National Park (on the Pacific Ocean)	Manuel Antonio National Park (on the Pacific Ocean)
Sun., Jan. 9	Manuel Antonio National Park (on the Pacific Ocean)	Manuel Antonio National Park (on the Pacific Ocean), transfer to Flamingo Beach	Arrival at Playa Flamingo, meet host families
Mon., Jan. 10	Trip to Conchal Beach (picnic on the beach), snorkeling, swimming	Spanish classes	Game night at hotel
Tues., Jan. 11	Service Learning project at primary school	Spanish classes	
Wed., Jan. 12	Service Learning project at primary school	Spanish classes	
Thurs., Jan. 13	Homework session at resort/swimming at pool or beach	Spanish classes	
Fri., Jan. 14	Homework session at resort/swimming at pool or beach	Spanish classes, posttest	Dinner on the beach
Sat., Jan. 15	Transportation back to airport		

CHAPTER

8

An Appalachian Example: Issues of Social and Economic Justice

Susan Kiss Sarnoff

You better listen to the voices from the mountains tryin' to tell you what you just might need to know.

—Gorton (1996, p. 206)

In less-developed regions, social workers tend to focus on assisting consumers to address such basic needs as obtaining food, potable water, shelter, and, if they are lucky, security against hunger and violence. This assistance reflects Abraham Maslow's (1971) theory of the hierarchy of needs, which suggests that until such basic needs are met, people are unable to set their sights on higher-order goals. It is not meant to suggest that people in these regions do not require that health, mental health, or other higher-order needs be met but acknowledges that people who lack basic needs will continue to prioritize them over—and often to the exclusion of—other needs.

The author wants to thank Michael Harrington for making her aware of Appalachia; Rich Greenlee, Donna Wilson, Freve Pace, Linda Schoeppner, and Deb Pack for helping her to understand the culture of Appalachia; and, most of all, Carolyn Tice, for introducing me to my new home in the hills.

161

Although Appalachia is situated within the richest nation in the world, the term "Appalachia" connotes poverty (Precourt, 1983) to such a degree that to this day it reflects many of the features of less-developed nations (Blauner, 1969; Lohman, 1990). In fact, Volunteers in Service to America (VISTA), the domestic version of the Peace Corps, was developed to serve the region (Lewis & Billings, 1997). This chapter introduces the social work mandates that address the promotion of social and economic justice and then describes Appalachia in the context of characteristics that engender social and economic need. An examination of a marginalized community within an economically oppressed region of Appalachia provides an example of a century-long, and finally successful, struggle to address a basic need long thought to be met in the United States. The chapter concludes with suggestions to promote social and economic justice to residents of such regions.

FOUNDATIONS OF SOCIAL AND ECONOMIC JUSTICE IN SOCIAL WORK

The National Association of Social Workers' (NASW) *Code of Ethics* (NASW, 2000) framed social justice in terms of social change:

> Social workers pursue social change, particularly with and on behalf of vulnerable and oppressed individuals and groups of people. Social workers' social change efforts are focused primarily on issues of poverty, unemployment, discrimination, and other forms of social injustice. These activities seek to promote sensitivity to and knowledge about oppression and cultural and ethnic diversity. Social workers strive to ensure access to needed information, services, and resources; equality of opportunity; and meaningful participation in decision making for all people. (p. 5)

The Council on Social Work Education, which accredits schools of social work in the United States and Canada, identifies the core competencies required for the practice of professional social work in its *Educational Policy and Accreditation Standards* (2008). One of these is "to advance human rights and social and economic justice." The description continues in this way:

Each person, regardless of position in society, has basic human rights, such as freedom, safety, privacy, an adequate standard of living, health care and education. Social Workers recognize the global interconnections of oppression and are knowledgeable about theories of justice and strategies to promote human and civil rights. Social work incorporates social justice practices in organizations, institutions and society to ensure that these basic human rights are distributed equitably and without prejudice. Social workers

- understand the forms and mechanisms of oppression and discrimination;
- advocate for human rights and social and economic justice; and
- engage in practices that advance social and economic rights. (p. 5)

Similarly, the *Statement of Principles* of the International Federation of Social Workers and the International Association of Schools of Social Work (2004) states:

Social workers have the responsibility to promote social justice, in relation to society generally and in relation to the people with whom they work. This means:

1. Challenging . . . discrimination . . . on the basis of ability, age, culture, gender or sex, marital status, socio-economic status, political opinions, skin color, racial or other physical characteristics, sexual orientation, or spiritual beliefs.
2. Recognizing . . . and respect[ing] the ethnic and cultural diversity of the societies in which they practice, taking account of individual, family, group and community differences.
3. . . . Ensur[ing] that resources at their disposal are distributed fairly, according to need.
4. Challenging unjust policies and practices . . . [by] bring[ing] to the attention of their employers, policy makers, politicians and the general public situations where resources are

✎ Reflection Exercises

1. Review codes of ethics of the National Association of Social Workers (http://www.socialworkers.org/pubs/code/code.asp), the International Federation of Social Workers (IFSW) www.ifsw.org/en/p38000324 .html), and the International Association of Schools of Social Work (IASSW) (www.ifsw.org/en/p38000324.html) in terms of language and statements describing social justice. Identify commonalities and differences in terminology.

2. Consider how the social work education program that you attend(ed) imparted education and promoted skills for advancement of social and economic justice. To what degree did you learn about international issues and the strife of specific marginalized populations in the United States? Were examples rural or urban in nature?

---

inadequate or where distribution of resources, policies and practices are oppressive, unfair or harmful.

5. Working in solidarity—Social workers have the obligation to challenge social conditions that contribute to social exclusion, stigmatisation [*sic*] or subjugation, and to work towards an inclusive society. (p. 3)

Clearly, social work professionals, in the United States and internationally, learn to recognize economic and social injustices during their professional training and learn skills to promote economic and social justice. All social workers are, therefore, obligated by preparation and mandate to actively promote social and economic justice, regardless of their roles, settings, or other factors. Moreover, social workers must understand the priorities of their consumers and help them meet those needs that the consumers themselves consider most vital. Only then will social workers gain the trust of their consumers that will enable them to be accepted as helping professionals.

OVERVIEW OF APPALACHIA

One must understand the history of Appalachia and its residents to understand their poverty, their culture, and their similarity to the global South. This history begins with the incursion of white settlers into what was formerly the tribal land of the people, primarily Cherokee and Shawnee, who were indigenous to the region long before Europeans arrived. Early agreements with these tribes set the Appalachian Mountains as the boundary between European settlers and the indigenous people (Linklater, 2002; Miles, 2005). However, as the new United States struggled to maintain its independence and maintain an army, it paid soldiers in deeds to land west of the Appalachian Mountains (Stock, 1996). Only those retired militia members who had no other resources chose to settle that land, which, despite paper ownership, had to be wrested from the tribes by force (Linklater, 2002). Most soldiers chose to sell their deeds, often to speculators who resold them, adding additional levels of complexity to land claims, a problem exacerbated by inconsistent laws and poor surveys (Blee & Billings, 1996).

Lack of a stable monetary system encouraged the production of whiskey in the region, as it was one of the few products that could be stored for long periods without deteriorating. Resentment against the perceived elitism of Easterners rose when steep taxes were imposed on whiskey, considered a luxury by those who enjoyed a safe money economy, eventually leading, from 1791 to 1794, to the Whiskey Rebellion (Stock, 1996). Mistrust of government and capitalists from the East began during this period, reinforced by subsequent experiences (Erikson, 1976; Gaventa, 1978). In fact, Blee and Billings (1996) found that the stereotype of "mountain feuds" resulted from the varied perceptions of residents that the courts were either ineffectual or corrupt, compounded by overlapping jurisdictions and the consequent venue shopping that furthered the appearance of government irrationality—or worse.

The white settlers of Appalachia were overwhelmingly of Scots-Irish descent, a fact that further influences our perceptions of Appalachians. Clearly selected for their fighting spirit, which made them outstanding soldiers (who have been overrepresented among the military in every American war), the Scots-Irish were also perceived as second-class citizens by other Europeans, especially those from Great Britain, who viewed them as a landless group unwelcome in either Scotland or Ireland (Cunningham, 1991; Drake, 2001; Webb, 2004). In other words, the U.S. government relocated the most despised group of British settlers to the disputed territory, knowing that their desire to be landowners would moti-vate them to fight off the Shawnee and Cherokee and that their feistiness would make them strong adversaries of the tribal members. The white settlers carved out a place for themselves in the region by force, learning how to survive there from the very indigenous groups with whom they alternately battled and forged alliances (Linklater, 2002). They farmed the region successfully, although the lack of transportation and the very literal barrier of the mountains made it costly, if not impossible, to trade with the East (Precourt, 1983).

During the 1830s, the national government drove the remaining tribal members from the Appalachian region, making it safer from attack and thereby attractive for development by Eastern capitalists (Miles, 2005). Already looked down on as inferior, Appalachians were then depicted as "ignorant hillbillies," (Shapiro, 1978). This depiction enabled first lumber and then coal companies to move into the region, ostensibly to assist the local populace by "modernizing" it. Excessive timber removal soon depleted the soil, making it more difficult to farm (Shannon, 1981). Then coal com-panies moved in en masse, buying land that had become less arable and using various forms of subterfuge and illegality (forgery, bribes, and force, among others) to expand their landholdings, until most of the region was owned by corporate entities back East (Gaventa, 1978; Wright, 1978).

Coal company control was extensive; employees even were paid in scrip that could be spent only at the company store (Drake, 2001; White & Marks, 1999). Low wages forced families to send women and even young children to work in the mines alongside adult males (Bettman, 1974). Poor conditions led to efforts to unionize. The coal companies met these efforts with violent backlash, hiring scabs to replace striking workers (Murolo & Chitty, 2001). Perhaps the best evidence that Appalachians were considered inferior to other Americans is the fact that the federal government intervened in some of these strikes, including the Matewan Massacre (Scott, 1995) and the Battle of Blair Mountain, the latter of which was the only instance in which the government bombed its own citizens (Lee, 1969).

Due to the extent of nonresident ownership, there was a limited (and uncaring) tax base to support schools (Duncan, 1992, 1999) and other local infrastructure (Fitchen, 1998). A poorly educated populace made it difficult to attract business to the region, while poor roads and nearly nonexistent public transportation made it difficult for residents to commute to better jobs nearby.

Harrington (1963) brought attention to the shame of "poverty amid plenty" and raised awareness not only of Appalachian poverty but of the invisibility of the poor when they exist in a larger society of greater affluence. Arcury and Porter (1985) observed that long-term, unmitigated poverty such as that found in Appalachia (Adams & Duncan, 1992) destroys aspirations. Especially when it is not pervasive throughout the larger society, it encourages the internalization of a sense of inferiority (Rolland, 1999).

The fact that Appalachia may reflect greater poverty and other problems than the rest of the United States must be attributed to the area's unique history. Appalachians have been ignored, marginalized, ridiculed, and exploited for so long that it should be no surprise if some residents internalize the attitudes projected onto them and consider themselves inferior and undeserving of better treatment, and are unwilling to believe that government or corporate entities, on the rare occasions that they proffered help, could be trusted.

Reflection Exercises

1. What were your perceptions of Appalachia prior to reading this chapter? How did you develop these values and beliefs about the region?

2. What did you learn in elementary and secondary school about the "settling" of the West, Indian "migration," the Whiskey Rebellion, and rural poverty? How did your education confront or support stereotypical images of the Appalachian region?

3. Locate the Appalachian region on a map (http://www.library.appstate .edu/appcoll/maps.html). How large is the Appalachian region? What state is entirely in the Appalachian area? Describe the geographic composition of the Appalachian region. What three impressions did the map have on you?

4. There is no single Appalachia or Appalachian culture; however, numerous stereotypes are associated with the region. Where did these stereotypes come from, and why do they persist? Read

the cited article or other articles pertaining to the region when you consider your response (http://www.appvoices.org/index .php?/frontporch/blogposts/hey_media_lay_of_appalachia).

5. The Appalachian Women's Alliance is a network of women and girls in Appalachian communities who are raising consciousness and self-esteem, sharing leadership and power, developing a collective analysis, creating a common vision, and taking collective action. Visit http://www.appalachianwomen.org and consider what roles social workers could use in support of the alliance.

SOCIAL SERVICE SYSTEM OF APPALACHIA: POOR SERVICES FOR POOR PEOPLE

It is axiomatic in social work that "poor people get poor services." As noted, Appalachia has poor schools, healthcare, and other institutions and additional forms of inferior infrastructure, such as roads, public transportation, trash removal, water and sewer service, high-speed Internet service, and cell phone towers.

Jensen and Royeen (2002) further observed that people who live in rural areas have difficulty accessing services; problems include an inadequate supply of providers, low incomes that create challenges to affordability of services, and significant distances to services and inadequate public transportation (which are further exacerbated by the increasing costs of fuel). Rechovsky and Staiti (2005) further observe that rural residents, because they tend to be older, in poorer health, and less likely to have private insurance, experience greater needs for programs and services than residents of other regions. Rural residents also reflect greater levels of stress and high rates of suicide, alcohol abuse, chronic illness, and disability (Helbok, 2003; Singh & Siahpush, 2002).

Providing services in rural regions is also challenging because rural residents often require outreach and advocacy and value face-to-face communication (Jensen & Royeen, 2002), which are not skills taught to many service providers. In addition, rural service provision especially challenges social workers to avoid inappropriate dual relationships and confidentiality breaches, which present particular difficulties due to the localized nature of rural communities (Helbok, 2003; Nickel, 2004).

Appalachians, even more than most rural residents, highly value independence and perceive any form of reliance on others as weakness, which makes it difficult for them to accept any forms of assistance (Browning, Andrews, & Niemczura, 2000). In addition, Appalachians tend to be fatalistic, believing that they have little control over their lives (O'Brien, 2001), which makes seeking assistance appear to be futile. Add to these experiences the long-term internalization of feelings of being second-class citizens that result from lifelong experiences with inadequate or nonexistent services, and it is not difficult to understand why many Appalachians fail to expect anything more than their current lot in life.

However, poverty, unemployment, low wages, and work in the underground economy should not yield an interpretation that Appalachians are lazy or less law-abiding than other citizens. Indeed, a common drug problem in Appalachia involves prescription drug abuse, and a frequent cause of abuse is unintentional addiction while using prescribed drugs appropriately. These scenarios suggest that Appalachians break the law out of financial desperation, as do many poor people. In addition, one of the common effects of hard physical labor is injury that leads to disability and early, forced retirement—which is yet another contributing factor to the poverty of Appalachia. Interestingly, a recent report by the Appalachian Regional Commission on drug production and use in the area identified Appalachia as the source of considerable methamphetamine production and marijuana farming; however, these drugs are rarely consumed in the region (Zhang, Infante, Meit, & English, 2008).

Reflection Exercises

1. Discuss the phrase "poor people get poor services." What empirical evidence exists to support or refute the axiom?
2. Examine http://www.city-data.com/city/West-Virginia.html and examine Moundsville, West Virginia's demographic composition and annual income. What does this information tell you about the city and the standard of living for its citizens?

3. Consider how Xavier, an international social work student, traveled to a university in the Appalachian region to engage in a community-based effort:

After viewing the video http://viewfromthehill.org/?p=92, Xavier became interested in community organizing. Xavier, raised in a rural community in Spain, saw a relationship between the people of Appalachia, who were described as living in a "colony" in the United States, and his family and neighbors, who resided in a remote and often-forgotten area of southern Spain. Through a social work program in a university located in Appalachia, Xavier was assigned to work with the Appalachian Community Fund (ACF) (http://www.appalachiancommunityfund.org). Since its founding in 1987, ACF has awarded over $5 million for community organizing and social justice work to more than 300 grassroots organizations in Central Appalachia. ACF's motto—Change, Not Charity™—reflects its vision to support social change organizing through partnering and community collaborations. Xavier agreed with this perspective and looked forward to his 3-month internship with ACF.

After flying from Spain and making a flight connection in Washington, DC, Xavier eventually arrived at a small airport in Bluefield, West Virginia. From there he and a member of ACF traveled across mountainous terrain 4 hours by car to War, West Virginia. It was in this small town in southern West Virginia that Xavier would work with teenagers to help prepare them for college admissions. Xavier was surprised to learn that these teens grew up in the sixth poorest area in America, where 49% of all adults in the county dropped out of high school. The economic and educational status of the teens shocked Xavier, who assumed that Americans were wealthy and had immense educational opportunities.

On a daily basis, Xavier tutored teenage girls and boys in math and science. He also organized trips to the county library, assisted with computer classes, and facilitated a weekly book club. When not working with the teens, Xavier played basketball, hiked, and fished at the local lake. In time, he made friends with some residents of War, including one of the students he worked with, Molly. In fact, soon Xavier and Molly began dating, a relationship that Molly's parents were less than pleased with since Xavier was not well known and seemed very "foreign" in terms of his accent, religion, dress, and eating habits.

Xavier enjoyed Molly, knew their relationship probably would be short term, but recognized that he was terribly lonely without her. Members of the ACF told Xavier that people from Appalachia are often wary of "outsiders."

a. Locate Moundsville, West Virginia (http://www.city-data.com/city/Moundsville-West-Virginia.html) and describe the area surrounding the small town. What has been the role of coal mining in the south-ern West Virginia communities like Moundsville and War?

b. What are the social justice issues involved in War, where the teens grew up in the sixth poorest area in America and 49% of all adults in the county dropped out of high school? Given these statistics, what issues face Xavier when he works with teens and parents in their home community?

c. Review information describing the Appalachian Regional Commission (http://www.arc.gov/index.jsp) and list five new facts you learn about the Appalachian area. Given what you have read, are you surprised that Molly's parents are unhappy with her rela-tionship with Xavier?

d. What do you think Xavier should do regarding his relationship with Molly? Is Xavier violating any professional ethics, as defined in Chapter 3, by dating her? If so, explain why. If not, support your position.

4. Xavier is far from home with no community affiliations other than his participation with members of the Appalachian Community Fund. If you were involved with the ACF, what would you do to support Xavier?

5. Xavier's work with teens is designed improve their recruitment and retention into college. Discuss a program evaluation project that could be implemented to measure the outcomes of the tutoring program. What "evidence" would the research project generate?

RACISM AND RACIAL INCLUSION IN APPALACHIA

As you have learned, Appalachia runs the length of the United States from northern New York State to southern Alabama and Mississippi (Drake, 2001). As a result, the racial history of Appalachia spans the states of the abolitionist North and the slaveholding South. The state of Ohio plays a significant role in this history, as it was the Ohio River that separated the slave-owning states from the free states, and it was the Ohio River that was likened to the River Jordan over which biblical slaves fled to freedom (Genovese, 1972).

Southern Ohio, bordered on the east and south by the Ohio River, was heavily settled by Quakers, who purchased land along the river in order to facilitate the escape of enslaved people. Similarly, free blacks settled nearby to assist the escape to freedom (Drake, 2001). However, slave catchers, who hunted escapees for the bounties earned for returning them to their "owners," also lived or hunted in these areas, which discouraged escaped slaves from settling in the region; consequently, most traveled through Ohio to the freedom of Canada (Franklin & Schweninger, 1999).

Appalachia's mountains were not conducive to plantation-style farming, and few Appalachian residents owned slaves, even in slave-owning states. In fact, the only state fully in Appalachia, West Virginia, was formed when it broke from Virginia over secession from the Union during the Civil War (Franklin & Schweninger, 1999). The independent nature of Appalachians make them accepting (or rejecting) of individuals rather than the groups to which they belonged, and as a result, there was initially little animosity between African American and white Appalachians. This began to change, however, at the end of the 19th century, when coal companies treated whites more favorably in order to create a rift between the groups in the hope of thwarting their joint efforts to unionize (Williams, 1985).

By the 1890s, reactions to Reconstruction had caused racial relations to deteriorate throughout the United States. Many Northern states, including Ohio, segregated schools after 1896, and many towns in those states passed "sundown laws" that permitted African Americans to enter certain towns only to work, requiring that they leave before dark. In fact, lynchings were as frequent in Kentucky and Ohio as in Southern states during

Reflection Exercises

1. What is the racial history of the community in which you live? What was its history during the first three decades of the 20th century?
2. The material you just read suggests that there is cultural and racial diversity in the Appalachian region. To understand more fully the influence of African Americans in southern Ohio, review http://www .angelfire.com/oh/chillicothe and http://www.angelfire.com/oh/chilli cothe/people.html, which detail lives, provide pictures, and present relevant history. What does this information tell you about the racial diversity of Appalachia and prevailing attitudes toward people of color? Relate your comments to specific issues of social justice including pay equity, accessibility, and legal rights.

3. What was the Underground Railroad, and how does it relate to Appalachia (http://www.lwfaah.net/oh/gray.htm). Who are the Quakers (http://www.ohiohistorycentral.org/entry.php?rec=2041), and what role did they play in the Underground Railroad?

4. Dionne is a social work major from a university located in the southern portion of the United States. Before agreeing to a field placement in Zanesville, Ohio (http://www.coz.org), Dionne knew little of the Appalachia region other than "hillbilly jokes" and other sarcastic comments regarding the people of Appalachia. However, after reading *Confronting Appalachian Stereotypes* (Billings, Norman, & Ledford, 1999), Dionne began to appreciate the relationship between economic insecurity and migration in the context of his home state, the Appalachian region, and the international scene. Provide a critical summary that weaves together economic insecurity and migration in a geographic area familiar to you.

---

this period (Loewen, 2005). The effort to prevent African Americans from residing in non-urban communities essentially prevented African Americans from residing in most suburbs, smaller towns, and rural areas, and may have been predicated on an unwillingness either to build separate local schools and other public institutions or to integrate the existing ones. As a result, even though the number of African Americans increased in Ohio as well as West Virginia and Pennsylvania, between then and the 1930s, the number of counties with African American residents actually decreased, and to this day, most African Americans reside in the few large cities in these states.

SOCIAL WORK PRACTICE EXAMPLE FROM APPALACHIA

As social workers learn through their classes, social and economic justice can come in many forms. For African American residents of the neighborhood of Coal Run Road, just beyond the Zanesville city limits in Muskingum County, Ohio, in 2004, those forms were hot and cold (Dao, 2004). That was the year that they finally obtained access to clean, treated, running water.

Prior to 2004, many of the residents of Coal Run Road had dug wells, a costly and imperfect solution because the water contained contaminants from local coal plants (*Kennedy et al. v. City of Zanesville et al.*, 2008). Residents who could not afford the considerable up-front costs of digging wells had to have water hauled to even less pristine cisterns—at a cost 10 times that of clean, city water available to white residents nearby (Ludlow, 2003). The local water is so full of sulfur that it runs red and stains clothes that come into contact with it (Suddath, 2008). The new plumbing includes new fire hydrants, which increase safety to all residents and lower their insurance rates (Ludlow, 2004).

It took decades of lawsuits for these residents to gain access to a resource that most U.S. citizens take for granted. East Muskingum County Water Authority officials claimed various causes for the delay: high costs (original estimates of $3 to $4 million were exaggerated, and the final cost was only $730,000); low water pressure (which is common to any mountainous region); lack of jurisdiction (the African Americans who won the lawsuit were able to demonstrate that the Water Authority had provided water over city lines for white residents in 1956 but refused to do so for African American residents); and lack of knowledge of residents' need for water (Ludlow, 2008).

A subsequent lawsuit, which was won and is now under appeal, used Geographic Information System mapping to demonstrate that original water lines had been laid around African American residents' property at far greater expense than it would have cost to run the lines past these homes, thereby permitting those residents to access the treated water (Parnell, n.d.). That lawsuit resulted in compensatory damages of $15,000 to $300,000 per resident, based on both the excessive costs for water that they had paid since 1956 and the pain and suffering that residents had endured between then and 2004, when they finally obtained water service (O'Carroll, 2008; Thompson, 2008).

Most of the refutations of the water company and the governments are ludicrous on their face value, particularly the statement in Muskingum County's appeal that some residents may not have running water "because the residents do not prefer running water" (City of Zanesville, 2008). Even plausible-sounding statements, such as Muskingum County attorney Mark

Landes's idea that "city water . . . is water that is supplied to people who live within the city" (Irwin, 2008), was contradicted by evidence that in 1956, the lines were run beyond Zanesville city limits to white families beyond the boundaries, but not to African American families as near or nearer (Suddath, 2008). However, the one postulation that carries a modicum of truth is the fact that some residents did not continually advocate for water, and in fact, some residents who eventually obtained water as a result of the initial lawsuit benefited despite the fact that they had never been parties to the class action lawsuit (Smyth, 2008). Landes claimed that the only recorded requests for water in the region were a 1973 petition and a 2001 public hearing (Suddath, 2008), although many residents stated that they had made additional verbal and written requests that were ignored.

Given the experience of most Appalachians, and African American Appalachians in particular, is it possible that some residents simply did not believe that any effort on their part would have a positive effect and that such a belief could be so demoralizing as to lead to inaction? Oscar Lewis (1959, 1966) characterized such inaction as reflective of a "culture of poverty," but it may be more appropriate to describe such apathy as a "culture of social and economic injustice" that is so ingrained in community residents that people expect nothing more. Alleging that residents "did not prefer running water" was absurd. Indeed, people in positions of power utilized many tactics to thwart efforts of others to garner needed resources. One way to discriminate against marginalized groups in general, and African Americans in particular, has been to hold the groups to idealist rules and standards, ignore verbal requests altogether, dismiss written requests not filed by attorneys or other authority figures, and make no allowances for failing to meet deadlines; Caucasian applicants were given ready access without strict conformity to guidelines.

The federal lawsuit was prosecuted by Ohio's Attorney General, Nancy Rogers, on behalf of the Ohio Civil Rights Commission. Attorney General Rogers later issued a statement noting "the importance of treating citizens with equal respect, regardless of race," which was reflected by the jury's verdict (Rogers, 2008). It can be hoped that such decisions demonstrate to the African American residents of the region that government attitude is not monolithic and that it, and times, can change.

It should be recognized that Zanesville is a poor Appalachian community. Prior to recent economic and financial woes in America, it had only 25,000 residents, with 1 of every 5 of its families living below the federal poverty line; in 2008 Muskingum County's unemployment rate was 7.4%, substantially higher than the national rate of 5.5% (Smyth, 2008). Furthermore, the civil rights lawsuit, which reflected $11 million in awards, or 15 times the cost of laying water pipes to all of Coal Run Road, was apportioned by the jury according to fault, assessing 55% of the damages against the water company, 25% against the county, and 20% against the city. However, the City of Zanesville recently purchased the water company, making it responsible for 75% of the legal damages (Smyth, 2008).

There is no doubt that the African American residents of Coal Run Road have a right to clean water, and have deserved it since 1956, when it was provided to their white neighbors. Despite appeals to the civil rights lawsuit, there is also little doubt that the rights of the African American residents were violated and that they deserve redress for maltreatment as well as for the costs they accrued during the delay in obtaining just treatment.

Unfortunately, the poverty of the community, coupled with the transfer of ownership of the water company to the city, cause reprimands for this situation to fall squarely on the city's citizens. In addition, mandated local responsibility for past actions could serve as an incentive for attempts to keep African Americans out of small communities in efforts to avoid the need for creating facilities and services. The irony is complete: Those communities that have changed enough to sit juries willing to award damages to victims of past discrimination will suffer to meet obligations, while those communities with citizens unwilling to recognize such injustices will avoid burden from financial retributions.

Perhaps, if federal or state government sources had been willing to provide support to communities that integrated during the first decades of the 20th century, the number and effects of sundown towns would have been diminished. In light of the lack of national support and other past inequities suffered by so many people in rural communities, it would benefit all communities if the federal government were to establish a fund for past discrimination and spread the burden of settlements of civil rights lawsuits more broadly, to a larger cross-section of society better able to absorb costs. Failure to do so will only perpetuate racial distrust, as poor people blame each other for unmet needs and high taxes, rather than blaming people in positions of power that created and benefit from oppressive circumstances and have refused to take responsibility for discriminatory actions. The availability of federal funds in settling lawsuits would support and reinforce community willingness to redress wrongs of the past.

Reflection Exercises

1. The unacceptable situation facing the residents of Coal Run Road caught the attention of a consortium of faculty from universities across the Appalachian region, who organized a community experience for students. The 7 students who enrolled in the 8-week experience lived with families in Coal Run Road. Their academic goal was twofold: (1) to gather community narratives (http://www.springerlink.com/con tent/c618574656467787) from residents of Coal Run Road and (2) to analyze the transfer of ownership of the water company. Consider these questions in the context of the community experience:

   a. Tice (2005) suggests that community narratives can be used to support and build on the strengths of rural communities. Explain how this could be the case in the Coal Run Road project.
   b. Review Chapter 3 on ethical issues and considerations and then identify or design an informed consent form for students collecting community narratives from residents of Coal Run Road to use. What elements are critical to include in the form, and why? What entity(s) should approve of any such form?
   c. In reference to the transfer of ownership of the water company, what are some of the intended and possible unintended consequences of that action?
   d. What aspects of the International Federation of Social Workers (IFSW)/International Association of Schools of Social Work (IASSW) principles and code of ethics, as outlined in Chapter 3, come into play by collecting community narratives and/or analyzing the transfer of ownership of the water company?

2. Students, international and national, might be unfamiliar with the discriminatory practices highlighted by the Coal Run Road community experience.

How would you propose to acquaint students with racial disparities in the United States? Consider http://www.msnbc.msn.com/id/15704759 as a starting point for your suggestions.

3. The students involved with the Coal Run Road project will reside with members from the community. Discuss how this could introduce a positive or negative bias in both the community narratives and analysis of the transfer of ownership of the water company.

4. Given what you know about strife in rural Appalachia and remembering the experience of Xavier, would you recommend that students from other countries participate in a university-based community immersion in Appalachia, such as the one described in reflection exercise 1, or as members of a study tour, as described in Costa Rica in Chapter 7? Identify three potential barriers for participation by students from other countries. Identify three ways in which social work students or social workers from another country could enrich such an educational offering.

SUMMARY

The 21st century has brought new challenges and concerns that may finally refocus attention on the needs of rural communities. National and international homeland security worries related to fears of terrorism and increased awareness of the effects of natural disasters have rekindled interest in the safety of water and food supplies. Rising fuel and food prices have also reawakened federal interest in maintaining and developing local resources and infrastructure, which further support protection of food and water supplies from terrorism.

Relatively new and underutilized, electronic information services and modes of program delivery and provision hold promise for reaching rural, remote, underserved populations and regions. Increased use of technology (cell phones, internet, and teleconferencing) potentially will enable people in small communities to reduce reliance on local service delivery while minimizing long-distance travel (McGinty, Saeed, Simmons, & Yildirim, 2006). Providing better education and training about community resources and enhancing coordination of services in rural areas also stand to affect availability, efficiency, and effectiveness in service provision (Jensen & Royeen, 2002).

However, throughout the world, a strategy traditionally employed by people living in rural regions and struggling with basic needs and employment has been to encourage migration to better, more fertile lands to obtain work and access services. This mentality not only ignores self-determination but also ignores the substantial costs and risks associated with commuting and/or relocation. This tactic also ignores the many advantages to living in rural communities, particularly if they are "homeplaces."

Not only does rural living permit people to offset low wages with home-grown food, but people learn to hunt and fish to augment dietary protein and cut wood for heating. When people have lived in any community for a long time, they develop social ties that provide not only emotional support but practical assistance in times of need (e.g., child care, meal preparation, and transportation). Indeed, when rural residents move from rural to urban areas to obtain employment, they lose informal forms of assistance and often require public services to meet the basic needs that had been informally addressed. In addition, they face new, unfamiliar challenges (e.g., friendship, loneliness, alienation).

Given the economic challenges of the day, countries around the world must discover new and better ways to provide infrastructure and assistance to keep rural communities "alive." For many people in the United States, the need for innovation and creativity to sustain or revive rural well-being could not be more apparent, and Americans can benefit from learning from others. For example, in Europe, it is common in certain areas for people to own country farms that lack nearly all basic services, with the exception of a shed to store tools and supplies to serve a picnic meal. However, in these instances, people have learned to reside in clustered housing, which makes provision of services (e.g., water) and social support more available and practical. As the people of the world learn to live more sustainably (e.g., by using wind, solar, and water to power homes), work-places decentralize and locate closer to residences, and nations learn to respect not only people's physical needs but their longing for familial and community relationships, it is only logical that transformation in modes of living will emerge, it is hoped with an emphasis on addressing needs and providing services in affordable, effective, equitable, and culturally appropriate ways.

REFERENCES

Adams, T., & Duncan, G. (1992). Long-term poverty in rural areas. In C. Duncan (Ed.), *Rural poverty in America* (pp. 63–93). New York: Auburn House.

Arcury, T., & Porter, J. (1985, Summer). Household composition in Appalachian Kentucky in 1900. *Journal of Family History*, 183–195.

Bettman, O. (1974). *The good old days—They were terrible.* New York: Random House.

Billings, D. B., Norman, G., & Ledford, K. (1999). *Confronting Appalachian stereotypes: Back talk from an American region.* Lexington, KY: University Press of Kentucky.

Blauner, R. (1969). Internal colonialism and ghetto revolt. *Social Problems, 16,* 393–498.

Blee, K. & Billings, D. (1996). Violence and local state formation: A longitudinal case study of Appalachian feuding. *Law & Society Review, 30,* 671–705.

Browning, D., Andrews, C., & Niemczura, C. (2000, May). Cultural influences on care-seeking by depressed women in rural Appalachia. *American Journal for Nurse Practitioners,* 22–32.

City of Zanesville. Answer to Kennedy et al.'s amended complaint. C2-03-1047 (D.C. Ohio 2008).

Council on Social Work Education. (2008). *Educational policy and accreditation standards.* Alexandria, VA: CSWE Committee on Accreditation.

Cunningham, R. (1991). *Apples on the flood.* Knoxville: University of Tennessee Press.

Dao, J. (2004, February 17). Ohio town's water at last runs past a color line. *New York Times.*

Drake, R. (2001). *A history of Appalachia.* Lexington, KY: University of Kentucky Press.

Duncan, C. (1992). Persistent poverty in Appalachia: Scarce work and rigid stratification. In C. Duncan (Ed.), *Rural poverty in America* (pp. 111–133). New York: Auburn House.

Duncan, C. (1999). *Worlds apart: Why poverty persists in rural America.* New Haven, CT: Yale University Press.

Erikson, K. (1976). *Everything in its path.* New York: Simon & Schuster.

Fitchen, J. (1998). Rural poverty and rural social work. In L. Ginsburg (Ed.), *Social work in communities* (3rd ed.) (pp. 115–134) Alexandria, VA: Council on Social Work Education.

Franklin, J., & Schweninger, L. (1999). *Runaway slaves: Rebels on the plantation*. New York: Oxford University Press.

Gaventa, J. (1978). Property, coal & theft. In H. Lewis, L. Johnson, & D. Askins (Eds.), *Colonialism in modern America: An Appalachian case* (pp. 141–159). Boone, NC: Appalachian Consortium Press.

Genovese, E. (1972). *Roll, Jordan, roll: The world the slaves made*. New York: Random House.

Gorton, R. (1996). Voices from the mountains. In G. Carawan & C. Carawan (Collators), *Voices from the Mountains* (p. 206). Athens: University of Georgia Press.

Harrington, M. (1963). *The other America*. Baltimore, MD: Penguin.

Helbok, C. (2003). The practice of psychology in rural communities: Potential ethical dilemmas. *Ethics & Behavior, 13*, 367–384.

International Federation of Social Workers and International Association of Schools of Social Work. (2004). *Ethics in social work: Statement of principles*. Bern, Switzerland: Author.

Irwin, K. (2008, August 12). Update: Coal Run, Ohio and the final water aftermath. *New York Times*.

Jensen, G., & Royeen, C. (2002). Improved rural access to care: Dimensions of best practice. *Journal of Interprofessional Care, 16*, 117–128.

Kennedy et al. v. City of Zanesville, et al. C2-03-1047, (D.C. Ohio 2008).

Lee, H. (1969). *Bloodletting in America*. Morgantown: West Virginia University Press.

Lewis, O. (1959). *Five families: Mexican case studies in the culture of poverty*. New York: Basic Books.

Lewis, O. (1966). The culture of poverty. In G. Gmelch & W. Zenner, *Urban life* (pp. 269–278). Prospect Heights, IL: Waveland Press.

Lewis, R., & Billings, D. (1997). Appalachian culture and economic development: A retrospective view on the theory and literature, *Journal of Appalachian Studies, 3*, 3–42.

Linklater, A. (2002). *Measuring America*. New York: Walker & Co.

Loewen, J. (2005). *Sundown towns*. New York: New Press.

Lohman, R. A. (1990). Four perspectives on Appalachian culture and poverty. *Journal of the Appalachian Studies Association, 2*, 76–88.

Ludlow, R. (2003, June 21). Racism colors water service. *Columbus Dispatch*.

Ludlow, R. (2004, February 18). Finally, water has no color. *Columbus Dispatch*.

Ludlow, R. (2008, July 10). Racism ruled, jury finds. *Columbus Dispatch*.

Maslow, A. (1971). *The farther reaches of human nature*. New York: Viking.

McGinty, K., Saeed, S., Simmons, S., & Yildirim, Y. (2006). Telepsychiatry and e-mental health services: Potential for improving access to mental health care. *Psychiatric Quarterly, 77,* 335–342.

Miles, T. (2005). *Ties that bind: The story of an Afro-Cherokee family in slavery and freedom.* Berkeley: University of California Press.

Murolo, P., & Chitty, A. (2001). *From the folks who brought you the weekend.* New York: New Press.

National Association of Social Workers. (2000). *Code of ethics of the National Association of Social Workers,* Washington, DC: Author.

Nickel, M. (2004). Professional boundaries: The dilemma of dual and multiple relationships in rural clinical practice. *Counseling and Clinical Psychology Journal, 1,* 17–22.

O'Brien, J. (2001). *At home in the heart of Appalachia.* New York: Anchor.

O'Carroll, E. (2008, July 14). Black Ohio neighborhood denied water for decades. *Christian Science Monitor.*

Parnell, A. (n.d.). *Maps used in support of the plaintiffs' argument in Kennedy et al. v. City of Zanesville, et al.* Retrieved from the Race Equity Project of Legal Services of Northern California, August 22, 2008.

Precourt, W. (1983). The image of Appalachian poverty, In A. Batteau (Ed.), *Appalachia and America: Autonomy and regional dependence* (pp. 86–110). Lexington, KY: University of Kentucky Press.

Rechovsky, J., & Staiti, A. (2005). Access and quality: Does rural America lag behind? *Health Affairs, 24,* 1128–1139.

Rogers, N. (2008, July 10). *Federal jury finds racial discrimination in Zanesville water case.* Columbus: Attorney General, State of Ohio.

Rolland, S. (1999). Valuing rural community: Appalachian social work students' perspectives on faculty attitudes toward their culture. In I. Carlton-LaNey, R. Edwards, & P. Reid, *Preserving and Strengthening Small Towns and Rural Communities* (pp. 326–334). Washington, DC: NASW Press.

Scott, S. (1995). *Two sides of everything: The cultural construction of class consciousness in Harlan County, KY.* Albany: State University of New York Press.

Segal, E. A., & Bruzy, S. (1998). *Social welfare, policy, programs, and practice.* Itasca, IL: F.E. Peacock.

Shannon, I. (1981). *Southeastern Ohio in depression and war: The disintegration of an area.* Columbus, OH: Ohio State University.

Shapiro, H. (1978). *Appalachia on our mind: The southern mountains and mountaineers in the American consciousness, 1870–1920.* Chapel Hill, NC: University of North Carolina Press.

Singh, G., & Siahpush, M. (2002). Increasing rural-urban gradients in US suicide mortality, 1970–1997. *American Journal of Public Health, 92,* 1161–1167.

Smyth, J. (2008, July 10). Jury: Black neighborhood was denied water service. WTOPNews.com.

Stock, C. (1996). *Rural radicals.* New York: Cornell University Press.

Suddath, C. (2008, July 14). Making water a matter of race. *Time.*

Thompson, K. (2008, August 2.) Appeal to be filed in Coal Run lawsuit. *Zanesville Time Recorder.*

Tice, C. J. (2005). Celebrating rural communities: A strengths assessment. In L. Ginsberg (Ed.), *Social work in rural communities* (pp. 95–107). Alexandria, VA: Council on Social Work Education.

Webb, J. (2004). *Born fighting: How the Scots-Irish shaped America.* New York: Broadway Books.

White, C., & Marks, K. (1999). A strengths-based approach to rural sustainable development. In I. Carlton-LaNey, R. Edwards, & P. Reid, *Preserving and strengthening small towns and rural communities* (pp. 27–42). Washington, DC: NASW Press.

Williams, L. Cited In W. Turner & E. Cabbell (1985), *Blacks in America.* Lexington, KY: University Press of Kentucky.

Wright, W. (1978). The big steal. In H. Lewis, H. Johnson, & D. Askins (Eds.), *Colonialism in modern America: An Appalachian case* (pp. 161–175). Boone, NC: Appalachian Consortium Press.

Zhang, Z., Infante, A., Meit, M,. & English, N. (2008). *An analysis of mental health and substance abuse disparities and access to treatment in the Appalachian region.* Washington, DC: Appalachian Regional Commission and National Opinion Research Center.

CHAPTER

9

Malawi and AIDS: Examining Diversity and Populations at Risk

DIANA ROWAN

The increased spiral of adult deaths in so many countries means that the number of children orphaned each day is expanding exponentially. Africa is staggering under the load. . . . It is now commonplace that grandmothers are the caregivers for orphans . . . but that is no solution. The grandmothers are impoverished, their days are numbered, and the decimation of families is so complete that there's often no one left in the generation coming up behind.

—Lewis (2003)

AIDS ORPHANS: A POPULATION AT RISK

Worldwide, it is estimated that over 15 million children have been orphaned by AIDS. More than 12 million of these orphans live in sub-Saharan Africa, where it is estimated that 9% of all children have lost one or both parents to AIDS (UNAIDS, 2006). More specifically in reference to the focus country of Malawi, the projected number of orphans for 2010 is 1,150,000 children, or 18% of all children (Republic of Malawi, 2005). In 2004, 48% of all orphans in Malawi were orphaned due to HIV/AIDS, with the majority of them being between 10 and 18 years old (Republic of Malawi, 2005).

Eight out of every 10 children in the world whose parents have died of AIDS live in sub-Saharan Africa; thus, this at-risk population is highly concentrated in this region. This chapter details how the AIDS pandemic is affecting orphans in one sub-Saharan country, the Republic of Malawi. The chapter explains the past and current sociopolitical structures and presents a specific example of a social work intervention through a social service agency. Reflective questions and exercises encourage readers to explore their own perceptions and ideas for interventions with this at-risk population and others like it.

PSYCHOSOCIAL IMPACTS ON HIV ORPHANS IN SUB-SAHARAN AFRICA

Children whose parents are living with HIV often experience negative impacts long before they are orphaned. Before their parent(s)' death, they are often the primary caregiver while at the same time they suffer from emotional trauma and neglect. This at-risk population in sub-Saharan Africa also suffers impacts such as lack of access to basic necessities, including shelter, food, clothing, healthcare, and education. In many cases, poverty drives the children to the streets to work, beg, or seek food.

Children orphaned by AIDS have lower school attendance rates than nonorphaned children (Bicego, Rutstein & Johnson, 2003). Out-of-home placement may cause their school enrollment to be interrupted or ended. Even if an orphan finds care with an extended family member, as frequently happens in this region, the guardian may not be able to afford costs associated with school, such as fees and school uniforms. Often orphans seek work instead of education, since they have a need to support ill family members or younger siblings.

Outside of school, AIDS orphans miss valuable life skills and practical knowledge they would have gained from their parents. Without these life skills or basic school education, children are more likely to face serious economic and health problems as they grow older.

As the AIDS virus continues to spread through the countries of sub-Saharan Africa, the number of HIV orphans also grows. Because of the severe nature of the epidemic, the traditional safety net of the extended family is unraveling. Families and communities can barely fend for themselves, let alone care for orphans. In these hard-hit regions, a generation of children is being raised by relatives or is left on their own in child-headed households or on the streets. AIDS has eroded the network of family supports and has overwhelmed the ability of local communities to absorb the costs associated with the death of parents with AIDS. Persistent poverty and medical and funeral costs have stressed the existing framework of social supports. The result is that many of these orphans become vulnerable to abuse and exploitation.

Reflection Exercises

1. Go online and read a recent newspaper article regarding the impact of HIV/AIDS on children. How does the article compare with what you know about HIV/AIDS in and around your community?
2. The Bill Clinton Foundation and the Bill and Melinda Gates Foundation focus on international healthcare, including AIDS. Visit the Web sites of these foundations and ask yourself the question: What role could social work play in the global fight against HIV/AIDS?

OVERVIEW OF MALAWI

Just as an understanding of consumers' families of origin or their early life events is helpful in understanding their dynamics, it is likewise helpful to understand the history of a nation, its people, and its land when seeking to explore its current status. The Republic of Malawi, a landlocked subtropical country situated in southeastern Africa, is roughly the size of the state of Pennsylvania, with a lake the size of Vermont. The Great Rift Valley traverses the country from north to south. In this deep trough lies Lake Malawi, the third largest lake in Africa (U.S. Department of State, 2008). The country's population in 2007 was estimated to be about 13.5 million people. In the southern part of Malawi, which is the focus of this chapter, fluctuations in rainfall there lead to 80% of households being food insecure for at least 3 to 4 months a year (International Fund for Agricultural

Development [IFAD], n.d.). Furthermore, all of Malawi is prone to flush flooding (a flood after a long dry spell that washes soil and organic particulates away) from prolonged torrential rains. With the distribution and consistency of rain being erratic and uneven, the whole of Malawi is also prone to drought (National Adaption Program of Action, 2007).

Malawi is ranked as the world's 13th poorest country with a gross domestic product per capita of US$160. An estimated 65% of rural and 55% of urban people live in extreme poverty, defined as earning less than US$1 a day (United Nations Development Programme, 2006). The nation's economy is predominantly agriculturally based, with tea, tobacco, and sugar being the main exports (Republic of Malawi, 2005). A HIV-positive rate of 14% in Malawi has impacted economic progress.

History of Malawi

Malawi has a lengthy history, with past and recent discoveries of archeological treasures making paleoanthropological field research and study in Malawi an area of international interest. Hominid remains and stone implements dating back more than 1 million years have been identified in Malawi (U.S. Department of State, 2008), and early human remains dating back 50,000 to 60,000 years have been discovered near Lake Malawi. The eyes of the world scientific community focused on the region when paleontologists Louis, Mary, and Richard Leakey conducted excavation work in the area in the 1950s. Stone Age and Iron Age settlements have been found in various parts of the country. From archeological evidence, it has been determined that Bantu peoples moved into the area in the first millennium (Pavitt & Pavitt, 2001).

Jesuit missionaries from Portugal are said to have visited the area of Lake Nyasa (now known as Lake Malawi) in the 17th century (Dolph, n.d.). The stunningly beautiful lake was probably not known to Europeans until Scottish missionary and famous explorer David Livingstone reached its shores in 1859. Livingstone drew European attention to ending the slave trade to the Persian Gulf region, which continued to the end of the 19th century (U.S. Department of State, 2008).

Most of sub-Saharan Africa was colonized by Western European countries. Northern African countries of the Sahara desert region have a different historical path, and many areas have a preponderance of Arabic speakers. The Francophone (areas of the horn and western Africa) and Anglophone (south and eastern Africa) countries of sub-Saharan Africa have welfare systems that reflect the ideologies and basic structures of their former colonial powers (Asamoah, 1995). To understand social welfare provision in modern-day Malawi, one must acknowledge its legacy as an Anglophone country initially settled by the English.

Great Britain proclaimed the land that is now Malawi as the Nyasaland Protectorate in 1891. The 1900s brought a number of unsuccessful attempts by native peoples and colonist descendants to obtain independence from the British. Eventually, a growing group of European- and U.S.-educated African elites became increasingly vocal and politically active. During the 1950s, Nyasaland was joined with Northern and Southern Rhodesia (now Zambia and Zimbabwe) (Dolph, n.d.; U.S. Department of State, 2008). In 1963, self-governing status was granted, and the Nyasaland Protectorate became the Republic of Malawi in 1964. Although independent of Great Britain, the influence of Britain is still identifiable in the contemporary political system (organized in parliament and ministries) and in the provision of social welfare.

Political Scene

The Republic of Malawi has had only three leaders in its postcolonial, independent history. First was President Hastings Kamuzu Banda, who led for three decades, until 1994. He ruled autocratically, arguably dictatorially, and was known to alienate other leaders in the region. This time period was marked by several significant factors and events:

- Sluggish local economy
- Growing foreign debt
- A nonresponse by the government to the 1992 drought, the worst of the century
- An influx of more than 1 million refuges from Mozambique during that country's civil war from 1985 to 1995, and Rwandan and Congolese refugees in 1996

Banda, who originally intended to be president for life, finally bowed to international criticism for his human rights record and rising domestic discontent. He allowed a multiparty election in 1994, and Dr. Bakili Muluzi, leader of the United Democratic Front (UDF) party, was elected as the second president. Muluzi did arguably little to address poverty and the growing HIV problem. The industrialization and infrastructure development that had begun under Banda did not continue; in many cases it deteriorated. Consequently, the urban areas of Malawi are still lined with empty buildings where factories once operated but were closed under the Muluzi regime.

After two terms as president, Muluzi handpicked UDF party presidential candidate Bingu wa Mutharika to succeed him, with the expectation that Muluzi would continue to exert his control over Malawi through a puppet-like leader. In 2004, President Mutharika took office as the third president and abruptly left the UDF party, disavowed his vice president, expressed his Christian faith, and alienated himself from Muluzi, a Muslim, and his parliamentary associates. Mutharika, a former economist, has been very proactive in addressing the severe AIDS epidemic. In 2004, he launched Malawi's first National AIDS Policy, with the goal of improving the provision of prevention, treatment, care, and support services.

Malawi's efforts to overcome poverty, AIDS, and famine are heavily dependent on international donors, with international development assistance totaling about US$400 million a year. In the past, there were concerns about political corruption and mismanagement of funds in Malawi under the direction of Muluzi. When President Mutharika took office in 2004, he vowed a zero-tolerance approach to corruption. Billboards bearing his picture prominently state this promise to the citizens of Malawi along the main roads.

Since 2004, international support for Malawi has increased. Important donors for HIV prevention and treatment include:

- World Bank (US$35 million)
- Global Fund to Fight AIDS, Tuberculosis, and Malaria (US$228 million)
- World Health Organization, which has contributed a supply of ARV (antiretroviral) medicines
- UNAIDS, which has also provided ARV treatments

- USAID (U.S. Agency for International Development) (US$70 million)
- PEPFAR (U.S. President's Emergency Program for AIDS Relief) (US$15 million).

Although Malawi is not one of PEPFAR's 15 focus countries, it still receives $15 million annually for voluntary counseling and testing, condom distribution, and programs to prevent HIV transmission from mother to child (PEPFAR, 2007).

As Malawi progresses in fighting corruption, improving fiscal responsibility, establishing a more transparent and effective judiciary, and nurturing Christian/Muslim dialogue and relationships, foreign aid will likely increase. The United States is the largest contributor to the World Food Program in Malawi, providing over US$100 million in food and emergency assistance. Beyond the formal monetary aid provided to the government of Malawi through PEPFAR and other U.S. initiatives are the numerous nongovernmental organizations organized and operated by U.S. citizens. Their missions are to assist in delivering prevention, treatment, and care services to the HIV-affected population.

Over US$2.9 billion in Malawian foreign debt has been canceled. The Malawian currency, the kwacha, however, is still weak in international markets.

Reflection Exercises

1. The location of a country is significant to its economic and political environments. Go on the Internet and find Malawi on a map (http://www.lib.utexas.edu/maps/africa.html). What strikes you as particularly interesting about Malawi's location in sub-Saharan Africa? What are Malawi's natural resources?
2. Visit the World Health Organization's website (http://www.who.int/en). As you explore the site, list at least five new facts about HIV/AIDS in sub-Saharan Africa and connect the information to social work practice and social welfare policy.
3. Define the term "government transparency" as it applies to Malawi's political system. What features are critical to "transparency" in any government?

4. Take a moment to read http://kristof.blogs.nytimes.com/2008/07/15/maternal-health-in-malawi/index.html, an article on women in Malawi. What impression do you have of life and role expectations for women in that country?

HIV/AIDS-RELATED SOCIAL SERVICE SYSTEMS

Roughly one seventh (14.4%) of the population in Malawi is infected with HIV (Malawi, 2007) with the rate in urban areas as high as 23% (Ministry of Health, 2003). Poverty, famine, and AIDS continue to exacerbate one another. The National AIDS Commission was established in 2001 to oversee AIDS prevention and care initiatives, including programs to provide treatment, increase testing, and prevent mother-to-child transmission of HIV.

Due to the prevalence of HIV/AIDS, a major challenge facing Malawi is the lack of human capital in the workforce. Many people are either caring for family members with AIDS or are suffering from the disease themselves. In many rural areas, medical support is beyond scarce. It is estimated that Malawi has just 1 doctor or nurse per 100,000 people, among the lowest number in the world (Avert, 2008). This has deeply affected farming communities, where access to HIV treatment is very limited. A local official in the Nsanje district was quoted by Associated Press reporter Claire Nullis as saying "We don't have machinery for farming, we only have manpower . . . if we are sick or spend out time looking after family members who are sick, we have no time to spend working in the fields" (Avert, 2008). Not only poor segments of society have been hard hit by the pandemic. In 2000, it was revealed that 28 members of Malawi's parliament had died of AIDS in just four years, and 100 important officers in the cabinet ministries had also died from the virus (Avert, 2008).

The AIDS crisis is one of a multitude of problems facing Malawi, alongside widespread poverty, food insecurity, and other diseases such as malaria. Even with governmental efforts and international non-governmental organizations (NGOs) working at improving access to healthcare, especially provision of ARV treatments, financial and human resource challenges are holding back healthcare improvements. Improvements also are needed in the areas of education and gender equality.

⬛ Reflection Exercises

1. Imagine that 80% of the population you, a social worker in the United States, serve does not have food security for 3 to 4 months a year. Since you cannot change the climate and therefore cannot modify the growing seasons, what are some micro and macro level interventions you could employ to address the issue of hunger?

2. Consider the implications of a political leader turning on those who placed him or her in power. President Bingu wa Mutharika changed his alliance with his political party; how do you think this move affected social welfare provision?

3. What would it be like to live in a country that has existed politically for only 50 years? In the United States, a relatively young country by international standards, Social Security and other policies of the New Deal era are 75 years old. The more recent programs of the Great Society, such as Medicare and Medicaid, are already 50 years old. From a social policy standpoint, how would the relative newness of social programs and procedures impact your social work practice?

4. Visit http://www.dd-rd.ca/site/_PDF/publications/globalization/food/food_malawi.pdf and read one article on policies that address hunger and the right to food in Malawi. What are the key features of the policy, including the intended consequences of the policy initiative?

ORPHANED AND VULNERABLE CHILDREN IN MALAWI

An important feature of Malawi's response to the growing HIV orphan crisis is a governmental strategy that promotes and supports community-based programs. In both rural and urban areas across Malawi, communities are encouraged to develop a variety of ways to cope with the crises of AIDS orphans. In many villages, orphan committees have been established to monitor the situation on a local level and take action in a collective manner.

The government of Malawi has demonstrated an awareness of and commitment to orphans and vulnerable children (OVC). In 2005, President Mutharika launched the National Plan of Action for Orphans and Other Vulnerable Children; its overarching goal is "to facilitate support for care, protection and development of OVC in a coordinated manner in order to provide them with an environment in which they realize their full rights and potentials" (p. 16). The plan aims to increase access to essential services, such as education, healthcare, nutrition, water, and sanitation. The president acknowledged in the foreword of the published plan: "The children of Malawi are under threat. Today's HIV/AIDS pandemic and severe poverty have put at risk the nation and in particular its children" (Republic of Malawi, 2005, foreword).

The plan identifies the typical harmful effects that may be experienced by children, women, and households as a direct result of the HIV/AIDS epidemic. Although these were conceptualized as relevant to Malawi, they are common themes occurring across the heavily infected regions of sub-Saharan Africa.

> *Fragmented households.* Orphaned siblings may not be able to live with one another because they may need to be placed in different households.
>
> *Increased child labor.* An estimated 1.4 million children are working in Malawi, and orphans are at the greatest risk of exploitation. With families' economic limits stretched, the burden of earning essential income falls on the children. In orphan-headed households, they bear the entire responsibility.
>
> *Wife inheritance.* Traditional cultural practices of the widow being inherited by one of her brothers-in-law or her father-in-law often further the spread of HIV/AIDS.
>
> *Property dispossession.* Relatives of a late father or mother may assume control of the house or property, leaving the surviving spouse and children with the option of participating in sexually risky behaviors in order to survive. When both parents die, the orphans may be left homeless and without possessions.
>
> *Increased number of child-headed households.* In African culture, when children are orphaned, the traditional safety net of families is supposed to provide some measure of security. The HIV/AIDS pandemic has taken so many lives that often there are no relatives alive or well enough to assume responsibility for care of orphaned children. Consequently, often these children are forced to assume adult responsibilities, including caring for younger siblings and working to provide income.

Increased risk of HIV infection. In order to ease poverty and cope with food shortages, children have opportunities to engage in commercial sex work, increasing their exposure to HIV and other STIs.

Dropping out of school. Some children, primarily girls, may be denied access to school in order to assume duties at home, including caring for the dying. Once children are orphaned, their new household may not support their right to an education.

Early marriages and pregnancies. To cope with a shortage of resources, families often encourage or force daughters to marry at a young age. The minimum legal age for marriage in Malawi is 18, although 15- to 18-year-olds can marry with familial consent. The median age at first marriages for women is 17.8 years old (International Planned Parenthood Federation, 2006). These young brides are denied access to school in order to assume household responsibilities. Along with early marriage come early pregnancies. Some pregnancies occur outside of the bounds of marriages, and many are the result of sexual abuse.

Increasing number of children living on/off the streets. Urban migration is evident among orphans who without the support of family find their way to the main cities of Lilongwe, Blantyre, Limbe, Mzuzu, and Kasunga in the hope of fending for themselves. An estimated 8,000 children are living without proper shelter and at least one meal a day.

Institutionalized children. Although the culturally preferred method of caring for orphans in Malawi is not in orphanages, the number of children in institutional settings is on the rise. These facilities are seen as a last resort for children, and monitoring and quality control of these facilities are currently inadequate.

Reflection Exercises

1. Review the list of factors just presented that affect orphans and vulnerable children in Malawi. Consider each one carefully and determine if it is a threat to orphans in the United States or other developed countries. Are there other threats to orphans in the United States that are not seen in Malawi?

2. Imagine that you are a child welfare social worker in Malawi. What might be reasonable goals for your work? Might your standards for determining success in interventions differ from those in the United States?
3. We learned that placement in orphanages is not the culturally preferred method of care for orphaned children in Malawi (and indeed in much of Africa). Yet in the United States we see fundraising film clips from international aid organizations raising money for orphanage-based programs. What do you think of this practice?
4. Children orphaned by HIV/AIDS in Africa are a seen as a population at risk. Answer this simple question: At risk of what?

BEST PRACTICES FOR WORK WITH HIV/AIDS ORPHANS IN SUB-SAHARA AFRICA

The world's largest orphan charity, SOS Children's Villages, a United Kingdom–based NGO, operates three orphan programs in Malawi and others in 122 various countries around the world. After surveying experts on the ground, it proposed a list of eight best practices for working with this population-at-risk. Its field workers recommended (n.d.):

1. Targeting the most vulnerable orphans first
2. Providing immediate support for their immediate survival
3. Using a holistic approach to service provision
4. Providing for their material needs
5. Implementing all services at the household level
6. Mobilizing the local community
7. Involving community stakeholders at every step of the process
8. Evaluating all interventions to ensure they remain relevant and effective

SOCIAL WORK HOME VISITATIONS

The next example is fictional yet is a composite of actual contemporary programs, policies, approaches, and interventions utilized by social workers in Malawi.

Mr. G. Y. Kwambiri is a social worker in the Chiradzulu region of southern Malawi. He has been a social worker for 10 years, after receiving his B.A. in social sciences from the University of Malawi. At the time, this was the only institution to offer a four-year degree in social sciences (or social work). Mr. Kwambiri is encouraged, however, because just two years ago a new university was opened on the outskirts of Limbe, a city nearby. The Catholic University of Malawi is scheduled to graduate its first cohort of social workers in two years. Most of these social work students are male, as are most social workers in Africa. Traditionally, women outnumber males only in the nursing and teaching professions (Asamoah, 1995). Mr. Kwambiri told the social sciences faculty that he was interested in supervising a student during the "attachment" semester, or field placement.

Agency

Mr. Kwambiri helps operate an orphans and vulnerable children training and apprenticeship program funded by the International Fund for Agricultural Development, a specialized agency of the United Nations (UN). IFAD funds US$14.8 million toward the total cost of US$16.6 million for the program over a nine-year commitment (International Fund for Agricultural Development [IFAD], n.d.). IFAD's mission is "to empower poor rural women and men in developing countries to achieve higher incomes and improved food security" (IFAD, 2007, para. 4). This UN agency is headquartered in Rome, Italy, but Mr. Kwambiri has never been to the office. He communicates with the funding source through electronic mail, when he has electricity. He is responsible for completing routine evaluations to measure outcomes. Positive outcomes mean extensions in funding. Although the program receives its financial support from the nongovernmental organization (NGO)—IFAD—it also operates under the supervision of the Ministry of Local Government and Rural Development. This means there are additional layers of bureaucracy to work under and more levels of oversight to keep informed. Mr. Kwambiri spends much of his time communicating with all of these systems.

Sustainable Livelihoods Approach

In his formal social work education, Mr. Kwambiri learned that macro system-level interventions at the community level effect more changes than at the micro or mezzo system levels. The program that employs Mr. Kwambiri is based on a specific approach to macro-focused work called the sustainable livelihoods approach (SLA). This new approach to poverty reduction emerged in the 1990s, using a different framework for understanding the complexities of poverty and a different set of principles to guide action to address and overcome poverty (IFAD, 2007). In this framework, people are the main concern, rather than the resources they use or their governments. The guiding principles of the SLA involve people centeredness; holistic thinking; building on strengths and opportunities, rather than problems and needs; promoting micro-macro links; encouraging broad partnerships; and aiming for sustainability. A community's vulnerability is assessed based on economic, political, and technological trends, and its assets are counted by looking at natural resources, access to education and healthcare, sources of credit, and networks of social support. Additionally, shocks, such as epidemics, natural disasters, and civil strife, are factored in, along with seasonal factors, such as prices, weather, and employment opportunities (IFAD, 2007).

The sustainable rural livelihoods approach acts on various levels of systems in a coordinated fashion called vertical integration. Micro-level interventions occur at the household level and are coordinated simultaneously with mezzo-level approaches, such as improvement in communication and transportation systems. Macro-level approaches are addressed in larger community systems and in national policy arenas (Blackshaw, 2004).

Rural Livelihoods Support Program

Mr. Kwambiri works for a program that provides training and apprenticeship opportunities to OVC; about three-quarters of its clients are children orphaned by HIV/AIDS. When orphans have no extended family with which to stay, they can end up in child-headed households. While this is not ideal, it has the advantage of allowing sibling groups to remain living together, supported and cared for by the oldest child. The training and apprenticeship program provides older orphans help in securing training in a variety of trades, which often results in a long-term, secure livelihood. In Mr. Kwambiri's program, children receive instruction in trades such as carpentry, tinsmithing, microbusinesses, masonry, tailoring, poultry farming, and construction. His responsibility is to monitor the outcomes of the program, to see if children who have completed the training become gainfully employed. He also handles referrals to the program. As he is educated, Mr. Kwambri is responsible for all of the administrative work, while less educated workers supervise the training. Needless to say, Mr. Kwambi is very busy and regrets that he does not have as much time as he would like to spend in case management activities with the children and villagers.

When working in the field, Mr. Kwambiri speaks Chichewa, one of the two official languages of Malawi. Chichewa is spoken by over half of the population in Malawi while English, the other official language, is routinely spoken by upper-class citizens in government and universities, and is used on public signage. The majority of middle- and lower-class and rural people speak one of seven tribal languages. Mr. Kwambiri interfaces with eight or more tribal groups on a regular basis.

Mr. Kwambiri knows that for tribal families, tribal affiliation is often more significant than their nationality. In this age of transportation and roads, people sometimes move to a different location to find work or land to farm. When a person retires or reaches old age, for example, the custom is to return to the land of one's tribe.

Typical Workday

After a breakfast of tea, biscuits, and fresh-picked bananas, Mr. Kwambiri dresses in trousers, shirt, and necktie and drives to his office on the outskirts of Limbe, a city that has paved roads and clean neighborhoods. His office is in a concrete block building equipped with electricity and running water. The frequent and recurring problem, however, is that the power supply is unreliable. Instability in the power grid makes it necessary to have battery backup for his desktop computer. Without electricity, there are no lights and no power for the pump that creates water pressure. Therefore, the ceiling fans are idle, the sink is dry, and the computer screen is dark.

Mr. Kwambiri checks his appointment book and sees that he is due to visit three families that require follow-up services. All three families live in the Namadidi village area on the outskirts of town. Mr. Kwambiri gets into his personal vehicle to make the trip. Malawi was colonized by the English, so automobiles have steering wheels on the right side and driving is on the left side of the road. Mr. Kwambiri passes through a few intersections with traffic managed by roundabouts. Throwbacks to the days of English colonization, these traffic circles eliminate the need for traffic lights. After only a few miles, the paved road soon turns into packed red sand. Mr. Kwambiri reduces his speed dramatically, as it is the rainy season and the road is deeply rutted and potholed. In sub-Sahara Africa, torrential rains often produce flash floods, which wash out bridges and large portions of unpaved roads, making them impassible for months at a time.

After a slow, rough ride, Mr. Kwambiri finally arrives at the Namadide village in the Chiradzulu district. He is welcomed by a group of young girls selling handfuls of peanuts. As he passes the girls, Mr. Kwambiri spots Saliza, a 15-year-old orphaned girl, at the *boho*, or community water pump. Saliza is pumping water to bathe her two younger sisters, ages 2 and 6. "Muli bwanji?" he asks, How are you? "Ndiri bwino," she replies, indicating she is fine and well today. Mr. Kwambiri stops to speak with Saliza regarding her failure to complete the apprenticeship training in carpentry. "I don't want to be a carpenter," she tells him in Chichewa, "I want to be a wife." "But as a carpenter you can earn money for food by making coffins and tables," he explains. "I will find a man," Saliza replies, "who is HIV positive and who will marry me and help care for these little ones. If he is HIV positive, he won't mind that I am, too." Saliza attended primary school until last year, when her father and mother both died from AIDS. Now she has sold her school uniform for a kitchen knife to use to prepare food for herself and her sisters.

Mr. Kwambiri makes a note to ask the wife of the area's tribal headman to speak to Saliza about her goals. He is concerned that the next time he sees Saliza, she will be pregnant. Unfortunately, his time is limited. Much of his job involves the macro-level interventions of checking on outcomes of programs, securing funding and working to expose corrupt or unskilled staff. When he can, however, he tries to intervene on a micro level to help effect change in the lives of the HIV/AIDS orphans. The frustrating part is that sometimes Mr. Kwambiri sees orphans make what he believes are shortsighted or wrong decisions, but as a social worker he understands and respects self-determination, even for children like Saliza.

A short walk brings him to the doorstep of Ndale, whose one-room home is made of masonry bricks, with an open square on two sides for a door and window, packed dirt floor, and a thatched roof. Ndale is a proud man who worked for years as a chimanga (maize) farmer. Now at the age of 42 he is dying of AIDS. Ndale realizes that even with AIDS, he is actually fortunate since the average life expectancy in Malawi is 41 years. The oldest of seven children, Ndale is the only sibling still alive. He speaks to Mr. Kwambiri about enrolling his oldest son in the apprenticeship training program. "Teach him to earn money, because I am too sick to get up and show him how to be a man." Ndale is very underweight, weak, and he knows that his life will be over in a short while. He was on antiretroviral therapy for a while, when an NGO funded by a European aid organization was active in the area. But Ndale's supply of medication was interrupted, and now he has developed drug resistance. Consequently, the affordable ARV treatments that are currently available to him would likely be ineffective.

Mr. Kwambiri fills out the necessary paperwork on his clipboard with Ndale's 13-year-old son Azibo, who has been in primary school for six years and is literate. However, through elementary testing procedures, Mr. Kwambiri determines that Azibo's math skills are too weak for a building apprenticeship. "If you can't enumerate, you can't do the calculations necessary for building," Mr. Kwambiri explains. As an alternative, Mr. Kwambiri suggests a placement with a chicken farmer. "You'll learn about layers and fryers," he explains to the boy. Ndale lifts his head from his cot on the side of the room and raises his hand, as if to concur.

Mr. Kwambiri's last stop in the village is at the home of Sabola, whose home is one room constructed with corrugated metal and grass thatch. Sabola is a recent graduate of the orphan training program, and Mr. Kwambiri is stopping by to invite him to be an instructor for orphans interested in micro business. "But I am only 17! I should not teach so soon," Sabola says. Mr. Kwambiri explains that because there is a missing generation due to AIDS deaths, there is a shortage of men to hire to teach the orphans. "We need you and the pay is good," he explains. Mr. Kwambiri knows that Sabola has recently married a 15- or 16-year-old girl who has a young child. She is still breast-feeding the child and appears to be pregnant with another.

Sabola is eventually enticed by the teaching offer and the thought of a steady salary. At 17, Sabola realizes that he will soon be responsible for himself, his young wife, children, and his wife's siblings. It is the custom that extended family members support each other, since the government is ill equipped to do so.

Mr. Kwambiri is offered a meal of mango, rice, and pumpkin leaves by Sabola and his wife. He stays to eat and drink chombe tea, a traditional English beverage, knowing that sharing a meal will help solidify a relationship with Sabola, his new micro business instructor.

After a bumpy, dusty ride back to the office, Mr. Kwambiri completes the paperwork necessary for reimbursement for the petrol he used by taking his personal vehicle. The funding resources are not always reliable, so he tries to submit his reimbursements promptly. The power has not yet been restored, and the air is stagnant and hot. Mr. Kwambiri mops the sweat from his face with a cloth and turns his attention to a letter he is writing to a building supply company in a wealthier neighboring country. One of the main challenges Mr. Kwambiri faces with the OVC training program is adequate start-up capital. There is demand in the marketplace for the skills the orphans gain, such as masonry, tailoring, and carpentry. What the children lack when leaving the apprenticeship program are the tools and materials of their trade. For example, one needs nails and planks to open a coffin workshop; another, a foot-powered sewing machine and yardage to make clothing. As of yet, Mr. Kwambiri has not found a solution to this perplexing problem.

Before the sun sets, Mr. Kwambiri heads home for the evening. He collects his clipboard and keys and rises from his desk chair. Mr. Kwambiri steadies himself for a moment and waits for a wave of dizziness to pass. Over the last few months, Mr. Kwambiri has been experiencing increased fatigue, weight loss, and a persistent cough. With a sense of reluctance and fear, Mr. Kwambiri knows he has put it off as long as possible; tomorrow he must be tested for HIV.

Reflection Exercises

1. Step outside of the U.S. framework for social work practice. Think about social work practice in a developing country. How would lack of electricity and running water and poor sanitary conditions impact both consumers and the working environment of social workers? How might these shortages affect day-to-day procedures for carrying out tasks and expectations?

2. Social work involves linking resources and mobilizing the community. How often do social workers in your country travel from place to place within a community or city to conduct their practice? How might social work practice be affected by the impassibility of roads and the lack of other reliable infrastructure, such as mail and telephones?

3. Review the description given previously of the sustainable livelihoods approach (SLA). What similarities does SLA share with practice from a strengths perspective and the ecological perspective?

4. Critique the manner in which Mr. Kwambiri engaged consumers in this case example. What elements of culture were used in his practice?

5. Visit http://web.worldbank.org/WBSITE/EXTERNAL/COUNTRIES/ AFRICAEXT/MALAWIEXTN/0,,menuPK:355878~pagePK:141159~ piPK:141110~theSitePK:355870,00.html and list at least three strategies the Malawi government, in conjunction with the World Bank, has implemented to improve the livelihood of it citizens. What values and principles are embedded in the strategies?

6. Would you like to work with Mr. Kwambiri? Why or why not?

SOCIAL WORK ETHICS

In 2004, the International Federation of Social Workers (IFSW), in concert with the International Association of Schools of Social Work (IASSW), identified four areas of challenge that appear consistent for social workers across the world:

1. Social workers often are in the middle of conflicts in loyalty.

2. Social workers must balance between being helpers and controllers.

3. Conflict exists between protecting the interests of individuals versus the needs of society.

4. Resources in society are limited. (IFSW, 2004).

As seen in this example, practicing social work in a developing country carries with it the burden of working with limited resources in an environment with severe levels of need. Mr. Kwambiri could not address the medical needs of the family he interfaced with, due to a lack of resources. He also was torn between spending time administratering the program and counseling the orphans.

The IFSW lists these principles addressing social workers' respect for human dignity:

- Respecting the right to self-determination
- Promoting the right to participation
- Treating each person as a whole
- Identifying and developing strengths

It further addresses promotion of social justice by social workers:

- Challenging negative discrimination
- Recognizing diversity
- Distributing resources equitably
- Challenging unjust policies and practices
- Working in solidarity (IFSW, 2004)

Does Mr. Kwambiri's work serve an illustration that social work practice in Malawi follows these guiding ethical principles? How might the lack of formal social work education contribute to possible breaches of ethical premises?

Reflection Questions

1. Cultural relevance is an important factor when assessing the value of a program or policy. In sub-Saharan Africa, child-headed households are common. In your opinion, how appropriate would Mr. Kwambiri's training program for orphans be in other nations of the world impacted by HIV/AIDS? Explain your response in the context of the ethical principles defined in Chapter 3.

2. Typically, what is the position of child protective service workers regarding children independently raising their siblings? Do international child labor laws support the underlying philosophy of Mr. Kwambiri's training program? Discuss how a country's political, economic, and social systems impact the policy and intervention strategies.
3. According to the NASW and IFSW/IASSW codes of ethics as presented in Chapter 3, would it be ethical for you to work for a program that encourages child-headed households and child labor?
4. Does Mr. Kwambiri practice from a strengths perspective? Explain your response by using details from the case example.

SUMMARY

Malawi, like many nations of the world, has few trained social workers, limited educational programs, and no credentialing or licensing body. The dearth of professionals is further complicated by the multiple layers of bureaucracy present in human service agencies and government offices. In Malawi, programs are funded and supervised by collaborative groups consisting of various funding sources and government ministries, each with an agenda. Corruption and the diversion of scarce resources cause frustration for social workers and consumers invested in making positive changes.

Like their neighbors in other sub-Saharan countries, Malawians are waging a battle against the scourge of HIV/AIDS. As the demand for HIV/AIDS prevention, treatment, and care increases, the role of social workers and other human services workers must be enhanced to meet the societal needs. Thus, the greatest challenges facing Malawi are the lack of human resources and overall capacity. When designing a national and international plan of action, one must make an effort to keep the faces of vulnerable Malawians in mind.

REFERENCES

Avert: Averting HIV and AIDS (2008). *HIV & AIDS in Malawi*. Retrieved January 24, 2008, from http://www.avert.org/aids-malawi.htm.

Asamoah, Y. (1995). Africa. In T. D. Watts, D. Elliott, & N.S. Mayadas (Eds.), *International handbook on social work education* (pp. 223–239). Westport, CT: Greenwood Publishing Group.

Beard, B. J. (2005). Orphan care in Malawi: Current practices. *Journal of CommunityHealth Nursing, 22*(2), 105–115.

Bicego, G. Rutstein, S., & Johnson, K. (2003). Dimensions of the emerging orphan crisis in sub-Saharan Africa. *Social Science and Medicine, 56*, 1235–1247.

Blackshaw, U. (2004). Sustainable rural livelihoods and the Chars Livelihoods Programme: Progression or new departure? Chars Organisational Learning Paper, Bangladesh.

Dolph, B.H. (n.d.). *Culture of Malawi.* Retrieved March 18, 2008, from http://www.everyculture.com/Ja-Ma/Malawi.html.

International Federation of Social Workers. (2004). *Ethics in social work: Statement of principles.* Adelaide, Australia: Author. Retrieved March 4, 2008, from http://www.ifsw.org/en/p38000324.html.

International Fund for Agricultural Development. (2007). *Sustainable livelihoods approach (SLA).* Retrieved March 14, 2008, from http://www.ifad.org.

International Fund for Agricultural Development. (n.d.). Rural livelihoods support programme. Retrieved March 18, 2008, from http://www.ifad.org/english/operations/pf/mwi/i565mw/index.htm.

International Planned Parenthood Federation. (2006). *Report card: HIV prevention for girls and young women.* [Brochure]. London: Author.

Lewis, S. (2003). UN Secretary-General's envoy for HIV/AIDS in Africa: Opening address of the XIIIth International Conference on AIDS and STIs in Africa, Nairobi, Kenya.

Malawi. (2007). In *The Columbia Electronic Encyclopedia* (6th ed.). New York: Columbia University Press.

National Adaptation Program of Action. (2007). *Improving Malawi's preparedness to cope with droughts and floods.* Retrieved April 13, 2008, from http://www.napa-pana.org/private/modules/knowledgebox/io/file.php?entry=893&field=22.

Pavitt, N., & Pavitt, N. (2001). *Africa's Great Rift Valley.* New York: HNA Books.

Republic of Malawi. (2005). *National plan of action for orphans and other vulnerable children in Malawi, 2005–2009.* Lilongwe, Malawi: Author.

SOS Children's Villages. (n.d.). *AIDS Africa Best Practices.* Retrieved April 14, 2008, from http://www.soschildrensvillages.org.uk/aids-africa/best-practice.

UNAIDS. (2006). *The impact of AIDS on people and societies*. (Report on the global AIDS epidemic: Joint United Nations Programme on HIV/AIDS). Geneva, Switzerland.

United Nations Development Programme. (2006). *Basic human development data on Malawi*. Retrieved April 14, 2008, from http://www.undp.org .mw/discover_mw.html.

United States President's Emergency Plan for AIDS Relief (PEPFAR) (2007). *2007 Country profile: Malawi*. Retrieved March 18, 2008, from http://www .pepfar.gov/pepfar/press/81881.htm.

U.S. Department of State. (2008). *Bureau of African Affairs: Background note: Malawi*. Retrieved March 18, 2008, from http://www.state.gov/r/pa/ei/ bgn/7231.htm.

10

Peru: A Focus on Individual Practice

Blanca M. Ramos, Mery L. Botton, and
Gary A. Wright

Peru is a place of brilliant hand-woven textiles and exuberant
celebrations, exotic animals, and fascinating peoples.

—Schlecht (2006, p. 5)

Social work practice worldwide is increasingly being shaped by current global trends that differentially impact on social welfare and
human service delivery. These trends include major economic and political changes, increased international social and economic interdependence, and an unprecedented migration of people who uproot to seek
employment or as political or economic refugees (Cox & Pawar, 2006;
Dolgoff & Feldstein, 2007; Estes, 1992; Ramos & Briar-Lawson, 2004).

The authors of this chapter thank the Centro Latinoamericano de Trabajo Social
(CELATS) for facilitating and inspiring the creation of an agency-based example
presented in this chapter. Deep appreciation and respect are extended to the women
who day after day diligently staff the *comedores populares* in Peru.

As global forces interact with individual historical and sociodemographic characteristics, the nature and scope of social work practice will vary across societies and countries. As a result, social workers in a given region or country may offer differential responses to seemingly similar universal social problems.

In the Latin American region, political turmoil, globalization, and deep economic crises have contributed to social unrest, conflict over human rights, and substantial inequality in the distribution of wealth and services (Minujin, 1995; Queiro-Tajalli, 1997; Ramos & Briar-Lawson, 2004). Social movements and indigenous activists concerned with the need to empower the most vulnerable have challenged social workers to shift their practice approach from "one that works on behalf of others and thereby represents their voice, to one that works alongside others who speak for themselves" (Paranda, 2007, p. 560). It is against this backdrop that social work practice takes place in Peru.

This chapter offers insight into how social work practice is implemented in Peru. It begins with an overview of social work practice as a foundation area in the context of social work education in the United States, followed by a brief discussion of the international context of social work practice. We continue with a snapshot of the country of Peru focusing on its sociopolitical history, sociodemographic profile, and ethnocultural dimensions that shape social work practice. An example for illustration and thoughtful analysis is provided. Potential ethical issues and dilemmas are discussed.

SOCIAL WORK PRACTICE FOUNDATION: SOCIAL WORK PRACTICE AND SOCIAL WORK EDUCATION IN THE UNITED STATES

In the United States, the Council of Social Work Education (CSWE), the accrediting body for professional social work academic programs, requires foundation curricula that prepare students for practice from a generalist perspective. As such, social work practice content is focused on knowledge and skills for intervention at multiple levels of human systems, including individuals, families, groups, organizations, and communities. Social work students are taught systems and ecological theories, the strengths perspective, practice-relevant research, advocacy, policy leadership, and a broad range of skills that follow an implicit problem-solving model. Master's of social work programs also offer specializations or concentrations for advanced practice organized by specific populations, problem areas, fields of practice, intervention methods, or practice contexts (Council on Social Work Education, 2001; Fortune, 2006).

The CSWE accreditation standards also mandate foundation curricula that include content related to diversity with an emphasis on vulnerable and at-risk populations. As a result, all practice courses must incorporate information on populations that have historically experienced oppression and on social and economic justice, including those that are distinguished by race, ethnicity, culture, religion, and/or national origin (CSWE, 2001; Ramos & Melecio, 2006).

Content related to immigration and recently arrived immigrants are sometimes taught in diversity-focused or specialized courses. Furthermore, reflecting the international nature and globalization of contemporary social work education and practice, CSWE requires that students be prepared to "recognize the global context of social work practice" (CSWE, 2001). Typically, international social work content is infused throughout the curriculum, in specialized courses, or both. Cox and Pawar (2006) further suggest that every course in the curriculum should include some specific international content. The internationalization of curricula has been one of the most fundamental changes in U.S. social work education (Estes, 1997).

INTERNATIONAL CONTEXT OF SOCIAL WORK PRACTICE

The far-reaching impact of global interconnectedness on human needs and human rights affords contemporary social workers diverse opportunities to practice within an international context. Consistent with the profession's long history of involvement in the global community, social workers, more than ever before, can play a pivotal role in addressing social problems that transcend national boundaries, such as mass population displacement and forced migration. Extreme poverty, war, natural disasters, political or religious persecution, and globalization are contributing to the large-scale movements of people around the world. For example, some of the dramatic social and cultural changes associated with globalization have had negative consequences on the livelihoods and survival strategies of indigenous peoples and the rural poor in some areas of the world, particularly Latin America. Large numbers of peasants have been forced to migrate from rural to urban areas and to other countries seeking jobs and better economic and social conditions (Ramos & Briar-Lawson, 2004). Social workers concerned with the welfare and survival of these dislocated populations can help mitigate their multiple social needs and facilitate their psychosocial adjustment to a new environmental setting.

For the United States, this pressing global concern translates primarily into an unprecedented influx of immigrants from the Latin American region. As a result, social workers and their agencies are increasingly called on to provide services to this population and to advocate on their behalf. To increase their effectiveness, practitioners must provide these services with cultural responsiveness and incorporate throughout the helping process factors related to the clients' country of origin, such as those that prompted the migration and predeparture, transit, and resettlement experiences.

Social work practice with immigrants is crucial to gain a clear understanding of the continuous interconnectedness between the clients' country of origin and the United States. In present-day immigration, clients often maintain ties to their countries of origin through economic and other type of relationships (Drachman & Paulino, 2004; Healy, 2004). Healey states, "[T]he international dimensions of social work with immigrants and refugees offers opportunities to improve practice and enhance the relevance of international social work to the profession" (p. 50). Cox and Pawar's (2006) integrated framework for international social work practice, which incorporates the global, human rights, ecological, and social development perspectives, is particularly relevant.

U.S. social workers interested in international practice in the field of displacement and forced migration can travel to Latin America and join local efforts to address the needs of the growing numbers of indigenous populations who have been forced to leave their homes and communities. In general, practitioners can draw on their own professional repertoire of knowledge, theories, and skills, but the way in which these are implemented and the nature and scope of practice in the host country will most likely vary, as social workers in Latin America may offer differential responses to seemingly similar universal social problems. Hence, it is imperative to keep an open mind, recognizing the Western roots of their social work training, which may not always be applicable to the host country's sociocultural traditions and realities.

The remainder of this chapter provides a glimpse into how social work practice is defined and implemented in Peru, a prominent Latin American country. An example illustrates international practice in the field of displacement and forced migration, as Peruvian social workers address some of the most basic needs among indigenous people who have experienced displacement and forced migration.

Reflection Exercises

1. Identify how international content is infused in your educational curriculum. What are some of the overriding considerations or premises guiding the inclusion of international content in your program's curriculum? Are specific courses dedicated to international content offered with the social work program or from other discipline-based departments? What are the advantages and disadvantages of course work offered outside of social work?

2. Even with the economic downturn experienced in the United States during 2008 and 2009 (e.g., stock market and banking problems), do you anticipate an appreciable decline in immigration from countries in Latin American (e.g., Peru) over the next decade? How many Peruvians live in your country and area? Is there an appreciable number of people from Peru in your community? Why or why not?

3. Are the terms "displacement" and "forced migration" familiar to you? With your classmates, attempt to identify examples of displacement and forced migration. What common elements do people who are displaced and forced to migrate to another geographical location experience?

OVERVIEW OF PERU

History

Peru, the third-largest country in South America, is approximately three times the size of the state of California. The Andes Mountains, which run parallel to the Pacific Ocean, divide Peru into three distinct geographic regions: the *costa* (desert) areas of the Pacific coast, the *sierra* (rugged range of mountains) or the central high sierra of the Andes Mountains, and the *selva* (Amazon rain forest), contributing to a great diversity in topography, geography, climate, and culture (U.S. Department of State, 2008).

The Instituto Nacional de Estadística e Informática (INEI) estimates Peru's population at 28 million, with 75% concentrated in urban areas; approximately 30% reside in Lima, the nation's capital (2006). The population is multiethnic, with 45% indigenous, 37% "mestizo" (a mixture of indigenous and Caucasian background), 15% European, and 3% African, Japanese, Chinese, and other ethnic heritages. Spanish is the principal language, although indigenous languages such as Quechua and Aymara are also officially recognized. Most Peruvians are Roman Catholic (85%); about 15% are Protestant, a number that is increasing rapidly, particularly among the urban poor and some indigenous populations (INEI, 2001; U.S. Library of Congress, 1993).

Peru has a rich traditional indigenous past extending back more than 10,000 years. Its *Norte Chico* was one of the oldest civilizations in the world, culminating with the Inca empire and its well-developed sociopolitical and economic systems exemplified by Machu Picchu, named one of the new seven wonders of the world (Wikipedia, 2009). With the arrival of the Spanish in the early 16th century, Peru rapidly became a crown jewel in the Spanish colonial empire, acquiring a prominent place in the New World due to its abundant plant, animal, and mineral resources. Unfortunately, by the end of Spanish colonialism, most of the natural resources had been depleted, its successful pre-Columbian social and economic systems had been largely dismantled, and a period of anarchy, internal wars, revolts, and social disorganization followed the nation's 1821 independence.

Peru has experienced democratically elected governments, military regimes, and the presence of one of the most violent radical guerrilla groups in the world. These continuous political upheavals have been accompanied by periods of stability and socioeconomic upswings followed by downturns marked by economic mismanagement, authoritarian abuses, and social and political unrest, where citizens lived in terror and human rights were severely violated. The painful experiences associated with terrorism have left long-lasting scars at all levels of Peruvian society today. Globalization and other international events have further contributed to the socioeconomic and political realities of modern Peru. Currently, Peru has a democratic government.

During the past two decades, Peru has experienced sustained economic growth due primarily to export revenues, with mineral exports generating over half of the nation's total earnings (U.S. Library of Congress, 1993). Worldwide, Peru ranks second in silver production, sixth in gold and copper, and contributes significantly to the world's supply of lead and zinc. More recently, the Peruvian economy has also made important gains resulting from increased investment and international trade agreements such as the U.S.–Peru Free Trade Agreement that is currently in effect.

Despite several encouraging economic advances and increasing safety and stability, the socioeconomic profile for Peru is disturbing, based on available statistics and population estimates. The poverty level is nearly 50%, and over half of the population lives on less than US$2 a day, which is significantly below the poverty line (U.S. Agency for International Development [USAID], 2008; U.S. Library of Congress, 1993). The average head-of-household income is about US$2,100, and this figure does not reflect the large numbers that endure extreme economic deprivation. Many Peruvians, particularly those residing in marginal-urban and rural areas, lack electricity, clean drinking water, and adequate housing and sewage control (Diaz, Drumm, Ramirez-Johnson, and Oidjarv, 2002; U.S. Library of Congress, 1993).

One of the major challenges for any government in Peru is to address effectively the profound socioeconomic disparities that exist across its three geographic regions, particularly between the relatively more prosperous costa and the remote sierra. Throughout the country, indigenous populations have experienced alienation and inequality based on racial and ethnic heritage dating back to the arrival of the light-skinned

⟨✎ Reflection Exercises

1. Peru is a country divided by geographical region, social-economic disparities, and cultural traditions. What kinds of considerations should be made when working with a person from Peru? List five questions you would consider asking a consumer of services from Peru in an assessment.
2. Given Peru's natural resources (e.g., metals) and popularity as a tourist destination, why has prosperity not spread throughout the nation?
3. Visit www.peruvianembassy.us, and examine the Web site for visitor information and warnings. Where is the U.S. embassy located? If you were traveling in a remote region of the country, what would be your plan of action during political unrest?
4. Racial and ethnic diversity in Peru can be viewed as both an asset and a challenge. Whom might one rely on for on-the-ground education and learning about racial and ethnic diversity? Examine formal and informal sources of information.

---

conquistadores nearly 500 years ago. European-indigenous upper-class mestizos continued the pervasive prejudicial attitudes and discriminatory behaviors that are still deeply embedded in the fabric of Peruvian society (Ramos et al., 2006).

By Western standards, Peru is considered a developing nation. This determination is made based on the developmental level of a country as measured by its industrial base, income, literacy, life expectancy, and educational attainment. As such, a once well-developed, complex society now finds itself in the process of social and economic redevelopment.

Social Services in Peru

As is the case in many other developing nations, the multiple social problems facing contemporary Peru are rooted primarily in its striking poverty and social and economic inequalities. For example, some of the poorest communities in Peru are the home of indigenous populations who often can barely meet their basic food and health needs for survival. Starvation and chronic malnutrition are pervasive and take a toll on health and well-being, particularly with child development and infant and maternal mortality, among the highest in Latin America. A lack of adequate sanitation services contributes to high rates of chronic health conditions and death rates from infectious diseases. Disparities are endemic not only in health status but also in access to basic primary healthcare (Foundation for Sustainable Development, 2008; U.S. Library of Congress, 1993). Furthermore, the forgotten, isolated nature of some remote areas in the jungle and highlands facilitates the transmission of HIV/AIDS, illegal growth of coca and logging, and drug trafficking, and provides a breeding ground for terrorist groups (USAID, 2008).

Throughout Peru's history, several governments have attempted to address poverty and social inequality, and their resulting social problems, primarily through decentralized governance and new social and economic policies. These include expanding policy that regulates the social welfare system in Peru to increase access to basic social services within available resources (U.K. Department for International Development, 2003). A number of public social agencies overseen by specific government units target populations in extreme poverty and the most vulnerable groups. For example, the Ministry for Women and Social Development (MIMDES) has in place various programs, benefits, and services for women and children that offer protection against family violence and attend to food and nutritional needs.

International organizations and some developed countries, such as the United Kingdom, Germany, Switzerland, and the United States, also provide financial and other types of resources for social programs delivered primarily through nongovernmental organizations (NGOs). The focus of these programs includes social development, economic growth, education, health, water sanitation, nutrition, and gender issues (U.K. Department for International Development, 2003). Yet, given the magnitude, longevity, and complexity of the social challenges, scare resources, and shrinking social welfare budgets, success has been limited, and great numbers of Peruvians experience multiple social needs that require immediate social services. These distressing factors provide the context in which social work practice takes place in Peru.

Social workers in Peru are highly trained professionals equipped with the knowledge, values, and skills to promote the welfare of the most disenfranchised sectors of society. Their educational training, drawn from social work and the social sciences, prepares social workers to contribute to the betterment of social and human conditions through education, community organizing, and social action. Most social work professionals have earned a bachelor's degree with a concentration in social work. Some social workers hold a master's degree in a related discipline. Peru's higher institutions do not offer master's programs in social work.

The accreditation body for social work education in Peru requires from practitioners an authentic vocation toward serving society, an ability to establish relationships with the areas of the country with the greatest need for social services, and inquisitiveness for understanding the nature of social problems, their causes, and possible solutions. Respect for universal human rights, the development of clients' potentials, and the human relationship with nature (such as current environmental global issues) are essential.

Social work professionals participate in the delivery of social services in public and private settings, usually in frontline service delivery roles or as program managers. Practitioners respond to social problems at the individual, group, and community levels, emphasizing macro interventions and clients' participation.

Reflection Exercises

1. Before reading this chapter, what had you heard about Peru and about its people? From what sources? What were your own impressions?
2. Research the Internet for information on cultural patterns characteristic of the three regions of Peru: costa, sierra, and selva. Compare and contrast these characteristics, and consider the delivery of social services in these regions.
3. If you were offered a job as a social worker in Peru, what characteristics of the country would motivate you to accept the position? Are there any features that would deter you?
4. As in the United States, the population in Peru is multiethnic and multicultural. List 3 ways these countries accommodate and respond to human diversity. Compare and contrast the similarities and differences.

PRACTICE EXAMPLE

Background

The impact of poverty, terrorism, and globalization are clearly reflected in the thousands of displaced rural indigenous Peruvians who, in search of safety, employment, and better socioeconomic opportunities, are forced to migrate to the main urban cities located along the Pacific coast, particularly Lima. Initially, during times of crisis and social unrest, migrant families would arrive without a place to live and would settle in open spaces along the outskirts of these cities. Scattered groups of shantytowns developed, known first as *barrios marginales* (marginal barrios), *pueblos jóvenes* (young towns), or *asentamientos humanos* (human settlements). More recently, shantytowns have evolved into more organized communities, known now as *distritos* (districts), where inhabitants do not merely occupy the same physical space but also share a similar history, social class, culture, and social reality with its accompanying opportunities and challenges.

In general, Peruvians in these districts experience deplorable living conditions and ongoing social exclusion, marginalization, prejudice, and discrimination based on race, ethnicity, and social class. The myriad psychosocial stressors that accompany poverty and unequal treatment are also present, generating or exacerbating social problems such as depression, substance abuse, and family, political, and social violence. For these disenfranchised communities, families, and individuals, social services to help meet even the most basic of physical and social needs are crucial for successful social functioning and, sometimes, survival.

Two of the most acute and pressing basic needs confronting these populations are hunger and healthcare. The urgent nature of the situation and the slow or lack of governmental assistance mobilized women in these communities to create the *comedores populares* (communal kitchens), which provide meals and health-related services to the poorest people living in urban-marginal districts throughout Peru. These communal kitchens are a unique example of mass women's collective organization, without parallel in other countries (Zibechi, 2007).

This example is partially drawn from the caseload of the Centro Latinoamericano de Trabajo Social (CELATS) and takes place in a communal kitchen in the district of El Yurinaqui in Lima. Isabela Gonzalez, a social work practitioner employed at CELATS, is assigned to provide services at a communal kitchen. She is a light-skinned, middle-class woman born and raised in the coastal region. She earned her Bachelors in Arts (BA) in social work from a major university in Lima. She has no previous experience working with migrants in shantytowns. The worker and names of consumers of services and some of the information presented are fictional.

Agency

CELATS is a nonprofit nongovernmental organization founded and staffed predominantly by social workers. It is located in the city of Lima. CELATS' mission is to contribute to an effective social work practice marked by social inclusiveness and equity, responsiveness to intergenerational and gender issues, and multiculturalism at the family, social, and community levels, where social work professionals provide intervention.

A few months ago, CELATS secured funding from an international source to design and implement an education program for the women in charge of and running the communal kitchen in the El Yurinaqui district. The project entails designing and facilitating a series of workshops and providing educators to work alongside the women serving food in the kitchen to help mitigate psychosocial needs and stress for workers and consumers of services. Isabela Gonzalez was charged with implementation of this project and, thus, was deployed to the communal kitchen in El Yurinaqui.

Geographic Setting

The district of El Yurinaqui has been in existence since 1965. It is located approximately 36 miles south of the city of Lima and is bordered by two main highways and the Rimac River. Due to a lack of financial resources, the houses are built in the foothills (*cerros*) and typically possess only the very basics of an infrastructure. Houses in the higher elevations face specific challenges, as the nature of the land does not permit the use of necessary building materials.

Social Work Practice in El Yurinaqui Communal Kitchen

When Isabela arrived at the site of the communal kitchen, she noted with distress the scarcity of resources for women to prepare and serve meals. The communal kitchen was a single, square room equipped only with a wood-burning stove. There was no running water on the premises. Water had to be carried uphill from a well in jars. The room had a single table without storage cupboards. The pots and pans were all severely blackened from being repeatedly heated by burning wood. Although the physical surroundings were bleak, Isabela was greeted effusively and warmly by the coordinator and other women in charge, who with wide smiles expressed their excitement about Isabela's presence.

Isabela quickly became familiar with the history of El Yurinaqui district, its people, the subculture, organization of the kitchen site, and the women in charge. For example, she learned that most of the first settlers were forced to migrate from the Andes without a specific plan or means for survival. Although they brought with them the cultural patterns and agricultural traits of their ancestors, upon relocation to the region, people had to adapt quickly to expectations and requirements intrinsic to the urban environment. Unable to cultivate the land to grow crops for consumption and as a means of economic income, most struggled to make ends meet and satisfy even the most basic of physical and social needs.

The main purpose of the communal kitchen is to fight hunger, although it also provides some health-related services and engages in capacity-building activities. The women running the kitchen are well organized. There is a management team comprised of a coordinator and various members responsible for education and recreation, finances, administration, cooking, cleaning, and distribution of goods. Each of these positions holds inherent responsibilities and is accountable to the general assembly, which makes the final decisions regarding the communal kitchen as an organization.

The female members of the communal kitchen rotate in shifts to cook, distribute meals, and clean. The kitchen is open from Monday to Friday. Isabela admires the dedication and tenacity of the women volunteers, as they diligently prepare and provide daily sustenance for many people while serving as a source of social support for each other in their quest to overcome poverty.

Over the past few months, Isabela has contributed in various ways to the well-being of the women who prepare the meals in the communal kitchen. For example, she has facilitated workshops on food handling, nutrition, empowerment, and family violence. The topics and the workshop contents were determined and designed in consultation with the CELATS management team. Isabela has created a space where the women can gain insight into their own strengths, needs, and challenges. She has also worked with women who reluctantly sought her assistance concerning issues of intergenerational conflict, child disruptive behavior, and depression. For instance, one day she noticed that Ms. Peralta was crying while cooking and serving the food. When she found a moment of privacy, Isabela asked her softly if there was anything she could do to help. With her eyes red and swollen, choking back her tears, Ms. Peralta thanked her politely and replied, "No, thank you, I have to make sure I take care of my father and my children and have no time for me; I don't really matter." Isabela kindly reassured Ms. Peralta of her self-worth and offered her unconditional assistance. Later on, at the end of her shift, Ms. Peralta approached Isabela and shared the difficulties she was experiencing between her children and recently arrived parents in the home.

Isabela teamed with community leaders to organize social activities highlighting Andean cultural traditions. She helped to prepare a presentation and accompanied members of the management team to give testimony at a legislative hearing on the need for government resources to support communal kitchens. Isabela has recently joined the national group Citizens United to Combat Poverty dedicated to raise societal awareness and take action steps toward the eradication of poverty in Peru. For years, she has been actively involved in an international human rights organization that advocates for displaced and forced migrant populations globally.

Isabela has now established a somewhat flexible routine of daily activities. Her day begins very early, because she does not have a car and needs to take public transportation. After riding in three packed buses, she arrives at El Yurinaqui. Isabela dresses professionally to convey respect for her clients and community members yet comfortably to accommodate a fair amount of walking and climbing to get to and from the kitchen site.

Considerations Prior to Entering the Experience

One day, while riding the bus to El Yurinaqui, Isabela recalls the moment when the CELATS' director asked her to provide services at the communal kitchen. On one hand, she was excited at the opportunity to realize her deep commitment to social justice and human rights through social work practice with one of the most vulnerable groups in Peruvian society.

On the other hand, she was concerned about her ability to function effectively within a dramatically new and different sociocultural reality and environmental context. Isabela recognized and fought back her initial fears and concerns about her own safety and well-being based on stereotypes and rumors about the dangers of the Yurinaqui area. She also felt insecure about whether she would be well received and accepted by the women in the communal kitchen and other consumers. Isabela approached the situation armed with a genuine desire to make a difference in the lives of her clients and their families, high levels of empathy, and an arsenal of social work practice skills, methods, and techniques. She strived to recognize and incorporate an appreciation for and understanding of the micro, mezzo, and macro system levels of the presenting situations. Of utmost importance, she had a passion for and was able to embrace the concepts of social justice and human rights and the salience of these notions in her clients' presenting situations.

Now, once the bus stops, Isabela disembarks and begins her daily walk toward the kitchen site to be welcomed and greeted by El Yurinaqui community members. They respectfully wish Isabela well and make her feel accepted. Her fears have vanished. She takes a deep breath and feels proud to be a social worker. She continues walking, ready to make a difference in the lives of many.

Practice Considerations

This example illustrates one of the many scenarios in which international social work practice takes place beyond the United States to help address a global social concern—displacement and forced migration. Here the social worker aligns herself with an organized group of women in their quest to mitigate, modestly but successfully, food and healthcare needs in their community. In a sense, her primary goal is to assist and contribute to the welfare of individual women and their families through education and psychosocial intervention; yet the social work practice situation calls for various levels of intervention, including intrapersonal, interpersonal, familial, organizational, community, and societal change. Thus, she expands her roles and contributions in response to related broader environmental challenges and opportunities.

As a social worker who received her professional training in Peru, Isabela Gonzalez was prepared to integrate micro, mezzo, and macro practice strategies, such as interpersonal skills, family counseling, linkage and referral, group work, social action, empowerment, and advocacy. This multilevel approach to practice is consistent with the generalist social work perspective required in practice foundation curricula in U.S. social work education. As noted earlier, generalist social work practice acknowledges the interplay of personal and collective issues and prompts practitioners to work with various human systems (Miley, O'Melia, & Dubois, 2004).

The example also describes a social work situation that calls for practice activities that promote social development. In her practice with the women in the communal kitchen, the social worker joins and initiates community efforts to act on some of the underlying causes of her clients' inability to meet their basic needs, namely, poverty, political and economic inequality, and social injustice. She includes a grassroots perspective for the development of plans for change, fostering clients' participation and empowerment. Funding is a continual concern; the communal kitchen relies on resources from many sources, including international efforts.

In the United States, social work frameworks for practice with racial and ethnic groups that historically have experienced oppression and populations at risk, such as recently arrived immigrants, have long emphasized the multilevel nature of their clients' psychosocial realities and presenting situations. Practitioners are directed to pay simultaneous attention to the micro, mezzo, and macro levels, in order to integrate individual and systemic change (Devore & Schlesinger, 1999; Lum, 2004). Furthermore, promoting social development is an essential component of direct social work practice with disenfranchised clients and the cornerstone of international social work practice (Estes, 1992).

The parallels drawn here offer an opportunity for reflection on the global nature of social work practice with disenfranchised populations. In some ways, the social and political inequality experienced by the El Yurinaqui people mirror that of racial and ethnic minorities and distinctions based on subculture found in the United States and other countries. These similarities—mainly respect for and understanding of racial, ethnic, and cultural differences—also exist regardless of whether international practice takes place locally or abroad or in a developed or developing nation.

✍ Reflection Exercises

1. Visit a soup kitchen in your vicinity. Identify five ways the needs of consumers and staff members coincide with Isabela's experience.
2. Would your community or an organization in your community (e.g., church or social service agency) consider forming an international partnership with an organization like the El Yurinaqui Communal Kitchen or CELATS? In a group, discuss how such a relationship could be formed. Identify available assets and challenges for such a venture.
3. It is difficult for Isabela, personally and professionally, to sustain her efforts. Identify four ways that Isabela can engage in self-care.

ETHICAL ISSUES AND DILEMMAS

The international code of ethics, developed by the International Federation of Social Workers (IFSW) and the International Association of Social Work (IASSW), suggests that ethical awareness is an essential element in social work practice. To guide international social work practice, this code provides three sets of broad ethical principles, recognizing that some ethical issues and dilemmas are universal and others may arise in specific countries. Two of these principles reflect the social work fundamental values of human rights and human dignity, and social justice (IFSW/IASSW, 2004). Similarly, the *Code of Ethics* of the National Association of Social Workers in the United States affirms these same ethical principles (NASW, 1999). It can be seen from the example presented that these ethical principles and tenets can be applied to and lay at the core of social work practice in Peru.

Practitioners working with displaced and forced migrants often encounter situations where their ethical responsibilities conflict with the law or policy regulations. Such is the case, for example, when clients or potential clients do not have the appropriate documents to reside legally in a given country or to settle on public or government-owned land. Cognizant of their dual responsibility to clients and to the broader society, social workers often face an ethical dilemma trying to uphold ethical tenets grounded in the profession's values of human rights and social justice.

Given the vulnerability of displaced and migrant populations, some social workers may be overprotective of their clients and thus have difficulty promoting the right to self-determination. Extending this logic, an ethical area of special concern is the sometimes-challenging nature of applying ethical principles to multicultural practice. At times, social workers may be successful in recognizing ethnic and cultural diversity yet struggle in differentiating their own values and beliefs from those of clients. As an example, cultural pride may severely limit a consumer's ability to receive goods and services; yet professional judgment suggests additional food and support is needed to sustain life. Horejsi and Garthwait (2002) offer important insight pertaining to these kinds of ethical dilemmas.

Morales and colleagues suggest the core of what bonds social workers globally are "beliefs about the inherent value of people and the responsibilities of societies to create conditions in which people can thrive" (Morales, Sheafor, & Scott, 2007, p. 174). The values, general ethical principles, and standards of professional conduct that underlie social work can also provide a unifying theme for social workers worldwide. The dedication of the profession of social work, across national boundaries, to core principles (e.g., human rights and dignity) can serve as a social glue to connect and unite practitioners, educators, and leaders in common causes (e.g., the eradication of hunger and exploitation of children).

Reflection Exercises

1. Isabela sees a growing expectation from funding sources to document the provision of food with such information as the characteristics (race, residency, and origin) of recipients. While this information can be useful, it can also be used to restrict who receives meals at the El Yurinaqui Communal Kitchen. With whom should Isabela discuss her concerns? Identify what you believe to be the most salient ethical principle for guiding her actions.

2. Isabela observes that some consumers of the communal kitchen place food in their pockets. She recognizes this action as an effort to acquire food for distribution to absent or ailing family members. To call out such a practice would create embarrassment and likely result in the person(s) not returning to the communal kitchen, to the detriment of themselves and family. Using ethical premises, identify and debate with others appropriate courses of action.

SUMMARY

This millennium brings new and exciting opportunities for social work practice within an international context. This chapter offered insight into some of the intricacies associated with social work practice in a developing Latin American nation, Peru. An example of practice illustrated a Peruvian social worker's experience with a disenfranchised population confronting the challenges of displacement and forced migration. The far-reaching social and economic implications of this global concern call for social work responses worldwide. A main thrust of the chapter was to contribute to a greater awareness of how direct practice is implemented in Peru and to provide opportunities for comparative thought. The authors hope this discussion will spark readers' enthusiasm and commitment to deepen their understanding of international social work practice abroad.

REFERENCES

Council on Social Work Education. (2001). *Educational policy and accreditation standards*. Alexandria, VA: Author.

Cox, D., & Pawar, M. (2006). *International social work: Issues, strategies, and programs*. Thousand Oaks, CA: Sage Publications.

Devore, W., & Schlesinger, D. (1999). *Ethnic-sensitive social work practice* (5th ed.). Boston: Allyn & Bacon.

Diaz, H. L., Drumm, R. D., Ramirez-Johnson, J., & Oidjarv, H. (2002). Social capital, economic development and food security in Peru's mountain region. *International Social Work, 45, 481–495.*

Dolgoff, R., & Feldstein, D. (2007). *Understanding social welfare: A search for social justice* (6th ed.). Lebanon, IN: Prentice-Hall.

Drachman, D., & Paulino, A. (2004). Thinking beyond United States' borders. *Journal of Immigrant & Refugee Services, 2* (1/2), 1–9.

Estes, R. (Ed.). 1992. *Internationalizing social work education: A guide to resources for a new century*. Philadelphia: University of Pennsylvania Social of Social Work.

Fortune, A. E. (2006). Multiculturalism and cultural competence in social work practice in the United States. In V. Fokine & R. Toseland (Eds.), *Social work and social work education in Russia and the United States: A comparative analysis* (pp. 132–139). Moscow: Russian Academy of Education.

Foundation for Sustainable Development. (2008). Peru: A Development Overview Retrieved from: http://www.fsdinternational.org.

Healy, L. M. (2004). Strengthening the link: Social work with immigrants and refugees and international social work. *Journal of Immigrant & Refugee Services*, 2 (1/2), 49–67.

Horejsi, C., & Garthwait, C. (2002). *The social work practicum: A guide and workbook for students* (2nd ed.). Boston: Allyn and Bacon.

Instituto Nacional de Estadística e Informática (2001). *Perú: Estimaciones y Proyecciones de Población, 1950–2050*. Lima: Author. Retrieved from http://www.inei.gob.pe.

Instituto Nacional de Estadística e Informática (2006). *Perú: Compendio Estadístico*. Lima: Author, 2006. Retrieved from http://www.inei.gob.pe.

International Federation of Social Workers and International Association of Schools of Social Work. (2004). *Ethics in social work, statement of principles*. Bern, Switzerland: IFSW.

Lum, D. (2004). *Cultural competence, practice stages, and client systems: A case study approach*. Pacific Grove, CA: Brooks/Cole.

Miley, K., O'Melia, M., & Dubois, B. (2004). *Generalist social work practice: An empowering approach*. Boston: Allyn & Bacon.

Minujin, A. (1995). *Cuesta abajo. Los nuevos pobres: Efectos de la crisis en la sociedad Argentina*. Buenos Aires: Losada.

Morales A., Sheafor, B., & Scott, M. (2007). *Social work: A profession of many faces*. Boston: Pearson.

National Association of Social Workers. (1999). *Code of Ethics of the National Association of Social Workers*. Silver Springs, MD: NASW Press.

Paranda, H. (2007). Social work in Latin America: History, challenges and renewal. *International Social Work*, 50, 560–569.

Quiero-Tajalli, I. (1997). Latin America. In N. Mayadas, T. Watts, & D. Elliott (Eds.), *International handbook on social work theory and practice* (pp. 51–59). Westport, CN: Greenwood Press.

Ramos, B., & Briar-Lawson, K. (2004). Globalization and international implications for social work. In A. Sallee (Ed.), *Social work and social welfare: The context of a profession* (pp. 355–378). Dubuque, IA: Eddie Bowers.

Ramos, B., Fernandez, J., Mera, A., Puican, G., Piscoya, L., and Pitsfil, P. (2006, August). A participatory action research project to promote child health in a rural Andean community in Peru. Paper presented at the 7th ALARPM and 11th PAR World Congress on Participatory Research, Standards and Ethics. Groningen, the Netherlands. August 2006.

Ramos, B., & Melecio, J. (2006). Multiculturalism and cultural competence in social work practice in the United States. In V. Fokine & R. Toseland (Eds.), *Social work and social work education in Russia and the United States: A comparative analysis* (pp. 132–139). Moscow: Russian Academy of Education.

Schlecht, N. D. (2006). *Frommer's Peru.* Hoboken, NJ: John Wiley & Sons.

U.K. Department for International Development. (2003). *Peru. Country Assistance Plan 2003–2005.* Retrieved from http://www.dfid.gov.uk/pubs/files/peru/CAP-peru/.

U.S. Department of State. (2008). Background Note: Peru. Bureau of Western Hemisphere Affairs. Retrieved May 20, 2008 from www.state.gov/r/pa/ei/bgn/35762.htm.

U.S. Agency for International Development. (2008). Latin America and the Caribbean: Peru. Retrieved June 2, 2008, from http://www.usaid.gov/locations/latin_america_caribbean/country/peru/.

U.S. Library of Congress (1993). *A country study: Peru.* Call Number F3408 .P4646 1993.

Wikipedia (2009). New seven wonders of the world. Retrieved from http://en.wikipedia.org/wiki/New_Seven_Wonders_of_the_World#Winners.

Zibechi, R. (2007, December 12). Comedores populares de Perú: contra el hambre y soledad. Programa de las Américas. Reporte. Washington, DC.

11

Lessons Learned from International Practice and Policy

DENNIS D. LONG AND CAROLYN J. TICE

Words not only affect us temporarily; they change us, they socialize or unsocialize us.

—Riesman, Glazer, and Denney (1955, p. 112)

Riesman, Glazer, and Denney's (1955) popular book of the 1950s,
The Lonely Crowd, introduced many Americans to the "other-
directed" side of character and self. The authors proposed that by looking
at examples of peers and contemporaries, in an other-directed fashion,
the modern-day learner begins to interpret life and meaning in newer,
creative, and more insightful ways. Many social scientists and historians point to this seminal work as a literary piece marking the origins of
an external, socially directed sense of self in American culture, derived
through social comparison and interpretation.

If, as suggested by Riesman et al. (1955), words comprise basic constructs for socialization and personal change, meaningful exposure to
language, practices, and customs from another country can constitute an
important, other-directed mode for defining and refining one's sense of

professional self in social work. As aspiring social workers, students often ask themselves: "Which population groups and types of program intervention and services appeal to me, and how do I best prepare for a career in social work?" Similarly, in everyday practice, social workers regularly reflect on professional strengths and areas for learning and improvement, wondering how they can keep their practice at the cutting edge and in tune with new and emerging population groups. Indeed, if a social worker loses her or his will and desire to learn, grow, and develop professionally, it is probably time to reevaluate and reconsider her or his professional status. Hence, social workers must have a profound and ongoing commitment to education and development of a professional self through participation in experiential and intellectual forms of social and cultural comparison, especially in relationship to human and societal diversity.

It is hoped that reading about and entertaining involvement in international social work policy and practice has spurred thought and a desire for additional knowledge and reflection concerning population groups, practices, traditions, and cultural aspects of countries around the world. Take a moment and ask yourself which of the preceding chapters was most interesting to you and struck a chord. What was it about a particular country and/or its people that was the most or least intriguing? Consider these dimensions:

- The foundation area (e.g., research or practice)
- The population being served (e.g. street children or traumatized women)
- The challenge of the physical and social climate (e.g., Malawi and Mongolia)
- The potential for making an impact on people's lives
- The notoriety or magnitude of a cause (e.g., HIV/AIDS)
- The nature of human needs and/or forms of oppression, familiarity, remoteness, and elements of natural beauty (e.g., Costa Rica, Appalachia, and South Africa)

As an example, some readers may have been especially moved by Isabela's leadership and grassroots efforts to address absolute needs (e.g., food) and support her staff members at a communal kitchen in Peru. For others, nomadic living in Mongolia could have kindled an interest to learn more about mobile, sustenance-oriented population groups. For those unfamiliar with regions in the United States, the examination of life, struggle, and resilience in Appalachia was likely informative and revealing. For social workers dedicated to promoting the rights and safety of women, reading about the strengths of women in South Africa could have been inspirational.

If you were afforded an opportunity for employment or study outside of the United States, where would you choose to go—Mongolia, Portugal, Appalachia, South Africa, Peru, Costa Rica, or the Republic of Malawi? Is the appeal of a country rooted in personal need or professional desire for growth and a passion and willingness to serve others? When motivations to engage in international practice and policy are needs based, a person is primarily searching for something (e.g., an adventure or form of escapism) or someone (e.g., possibly as a result of interpersonal conflict or loss) to fill a personal void in life. Social workers embracing international practice as a form of continued and professional development aspirations are less centered on their own personal-emotional needs; they direct attention and efforts on the plight and abilities of people and the potential for enhancing knowledge and refining professional skills.

Before engaging in forums on international practice and policy development, consider your impetus and motives, personal and professional. This type of introspection and reflection is an ideal topic for supervisory sessions with a direct superior or an academic advisor. Would you feel comfortable discussing aspirations for international practice with a supervisor or faculty member? If not, from whom might you seek advice: a confidant, friend, another social worker, or family member? How might both personal and professional feedback be helpful when contemplating your motivation(s) for engaging in international social work practice and policy? Try to be specific about investment behavior and what you hope to gain from an experience abroad.

Commonalities of Featured Authors and Social Workers

After you have read each chapter, it should be apparent that contributing authors possess several common characteristics. Foremost, each author is passionate about embracing the needs, strengths, and abilities of people in a particular country. Without exception, and regardless of motivation, social workers are excited about international social work practice and involvement in a specific country. A sign of professional success and satisfaction is when social workers are passionate about consumers and causes and look forward to each day's activities and effort. Aligning your work with personal and professional interests is very important and can sustain your development and career as a social worker.

For each social worker, life circumstances and employment opportunities are dynamic occurrences and subject to change. One's professional career is time limited. Therefore, it is important to maintain enthusiasm, attain satisfaction, and strive to make each and every day a source of stimulation and excitement in one's professional career. Coworkers and consumers of services alike can detect and know when a social worker is motivated or undermotivated about her or his practice. How might or does engagement in international social work policy and practice fit into your life course?

In addition to being passionate, chapter authors have been willing to move beyond comfort zones and inconvenience themselves in order to identify ways to share and exchange information, promote ethical practice, and empower consumers to actively engage in decision making. In one fashion or another, social workers highlighted in this book have shown initiative in negotiating and securing, with their place of employment or university, the opportunity to expand professional roles, expectations, and behaviors to include involvement in or with other countries. Structurally, this means that leaders in organizations (e.g., agency or university) have been convinced of the merits of international social work and exchange of information and expertise and are willing to allocate time and resources to the endeavor. Often social workers must exert initiative and innovation in convincing an organization of the benefits of international exchange and practice.

Finally, each author has a profound commitment to professional growth and development through experiential learning. In Chapter 2, experiential learning was described as "seeking out the meaning of encounters" and actively reflecting on experiences (Enns, 1993, p. 9). The examples of social work policy and practice depicted in this book were inspired by real occurrences and people; many examples were compilations of professional encounters, mixed with a bit of wisdom from the authors accompanied by occasional sprinkles of creativity. Chapters contain embedded questions and exercises to prompt thinking and reflection, recognizing that while in many situations there is often no single best answer or approach for addressing a situation or circumstance, social and cultural sensitivity, appreciation, and competency are always needed.

Piaget (1952) describes cognitive development that enables humans to entertain multiple dimensions and systematically and logically evaluate an array of perspectives and possibilities for understanding and influencing a situation, occurrence, or experience as a progressive form of thinking during *formal operations*. The practice of social work requires complex cognitive abilities. Irrespective of country, social workers are confronted daily with complex situations requiring reflection and advanced cognitive abilities that take into account a number of factors involving human and cultural diversity. It is hoped that this book, with its presentations of experiences of social workers from around the globe, has served as a conduit for complex and reflective thought concerning policy and practice and a realization that there is no universal research finding or one-approach-applies-to-all answers for addressing complex social issues and problems around the world.

Contemplate Gender and Examples of International Policy and Practice

If you have not already done so, now is an excellent time to return to Chapter 2 and complete the exercise featuring a cross-national analysis of the strengths and struggles of women. While oppression of and discrimination against women are fundamental forms of social injustice extending across the globe, it should quickly become apparent that conceptualization of the plight of women requires social workers to identify and consider a host of variables and conditions, especially concerning the fundamental nature of and cultural and social circumstances surrounding specific forms oppression, discrimination, and affronts to human dignity and the sanctity of life (Hughes, 2000, pp. 128–129).

The notion of power, the ability of men to influence and affect the behavior and actions of women, is often a cultural component, uniquely defined and implemented in a given social setting. As examples, the dynamics contributing to the exploitation of young female virgins in Malawi, the demanding expectations of women in Mongolia, and the violence endured by women in South Africa are grounded in tradition and long-standing beliefs and/or myths supporting male dominance. As an "outsider," recently or temporarily exposed to a nation's social conditions, social workers need to take care to avoid blaming the victims of male dominance. It is unrealistic and simplistic to expect women to rebuke male supremacy or that a society or culture, if prompted, will readily break with traditions and adopt different, more progressive postures and ways of doing. Instead, the challenge for the professional engaged in international social work is to assess the social environment and identify cultural and societal factors contributing to and supporting social relationships and realities that are detrimental to women yet amenable to social reform and change.

For social workers involved in international practice and cultural analyses, it can be helpful, in a deductive fashion (thinking from the abstract to concrete), to engage in a process of reducing society and culture into conceptual components. For example, as Meenaghan and Washington (1980) state, often "a question of particular interest to us is, How are people within a society to relate to and care for each other?" (p. 1). While an excellent initial question, practitioners frequently need to know how various roles (e.g., husband, wife, woman, man, consumer of services, social worker, etc.) and activities (e.g., affirming and oppressive behaviors) are defined, shaped, justified, and bound by specific societal values, norms, and traditions. Opportunities, barriers, and variations of rights for women in our examples of international practice and policy can be best understood in the context of societal values and norms. Furthermore, it is reasonable to expect that "each society, and even groups within a given society, will have somewhat different answers to these basic issues [role and behavior expectations], so that societies and subcultures will differ, that is[,] be somewhat distinctive" (Meenaghan & Washington, 1980, p. 1).

EXAMPLES OF INTERNATIONAL POLICY AND PRACTICE AS SNAPSHOTS

One of the realizations from reading country-based chapters describing social work policy and practice should be the inherent difficulties and challenges associated with learning about the complexities of a nation and its people, their strengths, needs, and ways, via a brief example or exposure. Often the intent of an illustrative example is to entice people to think differently and learn more about something or someone. This is why, often, intense study about and immersion in a country are important and necessary precursors to a decision to devote oneself to professional practice in a foreign land.

Many social workers would agree that a thorough analysis of social welfare as an institution in a specific country—or an emerging institution, as is likely the case of a developing country—is contingent on an examination of a variety of social institutions and their interrelations and interconnectedness (e.g., family, religion, government, political, education, and economic). While social workers can gravitate toward social, cultural, and economic dimensions and conditions, definitions of human need and care, typically manifested in policy development and service delivery, also occur in relationship to government agencies, political organizations, schools, and religious entities.

Look back and reflect on your readings in this book. How dominant is social welfare in each country? In other words, given what you have learned from each example of policy and practice, can you characterize social welfare as having dependency, equity, or primacy over other social institutions? The term "dependency" suggests that social welfare is less important than other institutions (e.g., family, religion, government, political, education, and economic); "equity" means that "social welfare is on equal footing with other institutions in society"; and "primacy" refers to social welfare having precedence over other social institutions (Meenaghan & Washington, 1980, p. 6). Consider for a moment the relevance and importance of social welfare (policy, programs, and services) in Costa Rica compared to Mongolia, Portugal, or South Africa. In Appalachia, did economics, family, and politics appear to be of greater importance than considerations concerning social welfare?

Given your snapshot of each country, how does the prominence and meaning of its social welfare system vary according to: urban-rural setting, availability of natural resources, political influence, level of economic development, and the absolute versus relative nature of need and poverty? Several countries hosted nongovernmental organizations (NGOs) that were supported by international organizations; does the mere presence of NGOs signify structural and societal commitment to and responsibility for human welfare? Or do NGOs reflect a minimal effort to care for the needs of people, found only when economics, religion, and family are ineffective in addressing human needs and problems? A quick litmus test concerning the primacy of social welfare in a country is to contemplate these questions:

- Are social welfare services and policy in a country or region viewed in a positive fashion and thought to be respectable?
- Are social workers valued and given recognition for their contributions and service. If so, how?

Need for Multilevel Intervention in Social Work Practice

While most examples of international policy and practice in this book affirm the need for social workers to engage in planned change across system-level sizes (e.g., individual, family, group, organization, community, and society) with people and the social environment, the research effort in South Africa is particularly memorable. In Chapter 6, Anna and her research colleagues sought to collect data and were able to document and describe the need for posttraumatic stress disorder (PTSD) screening at the time of intake at the foundation. But they also came to understand the plight of women as objects of violence in South Africa in relationship to culture, history, values, and norms.

Anna is convinced that until community and societal values and attitudes change, violence against women will be condoned and continue to be a problem in South Africa. And social service organizations will be consumed with identifying and treating the consequences of violence (e.g., PTSD) against women via micro-oriented interventions. She also realizes that for women to gain power in a society, men must relinquish power. At this point, women are reluctant to use services and programs at the New World Foundation, for fear of being identified and being retaliated against and persecuted by men. Promoting culturally appropriate ways to affirm the rights and dignity of women, especially in seeking services, organizing, and supporting each other, seems to Anna like a logical, macro-oriented starting place for social workers engaged in international efforts in South Africa. She seizes every opportunity available to inform others about and praise the fortitude of women at the foundation and credit them for her own awareness and sensitivity to the plight of women.

Social work is a profession dedicated to a duality in international practice throughout the world. Social workers have a "responsibility to individuals in need and responsibility for social reform and social change" (Healey, 2001, p. 80). This dual responsibility to addressing need and leading social reform and change is often what functionally distinguishes the social worker from other helping professionals engaged in international efforts. In international practice and policy, the social worker many times can be readily identified or perceived as an "outsider," complicating both responsibilities. Anna, for example, has learned to be very mindful and sensitive to the possible negative perception and ramifications of outsiders imposing different, even though innovative and helpful, ways. As suggested at the beginning of this chapter, while Anna has become more "other directed" and reaped the benefit of insight from social comparison and interpretation of people and events in South Africa, she acknowledges that many people are not at her same social and intellectual place.

Concerning Social and Economic Justice

Many social workers would agree with the basic premise that "needs are preconditions for human action, and . . . physical health and personal autonomy are the basic prerequisites for any forms of life" (Hughes, 2000, p. 129). For the most part, social workers around the world provide intervention and participate in programs and organizations that are in reaction to and, it is hoped, responsive to human needs. Each of the examples of international practice and policy in this book reflect remedial rather than preventive types of service and action. Generally, some kind(s) of human need has manifested and become apparent, and a group of people (significant in number or influence) has deemed the cause to be just and deserving of an organized community, societal, or international response.

Across the globe, and as demonstrated in this book, reactions to human needs and the promotion of human rights and dignity can occur in many ways and take various forms. International events and trends involving the global economy, military conflict, and sociopolitical dominance contribute to many of the problems endured by the world's people. For example, several of the countries examined in this book described "street children." Disturbingly, children are forced to survive by begging or selling goods and services in the streets of populated urban areas. The emergence of street children in a country is often a sign of poverty and disproportionate distribution of wealth and income in a national state, where children are left to fend for themselves and perhaps a few immediate family members in order to survive.

Lyons (1999) contends that "poverty is a universal problem rooted in structural divisions and personal differences in every society. But the concept of poverty has changed over time and means different things to different people, not least related to their national context" (p. 87). As you have read, poverty for children orphaned in Malawi is not the same as poverty in Mongolia, Portugal, Peru, Costa Rica, South Africa, or Appalachia. Nor are programmatic and service responses to the needs of children the same in the different countries.

For social workers, a useful theme that cuts across definition of need and organized response involves social work's long-standing professional commitment to social and economic justice. Two terms of particular interest and assistance in directing social work interventions are "distributive justice" and "relational justice." *Distributive justice* is commonly conceptualized and defined in terms of the fair and equitable distribution of social and economic goods and services throughout a society, whereas *relational (processual) justice* involves power and refers to the meaningful participation of people—dominant and subordinate groups—in important decisions impacting life, including rights, opportunities, and the distribution of goods and services (Long, Tice, & Morrison, 2006).

In many of the instances of international social work policy and practice found in this book, a primary emphasis was placed on distributive justice. For example, how can people acquire or attain in an equitable fashion needed goods or services? In Portugal (Chapter 4), you will remember Joaquin, a 33-year-old man with cerebral palsy. Much of the chapter focused on acquiring appropriate services and support for Joaquin, especially given his changing family circumstances. People in small towns in Appalachia struggling to secure and reasonably pay for water and sewerage services also exemplify distributive justice. Both instances involved fair and equitable distribution of services, care and water.

In many respects, relational justice involves a higher and sometimes more difficult standard in international social work. Promoting the ability of people to affect decision making concerning highly sought after and valued goods, services, and rights pushes the notion of competition between individual and group interests to the forefront. And, as Meenaghan and Washington (1980) point out, "whatever values tend to dominate in a social arrangement may be mere rationalizations of the needs and interest of the more powerful segments of the society" (p. 9). Indeed, rights and access to opportunities, services, and goods are often grounded in values and traditions benefiting and advantaging groups of people on the basis of gender, social-economic class, race, religious, ethnicity, and other factors. Hence, for the South African women highlighted in this book, oppression and interpersonal violence need to be seen as a form of social control. Relational justice will prevail when women fully participate in decision-making processes and are afforded rights and access to and consumption of goods and services addressing their self-identified wants and needs.

International Opportunities for Exchange and Equity

Finally, it is important to note that as social workers and social worker educators continue to embrace and engage in various forms of international exchange (e.g., practice, educational exchanges, consultation projects, and seminars and conferences), attention needs to be paid to a sense of equity and fairness when crossing national boundaries. For example, most of the examples in this book involve American social workers or social work students traveling to other, less-developed countries. The exception was Xavier and his experience in Appalachia (Chapter 8). Sponsorship for social workers to participate in international social work should be bidirectional with special effort given to extending invitations and support for social workers from less economically developed countries to travel to economically advantaged destinations. In the excitement and zeal for learning, it is common and likely ethnocentric to think about how I or we can travel to another country to study and promote human rights and dignity, as opposed to identifying individuals and delegations to visit our home country.

As found in this book, social workers who are engaged in international practice often gravitate and migrate toward countries where interpersonal or interorganizational relationships have been formed. As with the summer tour group in Costa Rica, thought needs to be given to sustainability and conscious and concerted effort must be paid to ensure that social workers are giving—intellectually, financially, and otherwise—as much as they are taking, in the true spirit of cultural and educational exchange.

At conferences around the world, social workers and other professionals are increasingly presenting papers and workshops describing course-based, research, and practice experiences in many of the countries highlighted in this book. Well-intentioned social workers are documenting and sharing important findings and observations. However, the ultimate outcome and standard for assessing international exchange in social work policy and practice should be twofold:

1. Ten years later, was the international endeavor able to sustain itself and document social-economic impact? Or was the net result a short-term project that yielded a one-time cultural exchange and documented insight (presentations, papers, and articles) but ultimately ended when key people were no longer involved?
2. Did the international exchange result in an investment behavior in a less-developed country or deplete and take advantage of precious time, goods, service, and commodities?

It is important to be conscious about, weigh, and document the social-economic cost and benefit of international exchange. As social workers professionals, we should be mindful in asking ourselves: Were people better off as a result of the venture? And if so, who, how, and by whose standards? As a practitioner, educator, or researcher, did I give more than I took?

STRENGTHS PERSPECTIVE IN INTERNATIONAL SOCIAL WORK

When considering the social work contributions offered to host countries and their citizens, the strengths perspective is applicable. What is the strengths perspective? As Saleebey (1997) states, the strengths perspective suggests a way of perceiving people in their immediate environment and/or broader world. Embedded in the perspective are five notions:

1. Every individual, group, and community has a unique set of strengths.
2. Challenges, difficulties or barriers may be threatening, but they also may represent opportunities.
3. The aspirations of people, groups, and communities must be acted on.
4. Consumers are best served through collaborative efforts.
5. People and their environments have a plethora of resources.

The strengths perspective creates a setting for international social work by shifting attention away from problems, barriers, and obstacles to the simple notion that each person, group, community, and country contains the capacity for transformative change. By understanding the strengths and resilience of people in their various environments, social workers challenge deficit or pathology models, allowing strengths and resources to flourish for positive growth. This is not to say that problems do not exist. Rather, problems are placed in their proper place as we recognize them in their proper context, explore them in similar ways, and devote less time and attention to them (Weick & Chamberlain, 2002).

Values

The practice base of international social work from a strengths perspective is supported by values. Values reflect a belief system about what is beneficial or desirable and what is not. Said another way, values are a cornerstone for the ethical codes as defined by the National Association of Social Workers, the International Federation of Social Workers, and the International Association of Schools of Social Work, as described in Chapter 3. For example, the value of self-determination suggests that social workers should not force individuals, communities, or countries to change. Rather, change is achieved as unique strengths and desired goals are recognized, values are embraced, and the rights and needs of others are considered (Compton & Galaway, 1994). Recall the situation in Chapter 9, in which Mr. Kwambiri attempted to secure employment for Saliza, a 15-year-old orphaned girl in Malawi. Although he knew what the future would hold for Saliza without employment, he did not force her to complete the apprenticeship training in carpentry. Instead, he attempted to understand her position and understand her desire to marry for the sake of her two younger sisters.

Another value related to the strengths perspective is confidentiality, a core element in social work practice that involves the negotiation between social workers and consumers on what information is to be shared and with whom and when. Remember Diane's dilemma with street children in Mongolia in Chapter 5, when she was unclear what interventions were being documented, shared with others, and monitored. From a strengths perspective, confidentiality is considered a resource that helps to build relationships, maintain boundaries, and recognize potential (Long et al., 2006). In highlighting resources, confidentiality adds to the development of support systems across consumer systems.

Social advocacy is a value that directs actions or activities to enhance the quality of life of individuals, groups, communities, and nations. From a strengths perspective, social advocacy challenges the status quo through mediation and consensus building. It is a method for elevating support systems, fortifying formal and informal resources, and expanding the horizons of people in their communities and countries (Kirst-Ashman & Hull, 1999). Social action was apparent in Chapter 4, in Portugal, where Pam advocated on behalf of elements in Joaquin's life to ensure that his support system acknowledged and addressed his grieving process. In the context of community, Chapter 8 described Xavier's internship as a tutor for teenage girls and boys in math and science. He also organized trips to the county library, assisted with computer classes, and facilitated a weekly book club. Thus, Xavier's work changed life as it had been in the small Appalachian town while increasing the life choices of teens.

Role of Social Workers

The values highlighted from the strengths perspective recognize the interaction of social work practice with policy and suggest roles for social workers. As indicated throughout the book, social workers typically assume more than one practice role as a function of agency demands, consumer expectations and needs, personal interest, and position or internship descriptions. Although not an exhaustive list, the next roles are found in the book and are matched with a principle from the strengths perspective:

- *Advocate: Interventions are based on self-determination.* In Chapter 4, Patrice and Pam prepare for a program planning meeting by gathering a comprehensive array of information from Joaquin and Mrs. Ferreira. Although Joaquin had limited speech, he made his wishes and ideas known through gestures. Using problem framing, strengths assessment, and a family system description, Patrice and Pam approach Joaquin's wants and needs in a holistic manner. They offer assurance that Joaquin's input will be followed by building a system of accountability and monitoring in the plan, all of which Joaquin agreed to during the interdisciplinary planning session.

- *Educator: The focus is on individual strengths.* Remember Diane, the social work student from Chapter 5? She considered the resilience of the Mongolian street children remarkable and their situation one that could not be ignored or forgotten. Consequently, she collaborated with nongovernmental organizations, while reflecting on her system of beliefs and values, to work with the children where they were and in an attempt to guide where they would go.

  The description of the Costa Rican cultural study tour in Chapter 7 highlights the use of experiential learning to enhance students' understanding about how human behavior actually functions in a culturally diverse social environment. While in language classes, in home-stays, and in painting murals in the center of a shantytown, students experience the norms, values, customs, symbols, thoughts, traditions, politics, religions, philosophies, material objects, and language of their teachers and host families. Often the students' preconceived views of human behavior change as they come to recognize the unique characteristics and qualities of lifestyles and cultural elements quite different from their own.

- *Researcher: Blending societal, programmatic, and consumer goals.* Chapter 6 introduced a quantitative research project designed to examine the frequency and type of domestic and community-based violence occurring in Lavender Hill, South Africa. An ancillary feature of the project explored the ensuing mental health issues associated with posttraumatic stress disorder and experienced by women. The New World Foundation (NWF), a strengths-based organization in which women are viewed as strong and empowered, is the described focal agency. At the NWF, the needs of women, the agency mission, and the reach agenda of social workers combine to generate evidence-based findings to guide change efforts from the individual to the national level of intervention.

- *Community organizer: The community is viewed as an oasis.* The Appalachian region of the United States was featured in Chapter 8, along with issues of social justice. Through a university-based social work program, Xavier was assigned to work with the Appalachian Community Fund (ACF). ACF has awarded over $5 million for community organizing and social justice work to more than 300 grassroots organizations in Central Appalachia. Its vision to support social change organizing is reflected in partnering and community collaborations. Through his community work, Xavier learned of the area's untapped resources and the potential of residents as well as his own. Further, he came to understand the concepts of boundaries, mutual reciprocity, and informal systems of support as they relate to social work practice.

- *Facilitator: People can learn, grow, and change.* In Chapter 9, Mr. Kwambiri helped operate an orphans and vulnerable children training and apprenticeship program funded by the International Fund for Agricultural Development (IFAD), a specialized agency of the United Nations, with the mission of empowering poor rural women and men to achieve higher incomes and improved food security. Mr. Kwambiri's close ties with people in their communities supports not only the work of IFAD but also the often unspoken wants of people to be recognized with dignity and respect. Against formidable odds, Mr. Kwambiri remains steadfast in his belief that if a door of opportunity is opened, a person will likely pass through.

- *Team member: The relationship is primary.* As you will recall, Chapter 10 on Peru examined a project that designed and facilitated a series of workshops and provided social work educators the chance to work alongside the women in a communal kitchen. Isabela Gonzalez, who was charged with the implementation of this project, attended to the development of relationships, assuming more would be accomplished in the kitchen and throughout the project through a spirit of cooperation and collaboration. Social workers recognize the importance of relationship as key to the success of any intervention. This does not suggest that social workers unconditionally accept all consumer attitudes, behaviors, or decisions. Instead, it implies that dialogue and critical analysis are important elements for making effective decisions and influencing change. Thus, as people came to depend on one another to complete tasks, the challenges of displacement and forced migration were placed in the context of human rights and human dignity and social justice that extended beyond the borders of Peru to the ethical tenets of social work practice.

Social Justice

The issue of social justice, or fairness in relationships, is a unifying force for the roles of social workers described in this book. The countries explored and the case examples provided portray dimensions of social justice, including dignity, opportunities, resources, and responsibilities. To engage in activities of international social justice, social workers must be familiar with a country's history, culture, and politics. Additionally, identifying and building on strengths requires sharing experiences and knowledge in a nonjudgmental fashion.

A social work framework for international practice that embraces social justice involves a critical review of attitudes and beliefs of oneself and environment; an increased knowledge of other people and places for critical thinking and action in various sociopolitical environments; and collaborative action taken for change (Gutierrez, Parson, & Cox, 1998). Therefore, social justice in the context of international social work is complex because it means different things to different populations.

Both a process and an outcome, social justice has many dimensions and components, all of which amplify people's voice regarding perceptions of problems, strengths, needs, and desires.

SUMMARY

The contributors to this book examine international experiences to encourage social work students and practitioners to envision themselves and people around the world as sharing common human needs that can be addressed through collective action. A major premise of the book is that the better social workers understand how people function in their communities and countries, the greater their likelihood of exerting influence over pressing issues associated with social justice, such as social and economic development and healthcare disparity. Further, the profession of social work is encouraged to incorporate in its liberal arts foundation, core curriculum, and field education program a strong sense of sociopolitical activism.

REFERENCES

Compton, B. A., & Galaway, B. (1994). *Social work process*. Pacifica Grove, CA: Brooks/Cole.

Enns, C. Z. (1993). Integrating separate and connected knowing: The experiential learning model. *Teaching in Psychology, 20*, 7–13.

Gutierrez, L. M., Parson, R. J., & Cox, E. O. (1998). *Empowerment in social work practice*. Belmont, CA: Brooks/Cole.

Healey, L. M. (2001). *International social work: Professional action in an interdependent world*. New York: Oxford University Press.

Hughes, L. (2000). Crossing, building, and breaking the boundaries: Social work in a global context. In E. Harlow & J. Lawler (Eds.), *Management, social work and change* (pp.119–132). Burlington, VT: Ashgate Publishing.

Kirst-Ashman, K. K., & Hull, G. (1999). *Understanding generalist practice*. Chicago: Nelson Hall.

Long, D., Tice, C., & Morrison, J. (2006). *Macro social work practice: A strengths perspective*. Belmont, CA: Thomson Brooks/Cole.

Lyons, K. (1999). *International social work: Themes and perspectives*. Burlington, VT: Ashgate Publishing.

Meenaghan, T., & Washington, R. (1980). *Social policy and social welfare: Structure and applications.* New York: Free Press.

Piaget, J. (1952). *The origins of intelligence in children.* New York: International Universities Press.

Riesman, D., Glazer, N., & Denney, R. (1955). *The lonely crowd: A study of the changing American culture.* New York: Doubleday Anchor Books.

Saleebey, D. (1997). *The strength perspective in social work practice.* New York: Longman.

Weick, A., & Chamberlain, R. (2002). Putting problems in their place: Further explorations in the strengths perspective. In D. Saleebey (Ed.), *The strengths perspective in social work practice* (3rd ed., pp. 95–105). Boston: Allyn and Bacon.

Author Index

Subject Index